The Box Closet

For Julia,
with best wishes from
the daughter of Margaret —
the middle
~~Sone~~ on the cover —

Mary Meigs

THE
BOX CLOSET

Mary Meigs

Talonbooks   •   Vancouver   •   1987

published with the assistance of the Canada Council

Talonbooks
201 / 1019 East Cordova Street
Vancouver, British Columbia
Canada   V6A 1M8

Typeset in Garth Graphic by Pièce de Résistance Ltée.,
printed and bound in Canada by Hignell Printing Ltd.

First printing: October 1987

Canadian Cataloguing in Publication Data

Meigs, Mary.
   The box closet

   ISBN 0-88922-253-3

   1. Meigs, Margaret. 2. Meigs family. 3.
Meigs, Mary. I. Title.
CT275.M45M4 1987   920.72'0974811   C87-091452-9

To Arthur, Wister, and Sarah,
and our parents whom we still share.

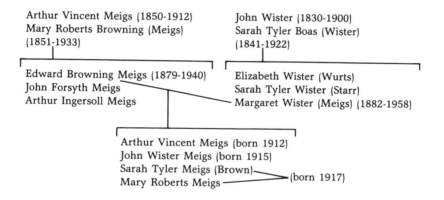

Arthur Vincent Meigs (1850-1912)
Mary Roberts Browning (Meigs)
(1851-1933)

John Wister (1830-1900)
Sarah Tyler Boas (Wister)
(1841-1922)

Edward Browning Meigs (1879-1940)
John Forsyth Meigs
Arthur Ingersoll Meigs

Elizabeth Wister (Wurts)
Sarah Tyler Wister (Starr)
Margaret Wister (Meigs) (1882-1958)

Arthur Vincent Meigs (born 1912)
John Wister Meigs (born 1915)
Sarah Tyler Meigs (Brown)
Mary Roberts Meigs (born 1917)

The Box Closet

The attic lay above the world of our house in Washington like a hot or frigid planet depending on the seasons. You groped your way up by the unlighted, dusty stairway and reached a door, like a shed-door, lifted the latch, pushed the door open. In the summer, you seemed to have walked into a blanket of dust-laden air, dry and oven-hot; a palpable heat enveloped you, made you open and close your mouth like a fish. Just behind the door, in front of you as you crossed the threshhold of the attic, was the wood elevator, with a high picket gate. It was like a big crate made of worn planks, worked by pulleys mounted on the roof, and long ropes that dangled all the way to the cellar and swayed eerily as the elevator descended into the dark shaft with an ominous rumble. You had to release the rope to stop the elevator and ease it down hand over hand, being careful not to let it plummet to the bottom. I remember the terrifying seconds of total silence one day after the wooden floor of the elevator hit bottom with a crash. A good way to get our seventy-four year-old mother in the wheelchair from floor to floor, we had thought, after a practice session, and she had gamely gone along with the idea, and had been wheeled into the elevator with Mrs. Chen, the nurse. Amelia, our laundress, was manning the ropes. The elevator began to rumble down, much too fast. "Let go, Amelia!" It was almost impossible to let go of the ropes when your strongest instinct was to hang on for dear life, and Amelia hung on, with a look of terror on her face, the lacy grey tendrils of her hair alive, it seemed, while I tried to wrench the rope from her grasp. The elevator hit bottom just as we released the brake; what had happened inside was hidden by its wooden roof. Silence. And then the sound of laughter—my mother's laughter. We galloped downstairs and found her and Mrs. Chen, who had hit her nose against my mother's head. "I hit my head," said my mother cheerfully; the downward flight of the elevator had propelled her and Mrs. Chen upward. I remember my mother's laughter breaking out at unexpected times like water from the rock that Moses struck.

Once perhaps, long before, my mother might have scolded Amelia for letting her drop, but now they were bound together by ties of love and mutual helplessness. Amelia's domain for twenty-five years had been the laundry room in the basement, where she reigned like one of the seven dwarfs. She was small and broad, sloping downwards in the shape of a Comice pear. Her mournful face would light up with a smile that shed warm rays of kindliness, or would petrify in a tragic mask. After my mother's first serious stroke, the laundry room began to be piled with mountains of unwashed sheets and bundles of linen (there was no washing machine or dryer, just set tubs and stretched cords for drying) with a half-empty bottle of whiskey hidden behind one of them. The accumulating sheets and the whiskey bottle were the visible sign of her grief and her inability to deal with it, her terrible nostalgia for my mother's daily visits and chats with her, and her unhappiness with Mrs. Willis, the brisk and super-efficient housekeeper, who would send the piles of laundry to be washed somewhere else. During the four-year period of my mother's illness, Amelia became part of the "System," which I describe in a 1954 letter (before Mrs. Willis' time)—"like a jalopy built out of ten different cars with different sized wheels. Amelia cooks four breakfasts, at 7, 7.30, 8, 8.30, and though I strove to think of a simpler method—I couldn't. Kathleen serves breakfast, Amelia serves lunch, Helen serves dinner. Something prevents Helen from doing something because she is allergic to dust. Amelia is allergic to stairs, and was so mad in general that she wouldn't go and see Mother for several days. When she did Mother wept for joy. 'Never leave me,' said Mother. 'It would take a policeman to get me away,' said Amelia.'' She stayed on and outlived my mother; her body seemed to shrink and broaden simultaneously, while the cloud of lacy hair on her head thinned and turned white. Her soul had flown out and touched my mother, confined with one leg in a brace, in the steel cage of her wheelchair. Amelia was confined in the white landscape of the laundry room.

The attic, isolated from the rest of the house, seemed determined to keep its dusty, frigid or stifling character, and discouraged efforts to turn it into something useful. It would outlive the time when a pool table was somehow hoisted up the stairs and set up in one of the rooms with dust-grey dormer windows that looked down on the street far below. For a while one heard the sharp cracking of balls and the duller sound of cue against ball, but with the departure of both brothers to college and the death of my father, the table died, as it were, and its elephantine body was carried down the stairs again. Ante-dating the table was a time of a magic lantern and a home movie-machine, with its heat and clatter, its flickering image and the smell of warm celluloid, the film that constantly broke, unravelled like flypaper. I see Harold Lloyd seated at a table with a white tablecloth that reaches to the floor; he keeps falling into wild fits of laughter and contortions of all his limbs. Under the table, unbeknownst to him, is a chimpanzee, tickling his bare feet.

But later memories prevail—times when my mother was sick and I would go to the silent attic for the comfort of its isolation and stubborn shabbiness. Leaning against the railing under the dust-covered skylight was a small painting which had been there since 1924, of a black and white steamboat in a green sea flecked by white-caps, with a blue sky above in which floated three clouds like three white sheep. When I looked at this painting I was consumed by jealousy. Once, when my twin sister and I were seven years old, our brother Wister, who was nine, had been invited to watch Mr. Comens paint Father's portrait three stories down in the living-room, and then to paint a picture of his own. My jealousy came less from the fact that we had not been allowed to watch the ceremony of portrait painting or invited to paint pictures, but because everybody praised Wister's steamboat to the skies. I remember that we were always hustled upstairs to the ''nursery'' when Mr. Comens appeared, and our exclusion seemed natural; we were too young to observe the sacred rite. We did not rebel, had been broken in by the edicts that proclaimed that our brothers had privileges that we did not have. But perhaps my jealousy was compounded by all the elements that went into the arrival of Mr. Comens: our banishment to the nursery, the idea of Wister being allowed to paint with real oil paints, the praise lavished on the steamboat, and my own latent ambition to paint. The little painting remained there in the attic leaning against the railing, grew dusty like everything else and disappeared after our mother's death, when the house was emptied and we resumed our separate lives.

One room in the attic, the box closet, was always closed, though that did not protect it from the invading dust. Inside, a dim light fell on boxes, trunks, old suitcases and shopping bags, some empty, some full of treasures which had been demoted to the attic and forgotten. The empty trunks were covered with hotel labels; they made ocean voyages with us, took up a few square feet of precious space in the stateroom. They owed their existence to the acknowledged fact that some people had trunks and other people carried them. A faint message of impatience, of huffing and puffing under the trunk's weight, comes back to me; I see a red-faced French porter with a leather strap around his forehead, his back bent under the trunk's weight. Today, trunks are almost as obsolete as the notion of privacy. They held our secrets, could not be slit open with a knife, were strong-boxes with keys. I still have my old Vuitton trunk with its iron-clad corners and hardwood braces running across the top and bottom, its beautiful iron lock and key.

If you had passed a stethoscope over certain shopping bags and shoeboxes in the box closet you would have heard the thump, thump of human hearts. They contained hundreds of family letters and disorderly piles of little leather diaries with their edges turning to brown dust. These, too, with their stiffening rubber bands that held the years together, had been assembled and kept by my mother, who never threw anything away. She knew that sooner or later, even random scraps of paper can be useful: bills, calling cards, theatre programs, announcements of shareholders' meetings or sales of stocks and bonds. Often she consecrated them by writing letters on the blank side so that they are now doubly alive. "Why did she do this? War shortages?" my editor asks. Not at all; it came from a deep strain of thrift in the Wister family, "the Wister stinginess," my sister Sarah calls it. "Don't you remember how Aunt Bessie's Christmas packages used to fall apart in the mail?'' Hoarding, mending and recycling were part of the family heritage.

Twenty-five years after my mother's death, my sister, who had kept the letters and put them in order, turned them over to me. I have held them in my hands, listened to their voices, and asked them a thousand unanswerable questions. In the benign heat of the box closet they were preserved like objects in a Pharoah's tomb, speaking of everyday life, above all of the great family network, enlarged by the marriage of my parents. Grandparents, parents, aunts, uncles, sisters, brothers, and children, all with the mystical sense of family that was inseparable from growing up in upper-class Philadelphia in the late nineteenth and early twentieth centuries. All these, as well as friends and relations in other cities, could be counted on to write letters on every occasion, for letter-writing was one of the pleasures and obligations of their lives. Letters did all the work of communication that is now done on the telephone in perishable words. The words of a letter that survives are alive and emit the energy of a living person. Reading my mother's letters, I feel that my hand is resting lightly on her hand, writing indefatigably in her unmistakeable handwriting, in which her steadfast and stubborn character is there for all to see. It had taken its form when she was thirteen years old and kept it until, when she was seventy-two, her right hand was paralyzed by a stroke. Even then, struggling to sign a legal document with her left hand, she tried to trace the old familiar letters. "Colonel Young, the lawyer, came with two papers for Mother to sign," I write in a 1956 letter. "She signed in such huge interlaced and illegible characters (a version of Margaret repeated three times) that I was torn between tears and laughter." She had signed her whole name, Margaret Wister Meigs, to thousands of letters, but had now reduced it to her essential self, the Margaret she had become when she was born.

Margaret-Persephone: The Engagement

My mother's letters to my father in the months before their marriage in June, 1910, fill a broken down black shoebox; it contains a small segment of time, part of the life and essence of a human being, and most elusive of all, my mother's love for my father when it was new and fresh, when it reached out, boldly or timidly, to test his love, like a sightless person who touches another person's face. The box holds, too, the material evidence that my mother wrote with a fine pen-point dipped in black ink on thick cream-coloured notepaper, crowding the margins with her large handwriting; she enclosed her letters in little 3 by 4½-inch envelopes and affixed on each a pink two-cent stamp showing George Washington facing left. The grey waves of the cancellation roll over his face, straight or undulating according to the office of origin: Broad Street or Germantown Station, and the postmarks show the month, day and hour as legibly as though it were yesterday instead of seventy-three years ago. Mails went out every few hours; there were several deliveries on Saturdays and Sundays, the letters seemed to fly between Belfield, the old family house in Germantown (near Philadelphia), and the Harvard Medical School, as swiftly as words on the telephone. Like all written words they had a peculiar power to hurt or to heal; once on the page and launched in the mail system that puts ours to shame, they could only be undone by subsequent unravellings, apologies, explanations that were likely to create new dramas.

The momentum of letters! It can derail a peaceful relationship and send it careening into a ditch. The gratuitous unhappiness caused by some injudicious or frivolous or careless word that, lightly written with a fine pen-point, might just as well have been carved in granite! Perhaps it was an unconscious sense of the danger contained in a single word that gave my mother's handwriting the look of a perfectly trained circus pony, trotting smoothly along, always making the same distance between steps, never breaking into a gallop. Even on a train, with a pencil borrowed "from a fat and florid gentleman across the aisle," her handwriting trots along at the same pace without any irregularity or tremor. (Evidently trains, like the mail system, went much more smoothly then than now.) The addresses of two envelopes, if placed one on the other, would coincide, and I wonder again at this most conspicuous of my mother's disciplines, her handwriting, which remained the same for sixty years.

My mother did not keep the letters my father wrote her during their engagement, though she kept all those before and after it. A mystery I am unable to solve, for if she kept her own, why not his? The handwriting of both has a changeless quality, as though their characters remained fixed, their emotions steady (but I know that their emotions were not steady). Edward's handwriting is modest, always legible with a flourish of capital letters, a curlicue in the E of Edward. His handwriting is more easy-going and yielding than my mother's, in which capital B's and M's have stiff little platforms over their heads like inverted L's. Reading both parents' letters, I have a strong sense of their handwriting as instruments of their presence, which they play without effort. My mother's letters between 1900 and 1909 are playful and sweet, full of little ironies, the news of engagements and marriages, luncheons, dinners, meetings with new people, travel, life on shipboard, or news of her commitments to the Girls' Friendly Society and other worthy causes. Her entire life, like that of all young women of her milieu in Philadelphia, was filled to the brim with volunteer work and with social and cultural activities; she learned French, read hundreds of books, went to concerts, the theatre and opera, made trips to Europe with her parents; she was kept in a perpetual state of happy non-concentration which subtly prepared her for marriage, trained her to enjoy fragmented days when the mind accepts interruptions almost as a pleasure. She was on a long leading-rein, led so gently that she scarcely felt the bit in her teeth. She was happy, for she was beautiful and quick-witted and loved by her friends, but she was being trained, was training herself to the stubborn discipline that was reflected in her handwriting.

Reading the 1910 letters, I am aware of a sudden jerk on the loose leading-rein that defines the space of my mother's freedom. My two grandmothers are there to pull my mother up short; they use techniques taught by their own mothers and have the authority of one live and one dead husband to back them up. "It is a hard thing," writes Margaret to Edward, "to have one's son, or one's daughter fall in love." At the most blissful time of their lives, a time when lovers now would be independent of their parents and free as birds, my parents found themselves prisoners, the victims of absurd regulations, of deliberate exercises of pride. The two mothers jockeyed like crowned heads, each with her rigid sense of her own duty and her family honour, to make life miserable for the lovers, to prevent them from seeing each other, above all to hedge with requirements the announcement of their engagement. The mothers were engaged in a ritual game of etiquette in order to display their authority. One feels it there in that "hard thing"—the stiffening, the determination to make it harder and to kill the dangerous happiness of the lovers. Their happiness spelled Mama's unhappiness-to-be, above all, her loneliness. Her two older daughters, Bessie and Sarah, had married years before, and her husband (Grandfather Wister) had died in 1900. Margaret had been her confidante and her constant companion, they laughed and cried and fought together. The change from unmarried daughter to married woman is inalterable; Mama could well imagine the new Margaret, Edward's wife, who was outwardly the same but had undergone a major operation—the rearrangement of her loyalties and the loss of her carefree single self. No wonder everybody wanted to cry! No wonder Demeter was frantic when her daughter Persephone, who had been joyously picking flowers on the plain of Enna, was carried off to the underworld by Pluto. Mother-goddesses were more powerful long ago, and Demeter struck a bargain with her son-in-law: Persephone would spend six months of the year with her mother. Poor Mama won no such rights; Persephone-Margaret seemed all too anxious

16

to go off with Pluto, and refused to live in Mama's house after her marriage.

Mama's first line of defence was to delay the marriage, to get up on her high horse, to find spurious reasons for outrage. There was something grim and slightly hysterical in her insistence on etiquette, only to be explained by the imminence of sex with its unstated rights of husband over wife in the kingdom of womanhood. (Remember that if Persephone hadn't eaten those pomegranate seeds in Hades, she would have gone back to live with her mother.) Mothers today lose their daughters slowly to men; sometimes the process of loss goes on under their eyes, in their own houses. Does this make it less painful? The ancient pain is reactivated in every generation, but mothers today have less power to delay it. The terror of her loss made Mama try to prevent it from happening as long as possible, until Margaret (writing to Edward) laughs in her despair: "My mother won't let our engagement be announced until she has seen your Mother and Father, and your Mother won't come to see me until it is announced. Thank goodness, the humor of the situation has just struck me and I feel better." I think again of her laughter that rang out so unexpectedly; it was always *saving* laughter.

"It is a hard thing." My mother states what is, in fact, a truth without questioning why it should be. *Why* is it a hard thing? Isn't the news of a friend's engagement a joyful thing, or is it? Did my mother really feel the joy she expressed in her letters when a girlhood friend was taken away forever by her new husband? It was the conventional joy she was supposed to feel, but her private feelings are expressed in an entry in her diary, October 19, 1906: "Have seen Amy & it seems more and more strange that she is engaged, not that it is less suitable in every way but it makes you feel queer to find her belonging almost to a man whom she only met last March." Amy, one of Margaret's dearest friends, did not marry until 1910; the usual procedure was to spend years getting to know a man, as Margaret did, and then to get engaged. Amy flouted convention in a way that made Margaret feel queer, made her take refuge in the conventions that kept sex firmly in the background. But she did not like the idea of belonging, sexual or otherwise. Perhaps she had begun to think for the first time in her life about the real meaning of "belonging," the unnatural right of ownership it gave to "a man whom she [Amy] only met last March." Margaret and Mama were both going to lose the

Persephone-person who picked flowers on the plain, and both were scared. The "hard thing" was the loss of Persephone and, as well, the literal reality of sex, which separates children from their parents and friends from friends. I remember my miserable unease when my brother fell in love with a close friend who had formed a trio with my sister and me, and how, later, something in me balked at my sister's falling in love and marrying. I wept bitterly on her wedding day. The unknown had yawned with its unspoken fears; my siblings had entered a world that detached them from their family ties and altered all their old relationships. Our friend, Camilla, would no longer be a member of our three-person club but would be forever joined by the bond of sex to our brother. I had so little knowledge of what sex was that on my brother's wedding day, at breakfast, I asked him, "What's an orgasm?" Somehow I had fished this word up out of my subconscious in ignorance of its meaning and with a real wish to know. I had graduated from Bryn Mawr College and still did not know what an orgasm was. What better proof of our family repression than the fact that my brother turned bright red and, without answering, rushed from the room. The taboo which had operated until then to prevent us from ever discussing the subject of sex with our brothers (or each other) is still strong, as though our mother were still there to enforce it.

Later in the summer of my brother's marriage, my mother spied him and Camilla swimming in the nude. They had sailed close to an island where we were having a family picnic and, still at a distance, had slipped into the water. They were stunned and angered (Camilla told me this forty years later) by my mother's outburst, sotto voce—"You should be ashamed of yourselves!" She was capable of moral outrage that could thrive on a starvation diet. The merest hint of sex, the nudity of my brother and sister-in-law even after they were married—nudity that might have been seen by an *unmarried* person (myself)—was this her fear, that I would get ideas? Or was it simply "not done," even if no one could see?

In her letter to Edward, March 29, 1910, Margaret describes Amy's marriage to Thornton, an artist. "I was scandalized, " she says, "by the groom's being at the house beforehand and seeing the bride, and I think they all went down to the church together. I never heard of such a thing." Margaret's moral world was composed of the things that she permitted her ears to hear and her eyes to see, an automatic screening perfected for the use of ladies and gentlemen. Stronger than "Well, I never!", "I never heard of such a thing" put an immediate end to further discussion. But on March 31st, Margaret writes again about the newly-married couple, now on their honeymoon on board a steamship. "A full hour before the boat sailed they were stretched out on their steamer chairs, the only two on deck, blissfully unconscious of the passing throng and radiantly happy. I still persist, to Sarah's disgust, in saying, 'Well, why not?' However I must admit that I am in a very detached state and view my own past behaviour with an astonished and scandalized eye." Sarah, her older sister, held high the banner of family morality and was disgusted by Margaret's laissez-faire attitude. But Margaret's happiness made her understand her friend's and detached her, for once, from judgement. As for her "past behaviour," which astonished and scandalized her, it probably consisted of the exchange of a few kisses. At the end of the letter she says that she "began to wonder why on earth I went to all the bother and general upsettedness of getting married, when I was perfectly happy unmarried!"

Do not make the mistake of thinking that Margaret's "past behaviour" or her wish to stay unmarried (in another letter, too, she says she wishes that the engagement period were longer) meant that she and Edward had been making love with each other. It was because she was kept in a delicious state of ignorance, because she was sustained by the great network of rules that made sex taboo and kept its menace at bay, that the period of her engagement with its ups and downs, its tribulations and deliberate dramas, could be so marvellous. She was the heroine of a fairy tale, with prescribed ordeals, one of which was *not to think*, not to talk, and to keep feeling within decorous boundaries. "Weddings are rather a forbidden topic down in these parts at present," she says in her March 30th letter, "and I am requested not to do anything about my bridesmaids for at least a month, and *not to mention thinking of being married*" (my italics). The preparations for a wedding were rigidly fixed by custom and the observation of all the meticulous rules was necessary to the moral well-being of every participant. Not to mention the financial well-being. The groom had to provide a written statement of his income, a dower, in other words, but the bride's dower took the form of her wedding presents. Just as Egyptian and Chinese noblemen and women were once buried with everything they could possibly need for the next life, so were well-to-do couples in my mother's time who passed through the portal of marriage.

On May 1st, 1910, a little over a month before the wedding, Margaret replies patiently to what seems to have been Edward's impatience. "There are several reasons why there is so much commotion about a wedding," she says. "In the first place it is supposed to be a joyful occasion, a feast, the happiest time of a girl's life, a family reunion, and in the second place, if there wasn't so much extra excitement there would be nothing but the sound of weeping in the house. All men are alike they hate weddings and I feel sorry for the poor things, but it isn't a bit good taste to elope." Margaret makes this statement about the sound of weeping without irony or reproof; it is natural for her family to weep, she thinks, but she sees her own tears, caused by her mother's exigence, as unnatural and selfish. "I must tell you how ashamed I am of the way I behaved when you were home this time," she writes to Edward, "to think that I should have treated you twice to tears. It was perfectly horrid of me, and I will try never to do it anymore." I remember times when I saw her suffering from the agitation of having suppressed her tears, when her face would become grim with the effort.

A month before Margaret's wedding, the sound of weeping gave way to the sound of the doorbell ringing, of presents being opened, of the almost continuous scratching of pen on paper, writing invitations and thank-you notes. Somehow there was time, too, for lunches, teas, dinner parties, theatre, opera, dances—and committee meetings, for the pleasures had to be earned by the observance of duties. The important thing was not to think. And weren't the whole monstrously top-heavy paraphernalia of a wedding invented to prevent the principals from thinking? To prevent them from weeping, Margaret said, and from asking themselves as Edward did, why? "The trouble with you is . . . you think too much and it's a great mistake," says Margaret on May 10th, a month before the wedding. "Who wants to know what anybody is like anyway. I hope to goodness I don't catch that habit."

Evidently he had wanted to know what *she* was like and she had taken refuge behind the idea that to think about "what anybody is like," much less to let someone else do it, is selfish and indiscreet. My mother arrived at her impressions of people directly, with spontaneous admiration or loathing, and did not want or need to delve. Delving to her was an invasion of privacy as distasteful as a physical examination by a doctor, and she guarded the privacy of others with as much determination as she guarded her own. In my view, since I, too, am a delver, Edward's effort to know her better was understandable, even laudable, but it made her squirm, and don't we all squirm if someone tries to explain us to ourselves? She did not like to be "looked at under a microscope," she told him. This form of self-protection is a time-honoured woman's way of keeping part of herself inviolate; its defensive weapons are irrationality and evasion. The disputes between my parents when we were growing up all bore witness to my father's tireless efforts to undo the knots in which my mother had tangled him. She seemed always to be armed with a net and he with a spear. Her net could baffle arguments; it could snare and hold sins so fast that she was unable to see the sinner in front of her eyes. Or rather the sin became the sinner as inexorably as Dr. Jekyll became Mr. Hyde.

Edward became Mr. Hyde just before the engagement was formally announced in January, 1910. In his happiness he had told some friends, and this had got back to Margaret and her mother who merged in their righteous fury. One wonders how Margaret could suddenly have forgotten Edward's face and the fact that she loved him, could now see only his petty mistake, bloated out of all recognition, and could have used it to threaten him. She and her mother were possessed by the patriarchal monster, What-is-not-Done, it, too, a Mr. Hyde, *the* Mr. Hyde, who creeps by osmosis into his victims.

During the months before her wedding Margaret's freedom to think her own thoughts and to make her own decisions was being deliberately curtailed by her mother, and though she laughed and suffered and chafed under the restraints, she was being gradually broken in to accept them. "If Papa had been living he would not have allowed me to write or see you until everything was settled," she writes before the engagement was announced, "but between ourselves, isn't it tiresome?" She was at a crucial point of her moral development, when love for Edward gave her the force to rebel, to be different from her parents. But as long as she lived in their house her life belonged to them, and particularly to the ghost-Papa, who required via the living Mama that evidence of an adequate income be produced before marriage could even be considered. In a letter to Edward on the subject of money (a Special Delivery stamp—10 cents in 1910—shows the postman

vigorously pedalling a bicycle to ensure "immediate delivery"),
Grandmother Wister stated the bride price, dictated by her dead
husband's ghost. "Since I wrote you last night, " she says, "I must
reconsider announcing the engagement until you can give me positive assurance of what you have to live upon. When my other
daughters were married Mr. Wister required that their husbands
should have an income of $3,000 *before* the engagement was
announced and until they were able to prove their possession of
this sum he would not only not consent to announcing the engagement but would not allow even a secret understanding." (How
could he have prevented this, I would like to know?) ". . . upon
thinking the matter over I have come to my final decision which
was my first one, that is that I will not allow any announcement
until you can produce the same sum as my other sons-in-law viz.
at least $3,000. My head must rule my heart in this matter." Her
heart relented to the extent of accepting Edward's $2,700 (his
income as an instructor at Harvard Medical School). Had she con-
sulted Mr. Wister's ghost again for instructions, or did that $300
represent the measure of her autonomy? Thus Edward's dower
was assured and in the fullness of his joy he must have thought
that he had the right to tell people he was engaged. Instead of
which he got a furious letter from Margaret's Mama: "Even in
my first letter," she says, "I did not give my consent to announcing the engagement before the 20th of January, therefore I am
exceedingly surprised that you should have told a number of persons. In view of your extraordinary conduct . . . " In view of
his extraordinary conduct, which was so natural and ordinary,
she refused to send out any letters announcing the engagement,
and forbade Margaret to mail any until she (Mama) had seen
Edward.

My recollection of this grandmother, who died when I was six
years old, is of a mild, sweet old lady dressed in black (though
Papa had been dead for many years) who sat beaming on the porch
of the old family house, and seemed so much more tractable than
my other grandmother. (*Seeming* tractability was peculiar, too, to
Margaret—until her eyes flashed fire.) Nor would you have
guessed from Mama's beautifully legible handwriting with graceful curlecues adorning the capital letters, or from the delicate
watercolour sketches she made on her travels, that an iron hand
was concealed under the velvet glove. Margaret loved her,
worried over her and mourned her death, she was even her

mouthpiece, just as Mama was Papa's mouthpiece, but she was rebellious. Margaret's diary, November 16, 1903: "Mama sighing steadily. I am absolutely unsympathetic because it irritates me so." March 10, 1907—a solitary entry for the whole year, which speaks volumes about life with Mama: " Never have I had two such weeks never have lived more or perhaps a better freer time with all my own way, I'm afraid that must be it. I'm a dreadfully selfish person & I've been doing all the small harmless things that rile Mama." What *were* they? She was probably flirting with all four of her suitors, for flirting was one of the great pleasures of her life, as we shall see. But now, in 1910, she was caught in the wedding-machinery, the rules that gave Mama the liberty to bully her, to tread on her spontaneous instincts like newly-seeded grass in the name of fear disguised as convention. "Isn't it tiresome?" she had confided to Edward, yet when it came to his "extraordinary conduct" she became one with Mama. On the day that Mama wrote her nasty letter to Edward, Margaret wrote an even nastier one. Her "isn't it tiresome?", so human, so frolicsome, had given place to hardness of heart. "Your method of announcing your engagement is singularly effective, and one with which I am quite unable to cope," she writes in her orderly handwriting, "but if you think that I love or respect you more for it you are quite mistaken. The fact that you promised me to tell no one, evidently weighs with you not at all. It pleased you to tell people and you have done so . . . All through this you have behaved to Mama and to me in a very inconsiderate and rude way and I wish to say now that the wedding date is not set." There! She has made the choice she was so often to make in her life between love and What-is-not-Done. She was unwilling to make any allowance for the happy imprudence that led Edward "to tell people." He had promised and Margaret felt betrayed but the real source of her indignation came from Mama, the games mistress and umpire. Edward had crept upon It in the game *Stop! No more moving,* and It had turned around and caught him and he had to go back to the starting-line. Margaret, the victim of the rules, was forced to play by them, even to believe in them. "My great desire in Life," says Mama in another letter to Edward, "is Margaret's happiness and I feel she could not bear the strain too long." She writes this as if it were not she, but Edward by his imprudent conduct who was imposing the strain on her daughter. And I want to cry out to Mama, "Let her be free! Stop tying her up! Why should she bear *any* strain?'' Why did they invent strains, spend their time perfecting strains in the name of their great desire in Life—their daughters' happiness? For Mama, convention and moral probity were identical and happiness had to be won by sacrificial offerings and strict obedience to custom. Or perhaps Margaret's happiness was unseemly, a breach of etiquette like that of the honeymooning friends in their deck chairs, in which lurked the suggestion that she would be glad to get away from her Mama?

Thirteen days go by after Margaret's severe letter before she writes again. Edward has sent her a bunch of violets and a gardenia so beautiful that people have stopped on the street to admire it. She runs into Arthur, Edward's brother, and says to him (as she writes to Edward), ''Isn't Edward nice? Look what he sent me to comfort me.'' And Arthur says coldly, ''But what has Edward to comfort him?'' ''So you see your family stand up for you,'' says Margaret to Edward. They have been officially engaged for four days. ''And this evening,'' Margaret says, ''my dear ring came back made to fit and with M.W. from E.B.M. 1910 inside, so you see everything is quite right.'' Edward's family had not shared the view that it was a crime for him to talk about his engagement; they must have thought it was ridiculous that Margaret was forbidden to see Edward until the engagement was announced. And what proud mother would like to see her eldest son humbled by the rival mother? Margaret, who was already a little afraid of her mother-in-law to be, was going to be humbled herself, and in the presence of Mater (as she called her) to wish for the comfort of Mama. Margaret ''belonged,'' the moment she was married, to her new family; she had lost her name (or pushed it back, so that it seemed to walk behind her new name like a Japanese wife), and when Mama's name became secondary, Mama's power over Margaret was transferred to Mater.

Two months before the wedding Margaret writes, ''I think everyone should be allowed to FIGHT WITH TheiR oWN ParentS, Don'T YoU?'' This unique and radical departure from the rules of her handwriting made me burst out laughing. This time the fight revolves around which of Edward's many job offers he is to accept, with the approval of his mother, of course. ''The last thing in the world I want to do is to have any disagreement with your Mother, '' says Margaret, gracefully passing the buck, ''I shall very bravely and nobly say that I really don't know much about it, but that you do.'' The others were interfering with everything:

with Edward's choice of a job, with his plan to spend the honeymoon in Japan and China, with his and Margaret's determination to rent a house for themselves instead of living with Mama. In every instance, Margaret stands firm. She wants to go to the Orient; above all, she wants her own house. She talks to Mama, who "seems to understand . . . but all the same it is hard. There is an atmosphere of gloom about a wedding that I never appreciated before, do not be deluded into thinking it is a gay and cheerful occasion. When you get home you will find out what it is like, your family will have suppressed misgivings and forebodings that will suddenly crop up at the most unexpected moments." I continue to think that the gloom that was spilled over a supposedly cheerful occasion was the gloom spilled by every spoil sport, in this case a mother who was jealous (as any mother would be) of the handsome young man who was taking her daughter away from her. So she handed out cheerfulness in little spoonfuls, alternating with hurt feelings. She could keep Margaret if she and Edward would only live with her, but Margaret refused to live with her. Margaret's will was as strong as her mother's, strong enough to give some extra courage to Edward, to help him to stand up to his own mother who had the power to reduce him to a state of nervous prostration. Margaret's obedience to the absurd rules of the engagement period was her last major concession to her mother's will. She, too, would follow the absurd rules when her own daughter married. Always law-abiding, she obeyed the law that turns daughters into their mothers, generation after generation, as soon as they marry and become mothers themselves. My mother believed in her own autonomy but in her heart of hearts she loved the absurd rules and her rebellion from Mama was about her right to observe them in her own way.

Looking back on that peaceful time, I think, how could they have made such mountains out of molehills? Evidently people without serious troubles have to invent them; they need reasons for being angry with each other, for setting up hierarchies and bureaucracies and rules of etiquette, the things that have been invented to keep women busy, above all to keep them from thinking about what really matters. Society is like an immense queen bee, faithfully tended by swarms of drones who do exactly what they must to ensure the next generation. And this takes time, it takes lifetimes. Privileged women then engaged help to free themselves to become better servants of the Queen Bee. Margaret, too, was in her thrall; her time was not her own but belonged to the demanding creature who made her scurry around and who had the power to shame and to punish. In 1910, people of Margaret's class lived happily on the slope of the volcano, unaware of the molten sea of violence that was going to burst out and engulf the whole world. They ignored the Threat, were unable even to see it, a new immanence not of God and life but of the multiple forms of death, the threat to life on earth which rolls now with uncontrollable momentum. Relatively speaking they had nothing to worry about, though the molten sea was stirring and grumbling underneath them. Their air was pure, their food was uncontaminated, their wild life was abundant. If thousands of snowy egrets were killed to adorn ladies' hats, if ladies' fans were made with eagles' feathers, if flamingo tongues were served at royal banquets—so what? There were plenty more. People then did not mourn the extinction of species. Nor did they think much about the welfare of their servants; there were comforting answers then to questions about class (if you happened to ask them). Margaret, too, believed in a chain of command, her right to command, and, in turn, her duty to obey. Obedience was loyalty, and loyalty was her great virtue and her great blind spot. Even before she was married she had pledged her loyalty to Edward's scientific work. "Don't worry about the monkeys," she writes him in 1909. "You must be thinking of the conversation we had up at Bessie's [her older sister] . . . and if you remember she was the one who didn't quite like the idea of killing things. For my part, I think that whatever you do in a scientific way is quite right, when I say you, I mean you, yourself, or your friends if you want to include them, so you see what confidence I have in you." Though Edward hated to kill things, he was in the exalted service of Science, and Margaret had confidence because she loved him. How would she have felt if she had seen today's photographs of monkeys being burned, shocked and poisoned in experimental laboratories ("in a scientific way") with expressions of anguish on their contorted faces? She did not know, as we know now; there was a world of horror that she could not even imagine. She had begun to prepare herself for her time-honoured role as loyal wife. "I pray that God will watch over you," she writes Edward a few days before their wedding, "and teach me the way to make you really, truly happy."

Imaginary Letter

Dearest Father and Mother,

Now that I'm eight years older than Father when he died and only six years younger than Mother when she died, do I have the right to call you by your first names, Edward and Margaret? I've outdistanced Father, who died too young, and am drawing closer and closer to Mother; I can remember you at my age, worrying about your weight, your high blood pressure, your swollen ankles. But you never complained; you merely looked in a puzzled way at your ankles which were bulging over your elegant shoes. In fact, they were a warning signal of the series of strokes from which you died. You always kept a distance between yourself and pain (ashamed, you say in your 1896 diary, when you wept at the dentist's), as though it were someone else's. Until you were paralyzed and defenceless, that is. "Poor Mama moans little moans for a good part of every day," I say in a 1956 letter to a friend, "clutches my hand, says, 'Don't leave me.' Nobody knows what hurts . . . This morning I said, 'Does something hurt?' and she said, 'Always.' " "Paralyzed," you had murmured after your first bad stroke. "I'd rather die." But you lived and struggled to get better for four more years.

Do you remember long before that, when you were much

younger and I was still a child, that in a fit of freshness I called you Margaret? Freshness was knowing that something shouldn't be said but saying it anyway—yet not knowing *why* it shouldn't be said. Unanswered why's and why not's were like tails attached to the mysterious rules of childhood; as time went by, some of them dropped off, but not this one—that one did *not* venture to call a parent by his or her first name. Why not? For it wasn't visibly (or audibly) a punishable offence like saying damn or hell. (In one of your letters to Father, you quote Arthur, aged four, commenting on the story of the Garden of Eden: "If that snake was the devil, I could say gosh darn to him, couldn't I?" Out of his childish mouth had come a marvellous logic that delighted you.) But I was old enough to know better and I had accidentally attempted the unthinkable, the turning of Mother into Margaret, someone close to my own age, without Mother's authority. I had discovered, but did not give it any further thought until now, that you had two identities: Margaret for Edward and Mother for your children, that you were two people. The Margaret-person had many shades of identity but the Mother-person was like the One Goddess, Mother and only Mother. Or Father and only Father, for I never tried calling Father Edward, or tried out the thought of your also being Edward. But here is Wister, in 1920 (aged five), stumbling into an entirely new identity. "Your story about Wister giving your name for me at Sunday School is certainly pretty sweet," you write to Margaret, "but I can't seem to remember that you really call me 'Dearest' very often." And yet Wister had heard "dearest" often enough so that it was the first thing he thought of. Do you remember how jealous I was of Wister? And no wonder, for he was universally adored. "Wister [aged three] is as smart as a steel trap and full of mischief," "dear little Wister," "Wister is the dearest little rat," and other encomiums are sprinkled through your letters. How I would have loved to be called a dear little rat! Be that as it may, Wister's name for Father recognized your identity as a Dearest, more importantly, recognized the love between you. What if I had said, "Margaret dearest," how would you have reacted? But I know without asking that you would have known instantly that this, too was freshness, i.e. impertinence.

Now that I've read your letters and diaries I'm so steeped in the reality of Margaret and Edward that Mother and Father scarcely exist any more. I compare the time before, when I groped for the truth about you, and *this* time with my new knowledge of you, when we have become friends beyond parenthood, and when I weep because we didn't live this understanding when you were alive. If you were here now I could say to you, forgive me for not having been present enough to you, for not having broken down the Father and Mother barriers and lived our love for each other. I've listened to you talking to each other, have heard your voices in your unchanging handwriting. You are there in those fragile and durable letters with their different postmarks and stamps: pink two-cent or purple three-cent stamps, Spanish, Greek, German, Moroccan, English, French, Italian, Chinese stamps, monarchs and palaces on them, travelling and arriving against incredible odds, determined pieces of paper, containing yourselves thrown out on the wind. They are my evidence of you that I can touch, and you left it, I think, so that I could get to know you better.

Your letters do not answer all my questions, of course. And they pose new ones—questions that you must have answered in conversations when you were together, the long conversations between husbands and wives after the children have gone to bed. But I discovered that when anything difficult had to be discussed Margaret and Mother were the same person; the defensive tactics you used with us were those you used with Edward. So Edward said things from the sanctuary of his letters that he couldn't have brought up in one of those long conversations without setting off a dispute. Why do face-to-face conversations so often turn into disputes, Edward wonders, just as his brother, Arthur, wonders in a letter to *him*. "It has often seemed strange to me," says Arthur, "that we write each other so fondly, so affectionately, so nicely, yet when we meet face to face, we have at times fallen to calling each other nincompoops." It seemed strange to Arthur because he could not see that it was he who, like a careless quadruped, trampled on Edward in a conversation, he who began to shout. Though he saw that a letter is a sanctuary, he didn't see that he wanted to put down the whole world, and particularly his brother Eddie. You, Father, suffered from all conversations that led nowhere, merely got the original subject into a hopeless tangle and ruffled up your clear mind. You depended on the written word and the insulation of distance to protect you.

Margaret's purpose in letters is to reach out and touch you with the day's news, whereas your letters candidly recount both your activities and the uneven voyage of your spirit. How homesick you were when you went off to scientific conferences in Atlanta, Syracuse, Indianapolis, Minneapolis, Chicago, longing for Margaret, longing for your children! Your need was a rubber band that held you and drew you back. You needed Margaret more than she needed you, or at least you were more willing to tell her so, for an aspect of her discretion was to give *less*, perhaps to keep your need alive. "To give them what they want would be to spoil them," Mother once said about presents to her children. One of your commandments was to hide your own wants and needs, just as you stoically hid your pain.

This self-denial of yours was a reproach during my period of obnoxious selfishness, when my sense of guilt weighed even heavier because you seemed so unselfish. Why did we never talk about what it's like to be a teenager, to want, to want, to be hard-hearted and rebellious? But that would have been Margaret talking, not Mother. Margaret would have said, "I used to quarrel with my Mama, I wanted my freedom and I *enjoyed* being selfish!" She would have remembered writing in her diary when she was fourteen, "Our trip is over, oh, it is horrible to think of it, and that nine months of my life with Mama and Papa and Sarah have gone by so quickly. If I had been at all good or grown any better in that time I wouldn't mind so much, but I haven't, and I'm just as selfish and as vain and conceited and as dissagreeable [sic] as I was when I left home. I'm going to try right away to grow better. I am given everything I want and yet I don't seem to be satisfied." But you don't get better for in 1904 (aged twenty-two) you write, "The trouble with me is I am too grasping. 'Every day and all day' seems to be my motto." And in 1907, in the only entry for the entire year, you give that cri de coeur that delighted my heart, which ends, "I'm a dreadfully selfish person & I've been doing all the small harmless things that rile Mama."

So you riled Mama and the things you liked to do were the very ones that riled her. And she riled *you*, for she was always putting the brakes on your freedom to have a good time. The high spirits of Margaret were pitted against the properness of Mama. Mama fussed, Mama was alarmed when, at Loèche-les-Bains, Margaret and Mr. Gallatly became good friends. "Now Mama has begun to fuss about Mr. Gallatly & absolutely tells me that I musn't lead him on! Imagine leading any man on, let alone one that has been pouring out his heart about someone else ever since you knew him." Do you remember that when you were anxiously waiting for a letter from Edward, Mama did nothing but fuss about Mr. Gallatly? Your exasperation with Mama erupts frequently in your 1904 diary. August 19: "A simply perfect day [this, too, with Mr. Gallatly] with a horrid ending need I add that Mama was the ending." And on December 29th, in the middle of Mr. Gallatly's visit to you and your family, "Anybody to get along amicably with Mama I defy, especially when she insists upon treating your guests like the dirt under her feet." No doubt, Mama thought that by this time, though your engagement to Edward was still three years away, your intentions were clear (at least to her) and you did not have the right to have such a good time with Mr. Gallatly.

Finally—the decisive struggle with Mama when you and Edward were engaged, punctuated by your comical cry, "I think everyone should be allowed to FIGHT WITH TheiR OWN ParentS, Don'T YoU?" Still, you behaved "in a very daughterly way to Mama," says Mr. Wheelwright (another suitor) in 1906; you loved her and were heartbroken when she died. The house in Germantown had lost its soul, you wrote Edward. But as long as you were unmarried, Mama had the right to fuss over her ewe lamb, who was required to be daughterly by iron-clad convention. When I read these entries in your diaries, I laughed and mourned. Daughters and mothers quarrel in every generation even though the mother may have vowed not to make the mistakes of her own mama. Surely you remembered your quarrels with Mama well enough to say, "I will *not* be like Mama!" It happened without your knowing it—your metamorphosis into Mama—not as fussy, perhaps, but just as watchful, just as determined to protect your daughters. There were new, much worse threats; in particular, sex, which had been kept decorously at bay, but now, after World War I, unleashed, as it seems to be by every cataclysm, had grown a hundred leering heads like the Hydra. About that, at least, you and Mama had seen eye to eye; your quarrels were not because Mama did not trust you, but because she cared so much about appearances. And though you were riled then by her caring so much about appearances when she knew she could trust you, you were fated to do the same thing with your daughters, fiercely protecting us, you thought, from greater dangers than any you had faced, from the Hydra heads that seemed to be staring through the windows of your own house. But you could not prevent your children from drifting away from you into secret realms, afraid

31

to talk, as you were sometimes with Mama. Supposing I'd con-
fronted you with your diaries, with that "Anybody to get along
amicably with Mama I defy." Could we have laughed together;
would, at that moment, mother and daughter magically have
become Margaret and Mary?

Tableau: The Wister Women

The Wister family was as matriarchal as it was possible to be in the days when patriarchs had all the authority. When Margaret's Papa died in 1900, he willed his authority to Mama, along with answers to difficult questions, and his ghost stood by to give counsel in practical matters. But as Great-aunt May Wister, another matriarch, said to my brother, Arthur, "The women wear the pants in the Wister family." "Oh, but I think Father wears the pants in *our* family," said Arthur. "Do you?" said Aunt May, "I hadn't noticed." Papa's death left a quartet of strong-willed women: Mama, Bessie, Sarah and Margaret. Bessie and Sarah had already proved Aunt May's dictum; they selected for husbands businessmen who were as much alike as Tweedledum and Tweedledee (or so it seemed to my childish eyes). Their names were Stewart and Jim; both had benevolent faces and handlebar moustaches, and, at parties, chewed on their cigars and listened to their wives. November 16, 1903: "Jim of course never speaks if he can help it," says Margaret in her diary, "speaking is against his principals." Writing to Edward in 1906, she reports a transformation in Jim: "Jim actually interrupts!" she says. But his little flare of rebellion was quickly extinguished and I remember only his good-natured silences while Aunt Sarah's tongue reeled out like a string with a colourful kite dancing at the end of it. Between Margaret and Edward, there was equal time for speech, yet Aunt May was right. Edward, without quite abdicating, gave the power he did not want into Margaret's hands. "Edward looks after me as if I were a piece of Venetian glass, not realizing that I won't break!" she wrote to Mama on her wedding trip. It took Edward time to realize that the Wister women were unbreakable, that only illness and old age could shatter their bodies and wills.

Mama and her daughters all had quick speech that could cut like a razor, and terrible tempers that struck with deadly force. They are there in Margaret's diaries and letters: Mama's tirades, Bessie's tantrums, Sarah's biting sarcasm. "As for my temper," Margaret says in her 1900 diary, "Beware, take care." She is proud of her temper, particularly useful in the art of flirtation. Her men-friends speak of it in their letters: "Margaret wrought up and in a temper," says Mr. Wheelwright; "I remember I brought down your reproof once,"says Mr. Gallatly. A leitmotif (if it can be called *light*) in Margaret's diaries is fighting; she fights with Mama, with Sarah, and particularly with Bessie. Afterwards, she is more or less contrite, and berates herself. "I know I am vain and conceited," she says in 1900. Evidently Bessie has told her so.

Margaret's diary, January 15, 1896: "Oh, it was perfectly horrible, horrible to say 'goodbye' to dear Bessie and all of them. How we did it I don't know but we cried and cried and I wished Bessie was with us . . . Oh, how I wish she was here. Dear, dear Bessie, we are a good way apart now." Margaret has just had her fourteenth birthday. Four years later, she has begun to be wary of Bessie's influence over her. January 7, 1900: "Bessie is worse for a person than could possibly be imagined. I believe she adores me & makes me think of nothing but myself all the time." For her sisters, Bessie became a lesson in how not to be and I think that Margaret's character was partly formed by her determination not to be like Bessie and to be as much like her dignified and noble sister, Sarah, as possible. If Bessie threw tantrums, Margaret would swallow her wrath; if Bessie gave parties that were famous for their density, decibels and fish-house punch, Margaret's parties would be graceful and decorous. She would try to restrain her inherited instinct to meddle, for she had only to remember Bessie, almost a second mother, hovering and pouncing during the months of Margaret's engagement period. Bessie needed to meddle as she needed to breathe; she succeeded in provoking everybody. "Jim spoke of Bessie as no gentleman should," remarks Margaret in her diary, October 25, 1903.

The death of Mama in 1922 marked the beginning of a thirty-year family feud, with Sarah and Margaret united against Bessie. Mama had left Belfield, the old family house, to Sarah, and $30,000 each to Bessie and Margaret, and Bessie, who wanted a share of the house, was determined to sabotage the orderly settling of Mama's will. In letters to Edward, Margaret speaks impatiently of Bessie's behaviour: "We worked all day and fought all afternoon." "We fought three hours this morning." "Another frightful fight." "Bessie stamps, roars and threatens." Bessie, hopping up and down in her childish fury, must have been driven almost insane by the solid opposition of her two sisters. She behaved so badly that her sisters stopped talking to her. Years later they came together at Jim's funeral, held in the little front parlour at Belfield. They were like three mourning queens, all in black widows' weeds with veils over their faces. Jim's death united them, after a fashion, but could not dissolve the old rancours.

In imagination, I see the faces of my two aunts: Sarah, with her dark, heavy-lidded eyes and ironic mouth, her look full of intelligence and humour, and Bessie, whose eyes snapped in her round face like raisins in a hot-cross bun, and whose little white teeth gleamed in a malicious smile. "Aunt Bessie is a baddie in my book," I said to my brother recently. "Oh, Mary, you should have let me read it. Aunt Bessie—in her way—was a wonderful woman," he said. "What about the thirty-year feud?" I asked. "Yes, but . . ." He had liked Aunt Bessie and her whirlwind energy, her legendary parties, when her calliope voice could be heard over the squeals, hoots, bellows and guffaws of the guests, and her bright eyes kept watch over the unruly flock. Even her funeral party was worthy of her. "I think the old girl would have enjoyed it, don't you?" said her son Johnny.

Thinking of "the old girl" and her virtues which I didn't appreciate (holding against her a memory of one of her parties when she had cornered me and said,"Why don't you get married? You're just an ordinary American girl") I remember suddenly that Bessie was, in Margaret's words to Edward in 1910, "the one who didn't quite like the idea of killing things." They had been talking about using monkeys in laboratory experiments and Bessie had thought not about the needs of science, but about the monkeys' suffering.

An invisible spring in her kept sympathy alive, and permitted her imagination to travel out to a monkey that was being tortured in the name of science. But loyalty to Edward forbade Margaret to think about the monkey, blocked her view and her sympathy as effectively as an asbestos shield, and pulled all her thought-cells like iron filings to a magnet. "Don't worry about the monkeys," she wrote Edward, "whatever you do is right." It was an impersonal loyalty, not so much to her future husband as to a husband acting in the name of science to "help mankind," a loyalty that is blinder than love. Deep in her character lay Margaret's loyalties: to the representatives of Science, Nation and God. Wearing any one of these labels, they could do no wrong.

What was it in Bessie, so conventional in matters of social standing, marriage, etc. that made her suddenly imagine the suffering of an experimental monkey? Perhaps it was merely opposition to Margaret that made her take the part of the monkey against implacable Science, which, in the person of Edward, could do no wrong. A kind of gratuitous disagreement. But this disagreement opened a little chink in the wall of Bessie's mind. Jealous of Margaret, she had started by trying to get at Edward, and at Margaret for her blind devotion. He is not a saint, he *can* do wrong, she wanted to say. But what started as contrariness opened a little window; it was a practice thought that led by chance to thinking about the monkeys. Perhaps she had been to the Philadelphia Zoo and had seen a gorilla, lying on the cement floor of his cage, alone in his cell, without a tree to climb, without a single plaything or a shelf to sleep on, curled on the floor with one arm hooked around his head, lying there in his miserable state of boredom that would go on until he died. Something like that would have been needed to focus her attention and release her heart from bondage, like a butterfly twisting and turning to get out of its lifeless shroud.

Bessie had had doubts about the means science uses to achieve its ends. Margaret had no doubts if the servant of science was Edward. "You or your friends," she said, for she included his scientific colleagues in the broad spectrum of her confidence. When I read this letter, it seemed to shed a bright light on the fatal nature of my mother's loyalty and to suggest a kind of compassion in Bessie that I had never noticed. Then I found a poem that my mother had written in 1940, just after my father's death.

To E.B.M.

He who woos Science
  Sees her pass unheeding
    Pure as a ray of light
    Ready to melt from sight,
Deaf to his pleading.

If he would win her,
  Follow where she's leading
    Up he must go and far,
    Struggle to reach a star,
Wears his heart feeding.

And when he's won her?
  Ah! that is all he's needing.
    He'll never count the cost,
    Health, life, are all well lost,
Toward truth he's speeding.

In Margaret's view, Edward was killed by his tireless devotion to science; in seeking after scientific truth, she suggests, he sacrificed his health and his life. It's as though after thirty years of fidelity in Edward's name to her great rival, Science, Margaret had turned against "her," for, interestingly, she makes Science female. "Look what you've done," she says. "You've killed him." That it was not Science who killed him but a disease (tuberculosis) for which Science was, the following year, to provide a cure, was irrelevant. Science gives life, and science kills. Perhaps Bessie had puzzled over the question, must science *ever* kill to give life? Margaret thought she knew the answer until in her state of bitter grief, she counted its cost.

Tableau: Loèche-les-Bains

November 6, 1985—A postcard from a friend arrives; it is a nineteenth-century photograph of indoor baths flooded with light from arched windows along one side. In the foreground: a couple, fully-clothed, up to their shoulders in water. The woman is moving a chess piece on a board placed on a round pedestal between them, another woman is swimming breast-stroke, and yet another lifts her arms to take a tea tray from a servant in black, with a white apron, leaning over the edge of the pool. Three women are reading books which they hold above water on the pedestals, beyond them, men and women are immersed up to their shoulders, while others in street clothes lean over a railing that runs the length of the baths. A bearded man in the foreground is holding a top hat and another nearby with a moustache has placed his bowler hat carefully on the railing. Both have serious, almost reverent expressions on their faces as they gaze at the scene below them. Near one of the big windows two dogs sit stiffly on their haunches, one snow-white with pricked ears, the other grey, shaggy with falling ears, their four front legs propping them up like crutches. They have the same grave stillness of attitude as the human beings, not one of whom is smiling. Time is arrested, though we know that the tea tray will move into the woman's

38

waiting hands, that a piece will be moved from the back of the chess board, and that the dogs, released, will rush to the photographer for their reward.

Something about this scene seemed familiar. Is it? Could it be? And looking at the back of the postcard I saw that it was indeed Loèche-les-Bains, the little Swiss village at the foot of the Gemmi Pass, where warm sulphur water bubbles out of the ground, where my mother's family and friends went for the baths in the early 1900s, where Margaret took her four children in 1928. The cool shadow of the Gemmi fell over the village in early afternoon; I remember this, the grass in the valley shorn by cows, the sound of little mountain torrents. I can feel the pebbles slipping under my feet when, armed with an alpenstock, I walked with Sarah and Miss Balfour, our governess, part way up the path that zigzagged to the top of the pass. Though we longed to, we were not allowed to go the whole way up as "the boys" (Father, Arthur, Wister) had done. But, with the twins on mules, the whole family climbed the Torrenthorn, up over bare, slippery shale to the very top, and I remember my mother sitting down on a rock, panting, and saying, "I don't care if I live or die!" And joining in our laughter. A walk to the top of the Torrenthorn, preferably in the company of several young men, was one of my mother's exploits every summer, as I realized when I read her diaries for 1903 and 1906. In 1928 this romantic excursion had become a family affair, and my mother, who appears to have clambered up mountains like a chamois when she was in her twenties, was, at forty-six, no longer spry and tireless.

The postcard captures the seriousness of all those who bathed in the magic waters. Apart from bathing, life at Loèche consisted of social activities at the hotel, playing tennis, walking and climbing. Even at age eleven, I was oppressed by the air of good breeding and polite conversation, and I developed a sulky dislike for mountains and alpine villages, which endured until I was grown up. In 1953, my mother went back to Loèche for three weeks. She wrote to say that she was lonely, but she got through her three weeks there with a stoicism that torments me now when I think about it. The ghosts of her Loèche men-friends and her mama haunted her there, and memories of being young, of long excursions, picnics, dances, and village fêtes, of the giddy delight of flirting. "And it was fun & gay & the moonlight on the Gemmi. Oh!"

39

Les Bains de Loèche. Here is another postcard of an eighteenth-century watercolour painted by Abrahams Fischer of Berne. A huge barnlike structure is built over the baths, with light pouring in from a triangular opening under the eaves. Up to their shoulders in the baths are elaborately-dressed women wearing bonnets with ribbons on top; they appear to be seated, for one dimly sees the body of a child on his mother's lap, immersed to his waist, and sharing whatever is in the pitcher on the tray in front of them. A servant in livery, wearing a powdered wig, a long-tailed satin jacket, tight satin breeches and white stockings, is bringing a tray with a similar pitcher to set down before a group of waiting women. Three women play checkers, two are reading; a gentleman, dressed in black like Benjamin Franklin, with a shovel hat, is standing at the railing with two other fashionably-dressed gentlemen and a lady who seems to have stepped out of a portrait by Gainsborough, with a great burst of black ostrich plumes on the top of her hat like the plumes horses wear in Neapolitan funeral processions. And there are three dogs, lean with drooping ears, hunting dogs which have followed their masters into the baths, higher bred creatures than the mutts in the later photograph. There is even a bird cage with a bird in it, hanging on one of the great beams that support the roof, and a miniature garden on one of the platforms in the bath. The clock with Roman numerals on the far wall says 8.20.

Clearly the heyday of fashionable Loèche was in the eighteenth century; at least the watercolour is suffused with an elegance and light-hearted charm one does not see in the photograph. But we must remember the stiffness required by the long poses of early photographs. And I know from my mother's diaries that the baths, which look so solemn in the photograph, had their hilarious moments. I recall her account of the ladies' hysteria when one of them touched a submerged object and thought it was a fish, the intrepid gentleman who dove in and retrieved a piece of sodden cardboard, and the general hilarity afterwards. Perhaps nothing much had changed, did not change until much later when the conventions that had made Loèche resemble the set for a musical comedy turned into wearisome decorum, unspiced by romance. Young people began to have more exciting things to do than to take the cures at Loèche and indulge in innocent flirtation. My mother, lonely there in 1953, must have felt that all the life had gone out of Loèche, not only because she was old but because the life she had known there was as extinct as some beautiful bird. It was bliss to be alive in the early 1900s (for her species) but now in 1953 she added Loèche to the list of dead joys. She had gone there to relive some of the old happiness and discovered that she felt further from her memories when she was there than when she was at home and could take them out of the safe places of her mind and look at them, far from the too-great contrast between Then and Now.

The Game of Flirtation

Go! tell the Human race that Woman's love
   is Sin, . . .
Forbid all Joy, & from her childhood
   shall the little female
Spread nets in every secret path.
                              William Blake, *Europe*

The six years between 1897 and 1903, when Margaret went with
Mama to Loèche-les-Bains for the first time, had given her plenty
of time to refine the art of flirtation. She was now living in the
agreeable limbo in which she gaily passed the time before marriage, for even in 1903, she knew that she was going to marry
Edward. The only problem, it seems, was to fall in love with him.
"Poor soul," she says about Edward in her 1903 diary, "he little
knows how his fate is being laid out." Her most intense flirta-
tions with other men were conducted over the entire period of
Edward's wooing (1898 to 1910) during summer holidays at places
of prescribed leisure; in particular, Chester, Nova Scotia, and
Loèche-les-Bains, each with a suitable background for romance—
sparkling days, moonlit nights, mountains or the sea. When Margaret was separated from her men-friends, letters flew between

them, which shook up the embers and kept the fire burning until the next face-to-face meeting. Margaret, so innocent and lively, with her genuine interest in other people and their lives, was like a Venus fly-trap for the lonely young gentlemen (unmarried, of course) who were vacationing in Loèche or had come to take the cure. James M. Gallatly, who never married, was an undergraduate at Magdalen College, Oxford, played varsity lacrosse, wrote songs and plays, above all possessed the necessary sweet saintliness of character and the wit to be a perfect friend, knew exactly the weight of attention he could put on Margaret without alarming or offending her. Their friendship was still alive in 1928 when they saw each other in London and Mr. Gallatly took the twins to the London Zoo. I still remember that day as one of the happiest of my life, when Mr. Gallatly, who looked like a tall bird with grey plumage, took us backstage, so to speak, and introduced us to the real Winnie-the-Pooh. We were allowed to hug her and to give her a little pot of honey, which she cleaned out with her long tongue in a matter of seconds.

Margaret's second friend was Ritchie Yeoman, a student at the University of Dalhousie, who was going to study for the ministry. The meeting place was Chester, Nova Scotia where Mama had bought an old house she called Wisteria. Like Mr. Gallatly, Ritchie was a friend for Margaret, and her disciple, too, for she had the moral power that virtuous women held then, and he looked to her for counsel. Even when she wrote telling him of her engagement, he showed, after a first flurry of bewildered hurt, no resentment but only regret and gratitude. "If I feel tonight more sick at heart than I have ever felt before, it is only because your dear letter was so like your old self, so kind and true." And at the end of this letter: "You have been far kinder to me than anyone else ever was, and I trust that you have, as I have, none but pleasant memories of our friendship." Margaret to Edward, January 28, 1910: "Oh, I've just had a letter from Ritchie, and I can't help having a heartache, not for myself but is it dreadful of me? for him,—for he wrote me the loveliest letter ever written, I believe." And in reply to Edward's answering letter of protest (I assume), she writes, "Poor Ritchie, I do like him, but I love you, so there's the difference. Now are you satisfied? I never saw such a man! Spoiled is no name for it!" And signs "Yours affectionately." How Margaret hated love's pressures! "I love you" was dragged out of her with a playful reproof to go with it. Poor yearning Edward!

It was possible then, when the rules were obeyed, for a man and a woman to be good friends. Margaret kept on writing to Ritchie, and just before her marriage she sent him a tie she had knitted for him. In 1913, three years after Margaret's marriage, Ritchie writes from Halifax, "I'd like to get down to Chester to see you all. As long as your Mother is there, it will be all right . . . . *She* will walk around the lake with me, and she never says I am not romantic. She knows Better." Still very gently playful, certain that he will not be reproved. For reproof is an important part of Margaret's arsenal, the ability to make each of her suitors say, "What have I done to offend you?" Part of love, the feeling of anxiety and guilt. Edward, too, was called to order. "Indeed I don't mind what you write," says Margaret, January 29, 1910. "You are the one who might mind, because I scold you so if I don't approve." It is always the fault of the lover. "I suppose that you are furiously angry at something that I have said," says Ritchie, November 9, 1909, "but won't you please tell me what it was? Then I'll apologize and you can go on writing to me." Margaret's young men took for granted that she had the right to scold, but her flashes of anger were sometimes as unexpected as lightning bolts in a clear sky. You could offend her in such unexpected ways! It was forbidden to say that you were bored, it was forbidden to say that someone was stupid (she claimed never to have known a stupid person); it was a serious crime, if you were out walking with her, to light a cigarette in the street. The young men went along abjectly with Margaret's notions of proper behaviour—to please her, of course, because she could be so irresistibly charming and attentive to them.

Sometimes, though, in letters in which ordinary conversational pinpricks turn to the wounds made by poison-tipped arrows, Margaret went too far. The third packet of letters is from Frank C. Wheelwright, who was in business in Bradford, England, who was brilliant and delicately ferocious. When he wrote Margaret he turned on his mind and let it spill out ideas, let his sentences run together, wrote an average of twelve pages on both sides of almost transparent paper, a more subtle and just as illegible version of the crossed handwriting people went in for in those days. I look at these letters and groan, unwilling to decipher them, refusing at times, yet they teach me how ladies and gentlemen played the flirtation game—in this case, in playful seriousness. It seems to me that Mr. Wheelwright got closer and closer to the edge of madness; his handwriting began by being legible with the words neatly spaced, and ended in scrawls of incoherence when the words came out too fast to give them order. He was too clever for Margaret and showed it in a slightly ungentlemanly way (the others never did this) by teasing her ("How funny that girls should attach so much importance to dress!"), by not letting her make him feel guilty, by laughing lightly at her reproofs: "And now in a moment of ennui on Easter Monday (this is not a promising beginning, I continue, I believe my ennui, or some bad trait of that sort brought down your reproof once)." It was not an apology, for he went on teasing: "So I made you a little cross, a thrill of 'crossness', with my cold-blooded remarks." Margaret seemed to have the idea that displays of "crossness" were one way to a man's heart, that she could tame even Mr. Wheelwright. "If you only knew what a vein of melancholy runs through me, " he says, "and how refreshing I find 'nonsense' you would not be 'wrought up and in a temper' & you would believe that after all it was I myself." One of Margaret's moral exercises was to tell her suitor that he was not being true to himself. The more humble ones agreed, but not Mr. Wheelwright. He would have much preferred to make her see him as he really was, for he saw her as *she* was: naive, a little frivolous in spite of her serious pursuits; he saw her small tyrannies as artificial, one of the many artifices that young women learned. He liked her when she was simple and nice.

There was something dangerous about Mr. Wheelwright and his piercing intelligence. If Margaret had married him he would have tortured her with his teasing tongue and smothered her in his melancholy. I wish I could see the two letters she wrote him that brought out the cat-person, simultaneously purring and lashing his tail in his letter of September 24, 1906. He had seen Margaret off on the train in Munich on September 11th and had given her a present of a box of red notepaper edged with white. Of this, Margaret says in her diary, "My but for once I was really frightened. The paper is red!!!!" Mr. Wheelwright had unwittingly committed a breach of etiquette that scandalized Margaret and she fired off two letters that gave him an entirely new and unpleasant view of her character. "This is to be a tête-a-tête," he writes September 24th, "and the question whatever made the child (for child she was, petulant and naughty, too) write the two letters in that way?" After getting it, Margaret notes in her diary, "Letter from

Mr. Wheelwright, who intended nothing by the red paper." She shows no remorse for having behaved like a "petulant and naughty child."

It was characteristic of Margaret always to be sure of the moral rightness of her anger. This time she had gone too far, but, as usual, she was forgiven, and I have the impression that except in this instance, when Margaret wounded his gentleman's amour-propre, Mr. Wheelwright relished her anger because he could make a joke of it. "You allow a jacket to be directoire but nothing else (Mama perhaps excepted)," he says in 1906. Margaret's anger did not work with Mr. Wheelwright as it did with the others who had to coax her back to "niceness." Though he fell in love with her, he could not be broken in; it was he who wanted to do the breaking-in, and in a subtle way, less loving than Edward's would be, he tried to educate her. He compares his seriousness with her habit of filling every day with a jumble of serious and non-serious busyness: "What books I've read, and since leaving school, I seem to have 'swotted' more than ever. . . . You do the same, don't you? Literature, French, German, partly because you have the taste, & partly to fill your time, you will excuse the egotism if I say, that I have the habit of work like the prisoner of Chillon, perhaps I should 'regain my freedom with a sigh.'" He wanted to find something like his own concentrated passion for books in Margaret and couldn't, was disappointed by her not quite paying attention to him. "You don't answer my letters, you reply to them," he says in his last letter to her. Was he replying to hers? One feels a plea in Mr. Wheelwright's letters and later in Edward's letters, "Please listen to what I'm saying and *answer*," for Margaret slid away from the subject and was impossible to pin down. Yet she was renowned as a listener. She listened both because it was part of being a lady and from a desire to give helpful advice. Listening to men could be a source of power, though it was more passive than attention that generated answers. It was this attention that Mr. Wheelwright was willing to give and asked in exchange. He wanted to understand the mystery of women, the uses of their inattention and inexplicable tantrums. "The only way would be to hold you tight the tighter the better & allow one's curiosity full play to see what would come of it," he says. Margaret's elusiveness was perfected by the flirtation-game; she hid behind her letters as women hid behind fans.

With each of Margaret's suitors the relationship was different, yet all were bounded by the same rules, as a canoe on a river is bounded by the riverbanks. It glides over calm shallow water; Margaret looks down, sees the pale forms of rocks just below the surface and feels a giddy joy; she is steering, enjoys heading into whirlpools with their little thrill of fear. (Mr. Wheelwright in 1907: "I can't imagine your doing housework, you don't seem like that, rather, sitting in the stern of the boat steering whilst a man made it go.") It is a trial run for marriage, but how different marriage will be, out in the open sea. Sometimes power changes hands, sometimes not. Above all, all those things that seem, in the period of courtship, so deliciously "feminine"—capriciousness, irrationality mingled with playful tenderness—begin to irritate and frustrate the man who has almost become "feminine" himself in his effort to understand his beloved. I can imagine Mr. Wheelwright, if he had married Margaret, saying (perhaps when the honeymoon was over), "Now, my dear, we're going to be *serious.*" And Margaret's little shiver of apprehension. How lucky for all of us that she chose for us not to be the children of Mr. Wheelwright, but of Edward, who held her tight but gently, patiently, and had no cruelty in his nature.

The upbringing of upper-class girls was designed to keep them so busy that they would not have time to question the vocabulary of seriousness. They were taught that marriage was serious, fidelity was serious, to go to church and to obey the Ten Commandments was serious. Books, theatre, opera, museums, these were serious. But so were balls, the buying of a Paris hat, luncheons and tea parties and the leaving of cards. The problem was even to imagine a hierarchy of serious things, to unmask, so to speak, the things that didn't matter. Mr. Wheelwright tried with teasing, "I remember now the plan of your life, so much 'going down to town' or up forget which, so many dances each winter, for how many? So much bridge & coming to Europe, et puis! pour ce qui est de l'avenir!" For Margaret was already in her twenties and life went on as giddily as ever. L'avenir was going to be more of the same. Mr. Wheelwright was in his early forties, Mr. Gallatly and Ritchie Yeoman were still undergraduates. They went to dances themselves; they delighted in women's hats. They were not "serious" any more than Margaret was, or rather they were serious in the same way. Whether in letters or in real ife their relation with Margaret was the same—a harmonious friendship of equals, with the acknowledged moral superiority of Margaret balanced by their greater experience of life. Yet even Mr. Wheelwright could say, "It is such a change after years of living intimately with men to seek a woman's criticism." He who did not accept it, sought it, perhaps to study a woman's soul rather than his own. He had found life to be essentially melancholy and boring ("business, mutton chop, beer, books & smoking, long walks on Sunday in the delicious country & having supper with married people") and his correspondence with Margaret, her unprovoked attacks which he countered like a skillful fencer, were an unexpected reprieve.

Any attempt by the suitor to delve, as both Mr. Wheelwright and Edward delved below the level that Margaret's ego could tolerate—resulted in disharmony. One of the objects of a young woman's education was to clothe her in the feminine armour that baffled all men's efforts to get at her, to make her serious. It was dangerous to stir up the conventional censures just below her surface, patriarchal ideas which had been taught along with female graces. Strange that her defences had been given to her by men, shaped to suit her and turned against them. They could not teach their idea of freedom to someone who had learnt her lesson by heart: a lady is this, a gentleman is that. A lady does not think about herself, a gentleman does not try to find out who she is (though the lady may pass judgement on who the gentleman is!). Margaret had learned a set of answers to life's problems that worked as long as the questions remained the same. They were good serviceable answers, tested by generations of "good" people and spiced with Margaret's natural good sense. But try changing the question to something she did not want to think about and she would panic; disgust, indignation, all those useful evasions of the truth were waiting to be used and seemed as truthful to her as a considered answer to the dreadful thing she could not look at.

Mr. Wheelwright, Mr. Gallatly, Ritchie and Edward all became more "feminine" while they were wooing Margaret than they ever would be again in their lives. Like bowerbirds. For male bowerbirds, when they decorate the bower with bottlecaps, blue buttons, flowers and feathers, are trying to please not themselves but *her*. Courtship is a kind of mimesis or empathy with the female creature, bird or human being, and her predilection for decoration, dancing and singing. Among human beings the roles are reversed with marriage; the woman then builds the bower while the man, who has merely pretended, during courtship, to share her interests, looks on.

Margaret was alarmed more than once when in spite of her skill she could not prevent her suitors from suffering. Suffering was not part of the game; it was too real, scared her and made her feel guilty. "You frighten me when you talk about burning letters!" she writes to Ritchie. "Was it really as bad as all that?" It is on the eve of her engagement to Edward, December 15, 1909, but she does not mention this to Ritchie. "You evidently are a very literal person," she says, "and think everything out thoroughly if you feel so strongly on the subject of 'My dear.' I am afraid up to this time I have taken those words too lightly, in fact I demand them at the beginning of all letters. Note, however, that after due deliberation I address you as 'My dear' simply because I can't help it, because you are one. Perhaps I should just say 'Dear Mr. Y . . . ' By this time you have discovered just what a horrid person I am about not writing, but please don't take it so hard, it worries me. At this very minute, for instance, I should be putting flowers in vases & hunting for dust, as we are going to have a dinner but you see what I am doing instead & you will have to take the consequences if there is dust and no flowers! . . . As usual I am shaking with fright, I wish you were here to hearten me up though I'm afraid our program-less dances wouldn't suit you & I'm sure yours with programs wouldn't suit me. I like people coming up a good many times of the evening for a dance here and half a dance there. You must be sure to tell me how the dances that you're going to come off. Your Exams must be over by now, well over I hope." (She had forgotten that Ritchie had told her the results of his exams a month before.)

It should be noted that when Margaret talks about addressing Ritchie as "my dear," she means "my dear Ritchie." And Ritchie, with one exception, always addresses Margaret as "my dear Miss Wister" until, upon her marriage, she becomes "My dear Mrs. Meigs." The exception is his letter of September 19, 1909, when he begins boldly, "My dear Margaret." "I must really refuse to call you 'Miss Wister' any longer," he says, "but please don't sit on me the way you did on Murray Watts. You and he were never great chums, were you?" He signs this letter "Ever yours, Ritchie." Evidently Margaret sat on him, for in his next letter he is back to "My dear Miss Wister" and "Yours sincerely, Ritchie

Yeoman." Margaret called Ritchie by his first name but this did not give Ritchie the same right. During the time of courtship a gentleman did not have the right to use a lady's first name unless he made it clear that he intended to propose marriage. In the exchange of letters, gears were shifted, from low ("my dear Miss Wister") to high ("dear Margaret"). Thus Margaret writes on August 23, 1905 (five years before her marriage!): "Had a letter from EBM beginning 'Dear Margaret!' So the die is cast." She herself had changed gears from high to low in 1902; before that she referred to Edward in her diaries as "Edward," "Edward Meigs," or "EBM." Suddenly, on the eve of his visit to her in Chester, N.S., she begins to call him "Mr. Meigs."

Ritchie must have thought that he would please Margaret by wanting to be closer to her, but without knowing it, he had stepped into Edward's domain. Perhaps a sharp reaction to any breach of a lady's rules of conduct was the only way she could remain "virtuous"; the lady lion-tamer, after all, has to be handy with her whip. And in the animal world, a male insect is routed and sometimes eaten alive if the female isn't in the mood to accept him. Only Mr. Wheelwright had the temerity to break Margaret's rules; on one occasion, to attempt to kiss her (this backfired) and on another to address her as "My dear." Anger had given him the right, and in the face of it, Margaret became meek and mild and placated him by sending him a copy of *The Rubaiyat*.

Margaret was twenty-seven years old when she wrote her hasty note to Ritchie. The material of it is the frivolous material at the top of her mind—dances, dust and flowers, anything to distract Ritchie, who was suffering. Later she would explain and Ritchie would forgive her. She liked to keep her suitors as friends, but liked, too, to play with fire. An element of flirtation is the woman's indifference to the pain she inflicts, or perhaps the pleasure she takes in it, for she takes it as a compliment; she can judge her power by his hurt. Flirtation gives the right to hurt, humbly acknowledged by all except Mr. Wheelwright. "Her imperiousness is making us a little meditative, is it not? We wonder if she will be the loyal companion of some man (she behaves in a very daughterly way to Mama & that is a good sign, been well brought up)," the cat-person says. Mr. Wheelwright's patience had indeed been sorely tried if he questioned Margaret's ability to be a perfect (i.e. loyal) wife. But she knew how to make amends, or to try, though Mr. Wheelwright was not going to let her off the hook so easily: "The Rubaiyat from one who can stamp and 'lay down the law'," he observes. The Rubaiyat for Mr. Wheelwright and a knitted tie for "poor Ritchie." Perhaps Margaret had learned the art of laying down the law from her sharp-eyed and censorious Mama and exercised it impartially in order to get even. Ritchie, Mr. Gallatly, Edward (I except Mr. Wheelwright) and her children, in our long sharing of our lives with hers, all submitted to her calls to order.

I see now (as Mr. Wheelwright had seen) that the calls to order were replies and not answers, reactions before Margaret gave herself time to think. Her replies came from Mama and Papa, and her answers from herself. All her young men valued her moral seriousness; all of them went to church with her and discussed the texts and sermons. "Please remember what I said about that text in the hymn-book," says Ritchie in September 1909. "We have gone to church together so often and you always had such a religious influence on me that I thought it rather appropriate." Margaret impersonated the ideal of the perfect woman, just frivolous enough to throw her moral seriousness into high relief. "Please give me some more talk about romance," says Ritchie, "or any other moralizing that you feel in the mood for, concerning anything from Purgatory to football . . . I believe in Purgatory, you know." Margaret's "moralizing" touched all subjects, including dusting, putting flowers in vases and the question of programless versus programmed dances. It was part of the art of being a lady, to get gracefully from football to Purgatory in a single sentence.

So with kindly evasiveness, Margaret tries to comfort Ritchie and keep him as a friend, for inexorable custom forbids her to tell him she is engaged until the announcement is official. Only then, when the fun and flirting of courtship have come to an end, is she able truly to imagine her rejected suitor's pain. "I can't help having a heartache." Poor Ritchie, poor Mr. Gallatly, poor Mr. Wheelwright, perhaps all doomed to a melancholy lifetime of mutton chops, beer and talking to married couples.

Mr. Gallatly

Margaret's Diary, Loèche-les-Bains, 1903

August 5: Only 3 days here and now I feel so at home and
not a bit strange. This morning I took my first bath in the big
basin, eleven ladies there were and we all breakfasted in the
water on little floating trays. It wasn't so funny to take one's
own breakfast as to see the other people breakfasting with
just their heads sticking out.

August 10: Rained most of the day. . . . Heard music at the
Kursaal. My friend Le Comte de Lapraderie who sits next at
table is a terror, the things he says beginning with the
"pantalons". The first night of our acquaintance tonight he
was talking about courtesans and asking me if I knew what
the word meant and I said no. At the end of dinner he asked
the gentleman opposite to translate, so that I had to say I did
know what it meant.

August 23: A sort of horrid indiscriminate day. Perhaps it is
the dance last night that makes me feel out of gear. Twice to
Church and then this evening what was I weak enough to do
but play cards and for money too, and worst of all I won. I

feel as if it was the worst thing I ever did.

August 24: Last night in my state I quite forgot to mention a letter from Edward Meigs, a most amusing description of Naragansett.

Loèche-les-Bains, 1904

July 12: Today the "monde" is actually arriving and the promenade was filled! Such an unusual occurrence in my experience of Loèche-les-Bains. There may be people here! . . . Mr. Gallatly, the young Englishman is rather nice, though of course upper middle class.

July 15: Mama and I rather fell out this afternoon and I am afraid it's going to happen often . . . To the Kursaal and Mr. Gallatly is so interesting. He knows such a lot about music and is trying to teach me to distinguish the different instruments. It is fearfully stupid how absolutely nothing I know about music.

July 19: Walked on Kursaal. Mama and I joined by Mr. Gallatly. . . . Then again to watch the haymakers . . . also the aforementioned gentleman of the party, who is quite the most entertaining and interesting and unget-tired of fellow I ever met. And laugh, we simply behave like two children. Today a second poem arrived with my hat as a subject. Am so stiff I can hardly go up and downstairs from our stroll on the Gemmi.

July 20: This afternoon went on a photographic expedition with Mr. Gallatly through the village. We took three pictures and the rest of the time sat and talked and he told me the story of his life. If you only have an afternoon it generally happens and then we had a disagreement when he asked me not to mention what he'd said. My feelings were really hurt. Is it complimentary or otherwise to have men tell you of the other girls they love? They will do it with me and I bear it as best I can. My poor blighted affections bear up however!!

July 23: . . . a walk to the ladders with Mr. Gallatly, who told me more. I wonder if anyone stops to notice that I never tell anything.

July 24: It is really getting to be funny how much Mr. Gallatly and I see of each other, particularly as we now sit by each other at meals and never stop talking for one minute except when he and Mama are in the bath and to make it funnier I'm not a bit the one! . . .

July 28: Promenade after lunch with Mr. Gallatly, who is a confiding soul. We do so much talking, at least I generally try not to, but was foolish enough to make a few remarks this afternoon. It never does to tell anybody anything.

July 30: As we were sitting on the balcony before lunch, who should step out, but Mr. Lewis. . . . He is really just the same only without a moustache and looked so much better-looking in dinner clothes. . . . Tonight was the swell concert for the benefit of the orchestra and a dance. Have some lovely flowers and oh how beautifully Mr. Lewis dances.

July 31: Mr. Lewis told me this morning that he had become a Roman Catholic and that was a shock, since then it has all been a strain. And now he says he is coming with us to Pontresina! I daren't tell Mama and I have carefully avoided every shaky subject, but give me my walks with Mr. Gallatly any day!

August 1: Mr. Lewis left this morning and let us hope that something will prevent his coming to Pontresina. This is Fête Day and the Grand Bain is decorated in red and white. Mr. G. and I went walking and the cat is out of the bag as to my age as it was bound to be sooner or later. Tonight were great goings on. Mama was awfully annoyed because I insisted on going into the Kursaal to see the rest of the goings on and we had to come home in the rain, but it wasn't much, but goodness gracious I think a person might have a little fun. Champagne at dinner and liqueur and coffee!

August 5: Played Halma with Mme Emedaz from lunch to

walking time and then Mr. Gallatly and I had milk at the
Paradis and climbed to the second waterfall's snow-cave and
I made a mistake, or I'm not quite sure whether it is or not,
but it serves him right at any rate. Played Halma this evening
too and am two games ahead, thank goodness. I never was
really glad, enchanted to beat anybody before, but she is
always so toploftical in everything.

August 6: Mama keeps telling me to stop worrying about Mr.
Gallatly so now I simply shan't mention him—if I can help it!

August 11: Walked with Mr. Gallatly. Still no letters. E.B.M.
would be most mightily surprised if he knew the excitement
he is causing! Poor soul, he little knows how his fate is being
laid out.

August 12: Now Mama has begun to fuss about Mr. Gallatly
and absolutely tells me that I mustn't lead him on! Imagine
leading any man on, let alone one that has been pouring out
his heart about someone else ever since you knew him. A
more absolutely harmless association with other interests
couldn't be imagined and if we are both amused by
it. . . . Poor fellow, he was discouraged today, as everything
has gone wrong, the leader wouldn't play his music, Madame
Tiers said his things were fearfully bad, the Dr. said he must
increase his baths and he got a horrid letter and now Mama
begins and I feel guilty.

August 14: Only a week more and then I must confess that I
shall be lost because six solid weeks spent in one man's
company must make an impression, despite a mutual interest
elsewhere. . . . Still no letter. Now I am having attacks of
indigestion.

August 17: Had a short walk with Mr. Gallatly and tea with Miss
Frick and two letters . . . one from E.B.M. eight pages long
saying nothing except to describe five dances.

August 18: Showery this morning, but cleared up enough
after lunch for a walk and returned for coffee, to which of
course Mama announced that she had not invited me! That is

Mama for you, if you don't come back she is lonely and if you do you are de trop. Unfortunately Miss Frick, whom she gets along beautifully with, is going away tomorrow and having tried to shove me off with everyone the whole summer, Mama now begins to sigh at the thought of my going off for a few days on Sunday.

August 20: A day spent in preparation for the great business of crossing the Gemmi tomorrow, which makes my heart rather beat at the prospect, expecially if you could see the faces of these good people on hearing that Mr. Gallatly is going to take me. My heart almost stops and I feel like crying, but it's no business of these cats. They don't know the manners and customs of the Far East! The telephone message that we sent from the Torrentalp Hotel to set Mama's mind at rest was never delivered and that was the cause of all the fuss last night.

August 21: Actually this Sunday evening finds me at St. Beatenberg and now that the cats at Loèche are left behind everything goes beautifully. Mr. Gallatly went on in boat to Interlaken. . . . I enjoyed the whole day. It was an experience and awfully nice. I know we both liked it and I felt most uncommonly blue when we both said "Goodbye". I've enjoyed this whole summer and no doubt am very selfish.

August 27: Everyone was much surprised at our sudden departure and the remaining friends . . . turned out to bid us goodbye . . . 3 watchcharms,—a sled, bell and chamois from Mr. Gallatly, awfully attractive, and nice of him.

September 6: A letter from Mr. Gallatly in this evening's mail. Well, it was a good summer to be remembered, of no wasted opportunities! And most selfish, I admit, but one full to the brim.

Belfield, Germantown, 1904-1905

December 12: In a week Mr. Gallatly will be here and now

the problem is rising what on earth shall I do with him every moment as there must be something doing to give him a good idea of the proper strenuousness of America.

December 13: Sewed and my blue velvet Assembly dress is gradually being evolved and as far as the waist goes ought to be stunning. Of the skirt I don't know. My diction absolutely shows the effect of Henry James' "The Wings of the Dove". Am wracking my brain for things to turn up to do for Mr. G.

December 22: Mr. Gallatly is actually here and today has gone swimmingly. . . . We sleighed tonight. He makes a favorable enough impression fortunately.

December 23: Things are really going rather well. . . . Took Mr. Gallatly to town and deposited him in Lardner Howell's hands, who took him to the Rittenhouse Club and has put him up there. I think it is perfectly adorable of him. . . . Mr. G. seems to be enjoying himself.

December 26: This evening I had my first talk with Mr. Gallatly and we half approached our old selves at Loèche but not really.

December 28: Mr. Gallatly . . . took the 2:30 train to town and went through the Biological Department of the University with Edward Meigs. . . . Mr. Gallatly feels he's had a rather full day. Everyone likes him so much that it is perfectly delightful.

December 29: Anybody to get along amicably with Mama, I defy, especially when she insists upon treating your guests like the dirt under her feet. Fortunately we are not in the house much.

January 2, 1905: . . . Oh, it's good to be dancing again and all my old friends were angels and danced with me. Mr. Gallatly loved it, too, and I saw him about once. On second thoughts I won't give up society just yet.

January 3, 1905: A great note when you start to a dance and it's so slippery that the horse can't get there. Mr. Gallatly and I left here at 6:30 and the horse couldn't get up the Bala hill and started to slide backwards, so we had to come home.

January 5, 1905: Can't realize that Mr. Gallatly's visit to us is actually over and has gone without a hitch.

Two Letters from Mr. Gallatly

Magdalen College—Nov. 6, 1904
Dear Miss Wister,
   Your letter arrived this morning for which many many thanks. I was glad to get it and so far from deploring its length, I should have been glad to double it. . . .
   It gave me quite a shock to find that the lady in the photograph was not you but your sister Mrs. Starr. The resemblance is almost horrible. I felt that I could swear to the hat, not speaking of features and pose. Do you all dress alike? or was the resemblance of the hat merely accidental? Anyhow it was bewilderingly like one of your hats—not *the* hat—at Loèche—that had little roses and things crawling round the brim. I have reason to believe the prevailing color impression to have been Cambridge blue but should not like to swear to it.
   By the way I hope *the* hat has not been 'broken up' yet and 'sold for firewood' or whatever is the equivalent period to a hat. It was an essentially feminine hat—never twice the same, whiles drooping in dank despondence, whiles fair preening itself with perky self satisfaction. It was like a drama in one act that hat. . . .
   I seem to remember your hats with some accuracy but cannot decide whether it is a compliment to you or myself. . . .
   It was great day on the Gemmi wasn't it? I remember it so well, from one man on the ascent whom we dodged with such skill, to the unpleasant landing place and disgusting funiculaire that closed our day.
   I had such a dull time the rest of my stay in Switzerland—a bad place, worse hotel, worst weather, and people who had

never learnt how to enjoy themselves. A formidable combination! I think I missed the daily walks and conversations and those inspiring meals. Take it by and large I should fancy we covered the majority of subjects for conversation during the six weeks. In spite of which I remain a regular Oliver Twist.

January 26, 1905

I can never tell you what a good time I had with you—you must just try to take it as said. I never believed that any family could be so fascinating, or 'come up to sample' in such a surprising way.

And you were about as good to me as it is possible to imagine, this side of Eternity, and have consequently implanted in me a most lively dissatisfaction of my ordinary existence. I was pleased too to see as much as I did of you yourself, to confirm beliefs. I always hesitate at including a new friend, but for some unearthly reason the hesitation disappeared in your case. So that I was a little nervous as once upon a time I made a bad mistake. I will write you again from shore.

Mr. Wheelwright

Margaret's Loèche-les-Bains Diary, 1905

July 17: . . . It just came over me that Mr. Gallatly wouldn't be back this summer and sure enough there was a letter on my return saying that he was going to start in with his newspaper work in a few days. To think that I won't see Mr. Gallatly again this summer perhaps not for years is too hard.

July 27: A letter from E.B.M. who is going to have a salary of $500.00 for his work at the University next winter. I am so glad to hear it.

July 31: Had a letter from Mr. Gallatly. He is not coming out. Well, I may never see Mr. Gallatly again—but I certainly did enjoy last summer and at the time, too, but I feel him as the near good friend slipping away.

August 11: Talked to my friends Mr. Wheelwright and Mr. French. I like them.

August 13: This evening down the Promenade, Mr. French and Mr. Wheelwright with us. I do like those two men.

August 14: After lunch we climbed still higher and Mr. Wheelwright and I went to a very hard grassy ascent, part way up he presented me with the seal off his watch.

August 15: Have spent a delightful day, mostly in Mr. Wheelwright's company and an awfully nice man he is. I imagine the best kind of friend . . .

August 16: After lunch 12:30 went for a walk down the Bois de Cythère with Mr. Wheelwright from which we returned at 4:30. Numerous stops I admit as it rained off and on and we stayed under trees. He made me such a nice ring for my little finger out of links from his watch-chain. I never knew a man talk more about matrimony, he seems frightfully afraid of it. Every now and then I find myself on ticklish ground but I do try to steer clear, but it does begin to worry me. Perhaps it is just as well that we leave as I wouldn't have the man misunderstand my feelings. I like him quite too much for that. But I haven't anything on my conscience, I don't think.

August 22: Had an angel postcard from Mr. Wheelwright saying he missed me dreadfully. Angel man and letter from Bessie.

August 26: Spent most of the morning composing a letter to Mr. Wheelwright and finished one at last and mailed it, but I am afraid it was not all that it should be, as now I am afraid it was too squelching for the circumstances and that I took too much upon myself. Still I did not feel as if I ought to give even the slightest encouragement, as it would only make it harder for the poor man in the end. (Now of course I am simply dying for another letter—such is the perversity of human nature and wish the other letter hadn't been written. But my conscience says it was right.)

Loèche-les-Bains, 1906

August 18: We haven't had any home news for days, but this evening I had a letter from Mr. Wheelwright and imagine he is going to be in Munich!

September 5, 1906—Munich: . . . Then we came back and Mr. Wheelwright came and we went . . . to the Maximilineum, a place full of huge historical paintings. I disliked it intensely. He lunched with us and we found him the same but nicer. After lunch we took the same walk in the park and returned a much fooled and rather at ease person as I thought there would be something doing, but there wasn't. His conversation ran on wives but I wasn't fooled that time.

September 6: Went out walking with Mr. W. Poor man I felt sorry for him, he hovered about the subject like a moth round a flame, but I didn't give him the slightest encouragement, but he told me in a hundred different ways and yet he was afraid to come right out with it. He asked if he should come back on Monday, but I told him he would have to decide that for himself.

September 7: Must admit I half expected a letter from Mr. W. today.

September 8: No letter from Mr. W. perhaps it is a holiday.

September 9: No letter.

September 10: He came and seemed to have no idea of not coming. . . . Mama came home while Mr. W. and I wandered about a half rainy day. He now describes us as a "laughing friendship", but as he came very near to kissing me once and tried another time I'm not so sure, except that he hasn't told me he's in love, but plainly that he can't marry. So things have turned out very well.

September 11—Salzburg: A feeling of blaseness stole o'er me as I walked through it, as Mr. Wheelwright said "I've seen so many places and they're all alike . . . " Mr. W. came to see us off on the train and gave me a box of writing paper as a parting present. Said that when he was with me he could not think of what he wanted to say, but when I had gone he thought furiously, but decided that he had gone away unsatisfied on one particular, but he wouldn't have liked me any the better if he had got it.

September 25: No letter from Mr. Wheelwright.

September 28: Letter from Mr. Wheelwright.

Letters from Mr. Wheelwright

Loèche-les-Bains—August 31, 1905

The next best thing to getting a letter from you . . . is writing to you, 'you know I like you' and 'you have braced me up,' 'my, we will write lovely (substantive?) letters to each other' (all the above with comprehensive and expressive waves of the hands) . . . The first part of your letter, descriptive does not provoke any remarks except that in one little thing you were not true to yourself, you diagnosed me so well, it did me good to tell me that what I once said (forget what it was) 'did not ring true' and also that there was a phrase that I feared, both true but how did you know?

Saturday and Sunday last the guests at the Hôtel des Alpes became smaller by degrees and beautifully less, the attendance at Church on Sunday (16 morning, 4 afternoon, not including me) was fairly good. I think we were wishing to leave too, no nice and novel counsellor for me, and only the remembrances and the lengthening distance. Monday we left, one o'clock, the previous evening had played much billiards until 11:45 p.m. with an amusing young Swiss . . . whopped him too! alas how quickly one deteriorates without you. . . . When our letters are edited we must have a name for them in imitation of the 'Letters of a man in the making to his Sister', no! to Miss Wister (that rhymes with 'sister') but I don't like it, must be more interesting, we'll put it in acrostic. The first two letters of your name, the first initial of mine and seek the vowel in the end, or in the contrary way, you have three fourths in your name and I, the other.

December 18, 1905

That the year just beginning may be one of real happiness, of continued satisfaction to you, Mrs. Wister and yours is the hearty wish of your preux chevalier, Platonic friend, quondam pupil, that's me (regardless of grammar) . . . I should like to have seen you in the temper you write of, why can't such things be got up for some object, amusement, charity, etc. it would read so well, 'Miss Wister in her ancient part of a Temper' followed (by request) by 'The Bored State' (which of the U.S. is that?) . . . Am glad you had such an interesting jolly time electioneering. [See Margaret's speech which follows.] 'Philadelphia Corrupt and Contented' is distinctly good. It was time something was done, all our local rags had accounts (short ones) of Philadelphia depravity, am glad that you, (I mean the women) have made the millennium possible, it shall be known in the future as Philadelphia, Pleased and Policed. As you surmise, women play some part in politics, mostly local, not really successfully, if there can be any success in what has been defined as 'the science of the second best'. Evidently you were deeply interested in it, the account you give is so racy, you ought to write for the Philadelphia Ledger, I'm sure that journal wants stirring up, and you were Secretary, hola! vive la Secrétaire! et la Présidente et Philadelphia même! the earth still seems to be on its axis and the Gulf Stream warms us in the North! Did you ask the individuals their political creed (if any) or did you simply pin a button on and leave him a partisan, I don't know whether it would not be that really and if they did not want to be of the same City Party, what lies they would have to tell, what a shame to risk their souls after previously sticking pins into their bodies, I thought the modes of the Inquisition were long past. . . . I told you how I liked your photo, didn't I? It is really good, and the position so nice, were you laying the law down to some poor wretch? No, it's the tout ensemble that I like. Four months today since you left Loèche, wish (weather permitting) I were walking with someone in the Bois de Cythère . . . I hope all this arrives safely . . . and that the little chain (long enough to cross the Atlantic) will fit one of your fingers, they are so small, it is a simple thing but will give you pleasure I hope, will reach you just at the beginning of the new year, perhaps it will be a talisman, the quality is said to be good, and the wishes that accompany it are warm.

I am not really satisfied about the chain, it is a little clumsy and the small rings, to join it if you like, are not the same quality, am sending it registered for the sake of the recipient, its actual value scarcely calls for the precaution, neither is it ceremoniously enclosed in a velvet lined box, if it gives real, real, real pleasure then I am glad too . . .

Margaret Wister's diary, January 2, 1906: This morning received a registered letter of 12 pages from Mr. Wheelwright with a heavy gold chain ring enclosed, it is a trifle too massive to wear and so I have hung it on my watch chain. So I needn't have bestowed such hard words on his unoffending head.

Margaret's notes for speech about women's suffrage—1906: You'll wonder why I'm out talking for the City Party and I'll tell you why. I've never had a chance to do anything for my country or my state or my city till the other night & the chance came. A lady called me up on the telephone and asked if I'd work for the City Party and right off I said I could. You see we women haven't got a vote, you men are so used to it that you don't know what it is for a woman to have no say and to have to stand quiet and take bad government and not be able to do anything to change it. And when the suggestion came that the women could do something for the election they all caught on, so that's how I happen to be speaking to you tonight for the time has come when we can all do something for our country and state and city and we've all got to lend a hand. Do we want to sit by with bound hands while people from all over the world point the finger of scorn at us & say, Oh you're from Philadelphia, corrupt and contented. Why this summer I met a gentleman who said, "Philadelphia, oh that's the city where the people pay the taxes and the politicians spend them." But now we've got a chance to change all that & it isn't a remote chance either, we've got the power in the hollow of our hand to have good government and decent politics if we only use it at the polls. Who is such a careless businessman that he doesn't want to get what he pays for? You know the story, don't you, of the man who was asked what was the difference between a dozen lemons and an elephant and he said he didn't know. The other fellow said, "well, you'd be a good one to send to the store for a dozen lemons," and that's the way with the men who are voting for the gang, they don't know the difference between a dozen lemons & an elephant, they don't know enough to get what they pay for. They don't want schools and clean streets & order, they want to pay their taxes and get nothing for them. Is there a man among you if he was walking down Market Street and was buying some apples . . . Side by side were two men, the man he had generally dealt with and another. And suppose your friend's apples were rotten and the other fellow's good. Wouldn't you say, "Well, my friend, your fruit's too rotten today. I don't want any of it, I'll just have a try at this man's apples." You wouldn't be afraid of hurting his feelings, would you? and you needn't be afraid of hurting the Gang's feelings either, for in the first place its fruit is too rotten anyway and besides it never had any feelings, so try the good fellow with good fruit this time & see what he can do for you and vote the City Party ticket.

September 24, 1906—Frank Wheelwright to Margaret Wister
My dear,
    This is to be a tête-a-tête and the question, whatever made the child (for child she was petulant and naughty too) write the two letters in that way? We remember, don't we? the lovable girl at the Munich station, brown eyes, brown hair over her temples and such a pleasant expression under a very becoming hat, before that we had seen the nice girl as an admirable woman in the scene on the stairs when she said No Sir! Perhaps a likeness might be traced to the Dana Gibson picture as she sat one day on a seat in the Englicher Garten with Nobody looking at her gently, and now she does not write her name, nor Nobody's either, in fact he frankly asks why writing paper republican red or imperial purple nicely edged with white should be the cause. Of course it was different when he was smoking a cigarette in the street when the girl's opinion had just been expressed against such a proceeding, but it was not his fault that the shopkeeper had no writing paper with a monogram and she'd said she liked red, which for replying to girls' invitations or notes is a nice warm color a woman's weapon, but surely an unworthy one, as we remember her she did not seem cruel, no! at heart a gentle maid and he? And 'he' dare not accuse himself of 'deep

66

thought' lest the vanity should be withdrawn by the gods, and 'she ' after the first white heat had worn off (only as deep as the white edging of the notepaper, hoffentlich).

It was not a good practical joke, there is no such thing and the accused hopes to be always guiltless of that. And at school, she got the testimony of all as being the most popular and could not accept the opinion that she was a man's girl rather that a girl's girl. The only remark anent the republican paper was 'hochroth' of course in their German way it sounds like 'Hochzeit' "she could not describe her feelings". So no more little gifts must be offered. A Münchener 'Kindle', a spoon aus München, not even a quill in a case stolen from an hotel in Brussels, it's pointed and perhaps she'd hurt the giver. Are we tired of talking about her? Oh! another thing, she does not like Salzburg because it rained there (entre nous, the same reason would apply to the whole Earth) but she liked the Velasquez children and 'could have kissed them' we shan't know what to make of her, you and I, for instance, he the culprit took all the care he could to post two letters confided to him and 'that dear porter never did mail the letter'. She once made a little error in addressing a letter, 'Amourland', instead of Ammerland! it was Ammergam, however it reached the addressee, and amongst other things that have crossed his mind, he ought to have insisted, yes Madam insisted on her pronouncing his name three times, although a little distasteful to her, she has a jolly name and it shades into the same meaning as his.

Nobody does not like this style of communication and would she mean the tantalising nice things which must be true things from her or of no value? And a red sunset is a sign of fine weather, fine always we hope for the girl and for the man—what he deserves. What a curious discussion we have got into and all on account of our Dosia, Daisy, Marguerite, her imperiousness is making us a little meditative, is it not? We wonder if she will be the loyal companion of some man (she behaves in a very daughterly way to Mama and that is a good sign in the child, been well brought up) or will he be her slave (vide Daily Telegraph, Grumbling Husbands).

When our child has again grown into the nice girl at Munich Station one who is afraid will venture to address her in the first person, (singular). And now the afraid one is back at business, that will keep and we hope will improve by keeping, also any details of return journey if not too tiresome.

January 2, 1909

. . . Last year was a long one, not unpleasant to me. . . . from time to time an anxiety for others, for the future, for the unknown (the unknown includes you, I'm not certain that I know what sort of girl you are yet, by the way I began by saying what girls are, so you must write and tell me if you are a good girl now,—as children sent away into another room are asked, I heard the other day of a little girl who was banished to a drawing room her quietness led to the suspicion that she was in mischief and when someone was sent with the question, the reply was 'No! I am in misery', so little girls can feel deeply, although big ones can't).

. . . As I read your words about being lonely I wondered, and wonder is said to be the seed of knowledge, not that girls can ever be known . . . poor Margaret! had not a girl to talk to and had a lot of partners—men, peu de chose I admit, but there's nothing else . . . At this time of year I have to write to old and intimate friends and it does take it out of me, cards and things I can't be bothered with am getting crusty and feel the world is out of joint . . . We had severe weather between Christmas and the New Year, now it is just as mild, result with me a wretched cold in my head and feeling like that of the little boy who said 'I wish I were not I'.

Margaret and Ritchie

Imaginary Letter

Dearest Mother,

"Nulla dies sine linea (no day without a line)" says your five-year diary, a Christmas present in 1907. In fact, each day has room for five lines; you fill them faithfully in 1908 and 1909, then jump seven years to 1916 and end in Woods Hole on July 13th: "I really don't think I can bother with this old diary up here. There are so many nice people who I can see all the time, that I am quite bewildered." Perhaps that was the reason why you finally stopped writing diaries altogether; you had no time.

Those three years, 1908, 1909 and 1916, are like the stratified layers in a cliff face, except that the most recent layer is on the bottom. In spite of the invisible time-gap there is no change in your handwriting, yet 1916 records an entirely new life and new worlds to conquer. You are very far from the young woman who flirted with Ritchie Yeoman in 1908 and 1909. Ritchie's name is repeated like a series of fossilized footprints, traced on almost every summer day, doubled by the two years, one lying over the other. For instance: September 11, 1908: "Oh, such a moonlight paddle with Ritchie." September 11, 1909: "Ritchie home, such a surprise." September 13, 1908: "Feeling very low in my mind because I missed Ritchie at church this evening, but as Mr. Bent's text was, 'It is good for me that I have been in trouble', it comes in very nicely." (Did Mr. Bent mean your kind of trouble?) September 13, 1909: "Oh, Ritchie, Ritchie, this evening's conversation has driven from my head all thought of Halifax."

Your ignorance (deliberate?) of what was going on in Ritchie ended September 14, 1909 when he poured out his heart at last. "Ritchie to walk and I am hearing about it. Poor boy, why didn't he tell me all these things a little sooner. How was I to guess?" The next day you say, "Imagine me breaking anybody's heart. In a way it is encouraging as I never lifted a finger, but I don't want to hurt him, for he is a dear." Who can say if Ritchie, by being less of a dear, could have won you away from Edward? It was partly because of Edward's priority that you were unable to, or did not want to guess Ritchie's feelings. Ritchie was a dear because he was not "dangerous" like the mysterious "Mr. L." September 2, 1908: "He [Mr. L.] says I show the courage of ignorance in not considering him a dangerous man but life in his vicinity is precarious." September 6: "A slight scuffle. He did not succeed." Mr. L.'s failure made him angry, but on September 9th you write: "Two visits from my friend today. He seems to have recovered from the temper he was in and is still dangerous." The year 1908 was full of similar dangers, for on February 16th you speak of a certain C.C., who, you say, "really made me nervous. One word and he would mean business or else I'm mistaken."

"Danger" was the slightest hint of desire, and "one word" was the word both Mr. L. and C.C. hoped to hear, which you would never say, or it was one slight movement in body language. It was part of your maidenly pride never to lead a man on ("Imagine me leading a man on!" you say in 1906 after Mama's accusation), never to "lift a finger." Within that framework you felt free to see Ritchie every day, to go moonlight canoeing with him, to take obvious pleasure in his company and to write him regularly. There was obviously something safe and reassuring about your relationship with Ritchie that kept even Mama unalarmed, except when you got up at 5:30 A.M. to see him off on the train. "Mama thought I was quite mad," you say. "But I wanted to cheer him up a bit." This cheering-up, so kind and well-intentioned, must have made another big crack in Ritchie's heart, a crack as deep as his sense of loss.

Sometimes I wonder if Ritchie didn't berate himself for having been such a dear, for not having exhaled the slightest breath of the possessiveness that makes "being in love" so unmistakeable. Unlike C.C., Mr. Wheelwright and Mr. L., he was never "tempted to spoil a Platonic friendship." Of course he was right, for to "spoil" meant to lose forever. No wonder men in those days who observed the rules were so wary of the kind of direct statement or gesture that C.C. and Mr. L. made; no wonder that Mr. Wheelwright drew back from a real proposal of marriage, or rather, danced over the danger like someone skittering over hot embers. But for you, fire was your element. August 1, 1909: "I had to play with fire this morning Mr. L. again! Feel so cheerful."

In the course of growing up you had become a master strategist, so accomplished that playing with fire made you feel cheerful. Even at fourteen, you saw every dancing class as an occasion for triumph or despair, noting the numbers of boys—"I danced almost every dance with a boy," etc. In 1908 (you are twenty-six) you note on March 3rd: "Lay about in a low state of mind over the defection of a certain gentleman!" The day before you had been to dancing class: "the stickiest Class and I found it dull, probably because Dickie wasn't rushing me! I hate that!" January 12, 1909, a few days after you have seen Edward ("Oh, he is so nice, but Goodbye till Easter time"), you speak of a young man named "Hun"—"he is a dear. Tired of being virtuous." The next day: "Hun came this afternoon for an hour. Oh, those clear brown eyes." "Tired of being virtuous," i.e. of not indulging in the fun of flirting.

Flirting was to test yourself, to discover yourself through Them. They rushed you (or they didn't); they looked at you with "clear brown eyes." Without Them to define your charms, your beauty, you are not yourself, your spirits sink. What does it mean that a "certain gentleman" has defected? Are you losing your power? They have stolen your power. And Edward? Edward is there, patiently waiting. There is not the same urgent need to dazzle Edward, to see yourself in his reaction to you. By now you are sure of his reaction, different from Hun's, Dickie's, Ritchie's. He is your future, your safety. The flirtation-game will end with marriage; you will be defined not as a desirable woman (except by Edward), but as wife, mother, hostess, clubwoman. All the unconscious sensuality that went into flirting before your marriage will take another form, composed partly of fear—sex with its awful seriousness, so unlike the old dizzy fun of flirting.

Before your marriage your diaries are brimming with emotions which are released in tears, laughter, anger, released above all by art, a kind of safety basin which caught the overflow from life.

January 4, 1909: "Edward came and took me to see Julia Marlowe in 'The Goddess of Reason' and I suffered agonies from sobbing and hated it." (Hated having sobbed, of course.) Three days later you hear "Tristan und Isolde" and say, "I adore it. It floats me through space and keeps me rocking there." I remember your air of dreamy pleasure when you recounted a recurrent dream of floating downstairs without touching the bannister; it seemed to be the only dream you could remember.

Floating and rocking—you knew that sensation and liked it. If you had seen it as sexual, you would have condemned it to solitary confinement. You were alert to the slightest hint of sex; like spilled oil it had to be contained immediately. January 8, 1909: "Visit from T.C., an extraordinary person but if he isn't engaged to Amy *he ought to be*" (my emphasis). Quick! Quick! Bring out the booms of engagement and marriage, put them around Thornton and Amy, smother the fires that keep breaking out. Next year, observing Thornton and Amy blissfully stretched out in their deck chairs, you say, "Why not?" I've spoken already of your "why not?" born of your own happiness and the relaxation of your moral and physical being. It seemed a real metamorphosis—the dry cocoon of "why" hatching a living "why not?" Your heart beat hard in that year and a half before your marriage when you longed to follow your own instincts. But even then you felt that you had to submit them to review by inexorable judges of good taste and manners.

Do you remember when you went to hear Strauss' *Salome*? Your first reaction was to be stunned by its beauty. February 11, 1909: "To my mind there was nothing sacrilegious or immoral in it and it was the most wonderful opera that I have ever heard." And then They begin to get at you and to make you regret having liked *Salome*. They are explaining "the nasty parts of the libretto" which you haven't read. February 14, 1909: "Am worried now because I couldn't see anything wrong with 'Salome'. I suppose it shows how thoroughly depraved I am!" A week later, your friend Sally is "distant and detached, all on account of *Salome*." Then on

February 25th, you see Massenet's *Thaïs* and unload all your guilt feelings about *Salome*: "It was without exception the most unpleasant thing I ever saw and I never want to see it again." What a relief to be able to hate *Thaïs* and to be welcomed back in the fold again, for I'm sure that all of Them, including Sally, hated *Thaïs* too. Well, I hate *Them* for making you feel depraved and for hammering the lesson home: depravity is sex; it is the enjoyment of intense emotion, from the strange passions in *Salome* to the bliss of being in love.

And Ritchie? I've wandered far from Ritchie, dear boy, who held no threat even in a canoe drifting through the moonlight, gave no clue to his man's feelings even to Mama. Twenty-four years later, you repeated, perhaps word for word, the scolding Mama gave you when you returned with Mr. Gallatly from the Gemmi expedition. I thought of this and of your moonlight canoeing with Ritchie, startled to remember how angry you were when I got back late from a moonlight sail with another girl and a boy. Is it possible that you were angry not with us, but with the massed prohibitions and scoldings of your youth? At first you had felt dismay and outrage when innocence was seen as "depravity," and then gradually you began to accept Their definitions, to see them as good and useful, particularly when you had daughters of your own. But somehow these definitions were inseparable from your rage for they had to be enforced and this brought back memories of your smothered rebellion. Rage, a legacy from Mama, going back into the mist of patriarchal time.

At the time of your friendship with Ritchie your only responsibility was to keep something joyful and fragile inact in the bright setting of cloudless days, picnics "where we bathed and cooked and slept and sailed with the most glorious day and breeze." And evening picnics: "Jim and Rufus dug clams and tonight we ate Jim's porcupine. Oh, such a moonlight paddle with Ritchie. The air soft and warm, the moon hazy and Northern lights." What did Ritchie look like? Was he one of those old-fashioned boy-men, with a charming, loose-limbed body, a turned-up nose, brown eyes, straight hair, a disarming smile? He would go to Theological School, become a minister. He did not look like the angel Gabriel, as Edward did, or like a don-to-be (Mr. Gallatly) or a businessman (Mr. Wheelwright). He brought out the best in you; you suffered when he suffered. Ritchie reminds me of the bird of paradise which wears a blue feather shield on its breast. The tribesman who pursues it with a bow and arrow (like Eros) shoots it in order to make the shield the centrepiece of his headdress. The bird makes a gift of itself to the tribesman, it is said, who also takes into himself its valiant and lovely spirit. So Ritchie made a disinterested gift of himself, and you accepted the gift not as a trophy (you had plenty of those) but with appropriate sorrow at having had to kill something beautiful.

Ritchie's Letters

September 19,1909

I am sending you the new Hymn Book, in loving memory of a good many Sunday evenings last summer and this, and particularly of last Sunday night. Please excuse the hackneyed text that I put in it. You know that it is not used idly or in any profane way, for it comes from the bottom of my heart. . . . Think sometimes of old St. Stephen's and the good old Chester days. Bob says it was awfully good of you to come to see us off. But one expects you to do the nicest thing possible.

Ever yours, Ritchie

P.S. Sept 24, 1909—Please remember what I said about that text in the hymn book. We have gone to church together so often and you always had such a religious influence on me that I thought it rather appropriate.

October 6, 1909

. . . It is really only you that I have to thank for the summer's ending in such a blaze of glory, for not many girls would have been as nice as you were in those last few days. You don't realize how much your letters mean to me, for it isn't often that one finds a friend in whom there is nothing but good. As Browning puts it,

If you knew the light
That your soul casts in my sight
How I look to you for the pure and true
And the beauteous and the right.

You'd see one reason why I like so much to hear from you. But I'm getting up into the clouds and must come back to earth.

October 10, 1909

Your letter came this morning just as I was leaving for
college, and I read it twice on the way out and at least once
during each class, and have been quite delirious all day, it
was so nice. . . . If you will refer the people who say that
you have no heart to me, I'll tell them what I think about it
and about them. The longer I know you the surer I get that
you have the biggest and kindest heart in the
world . . . When you write again please give me some more
talk about romance, or any other moralizing that you feel in
the mood for, concerning anything from Purgatory to
football. . . . P.S. I believe in Purgatory, you know.

January ?, 1910

My dear Miss Wister, when I got your harmless-looking
letter this morning, I did not think that it was to mean so
much to me. Is it, then "un peu d'espoir, un peu de rêve, et
puis—bonsoir?" For foolish as I always knew them to be, I
have had my hopes and dreams as I sat by the fireside
thinking of the happy times that we have had together. But
when one aims as high as the stars, one must not expect to
strike his mark.

You know that nothing that you could do would hurt me,
and I understand perfectly why I have not heard from you
lately. If I feel tonight more sick at heart than I have ever felt
before, it is only because your dear letter was so like
your old self, so kind and true. I stayed home from the dance
tonight to perform the melancholy duty of telling you how
glad I am for your happiness, because the man of your choice
must be splendid, if not quite worthy of you, and you will
both be very happy. Is it to be a short engagement and will it
change your plans for travelling?

I am glad that it has been announced so near the beginning
of Lent, for I hope that when those six quiet weeks have
passed you will have found a model for your life which you
will always stick to.

If you have the slightest objection to my keeping your
photograph, don't mind telling me so, but I should like to
have it, not only as a reminder of our walks and sails and
canoeing, but as a symbol of all the goodness and purity and
liveliness that a girl can have, and of the greatest privilege I

have known, to be able to call you 'Friend'.

This is the day of our text and though we have come to a parting of the ways, it will still be my text. As I have asked each night that our friendship might ever increase and that I might be in some degree worthy of it, so now I shall always ask for your happiness and that when we meet again you will have no cause to be ashamed of one who always will be, as ever, your friend.

If I have written anything that perhaps I should not have, you will forgive me, or if this letter has been foolishly personal you will forgive that, too, for the sake of the old days. And now, before my last "goodbye", I hope and know that you will have every blessing and happiness in the years to come, for you deserve it all.

You have been far kinder to me than anyone else ever was, and I trust that you have, as I have, none but pleasant memories of our friendship.

Et enfin—bonsoir.

Ever your sincere and grateful friend,

Notes for a letter from Margaret to Ritchie, 1908: Are you A.R.Y.? Because as a portrait I don't find the postcard very satisfying, though I am delighted with the postcard as a picture of one of the very most attractive places on record. Do I make myself clear? Remember what you promised to send me. And the other postcard with the 'Canada', never shall I forget that night, I loved it. Wasn't the water & the moon and the clouds you to take me & everything, too adorable? And the fiddle in the forecastle, I musn't forget that. Yesterday we had more cricket and met the cricketers at tea afterward & they were most agreeable and had accents, and you know how I love an accent, but not one said 'rib!' I must stop because I'm working,—you needn't laugh—it's dusting books.

Love's Progress

On December 23, 1898, Margaret (aged sixteen) goes to the "Sophomore Dance," and, according to the program she saved, four out of twenty dances were with E. B. Meigs; the Lancers, two two-steps and a waltz. By 1902, though I could find no mention of Edward in Margaret's blurry handwriting, they were thought by some people to be engaged. April 17, 1902: "Ella said Dr. R. asked her if she had heard the report that Edward was engaged to me & she had. Wouldn't Mama have a fit if she heard it. Ella is a perfect love." Mama would certainly have had one of the worst fits of her life (we know what a fit Edward provoked eight years later when he blabbed about his engagement before it was formally announced), though it is certain that her eye was already fixed on Edward as a worthy son-in-law. The night before (April 16, 1902), Margaret had had dinner with her future parents-in-law and had a "lovely time. Having been asked most informally everybody was in gorgeous dinner dresses & diamond chains! Edward is a love. He nearly walked into the Ladies' Dressing-room & told me that his mother was never ready & he was just going to see if he couldn't help her along. It was so sweet." The Dressing-room, obviously, was not a place where the ladies dressed, but where they looked at themselves in the mirror, patted their hair for the last time, and adjusted their diamond chains. Ella (Margaret's first cousin) was "a perfect love," Edward "a love," Ritchie "a dear," Mr. Wheelwright "an angel man"; one scarcely knows how to weigh these terms of endearment. One must read the entries in Margaret's 1902 diary to learn that her feelings about Edward were not altogether positive. She seems to have begun to see the things she didn't like about him the moment she began to think about him as a possible husband. It was far from being an uncritical coup de foudre; she needed eight years to learn the art of loving Edward and, even a few months befoe the wedding, was still tormented by doubts.

In the summer of 1902, just before Edward went to visit at Chester, Nova Scotia, Margaret suddenly began to call him "Mr. Meigs," as if to keep him at a safe distance. She worried constantly about his being bored—"I don't want the poor man to have a horribly dull time," she says. A male guest was a responsibility that filled her with terror, to the exclusion of fun, it seems, for she couldn't flirt with Edward for the very reason that he was a guest. "It wouldn't be 'suitable'," she says. The whole occasion had something portentous about it, for it was clear that Mr. Meigs was a serious suitor, and now marriage, which once seemed so desirable, loomed as the end of freedom. And she makes a vow: "Not for 9 years do I marry," she writes in her diary. It turned out to be seven years—during which Edward got his medical degree, spent a euphoric year at the University of Jena, and started teaching at Harvard Medical School. While his thoughts were concentrated on Margaret, Margaret's fluttered about like a butterfly in a garden. He was the chosen one and yet, and yet. "I suppose he is nice," she says after his visit in Chester, "in fact I am sure of it, but there are things that I couldn't stand." It was like her not even to tell her diary what they were.

Margaret's August 28th letter after Edward's visit has all the lightness of tone that was missing in her meetings with him. "Being a thousand miles away I dare pay you a compliment without my having to undergo the ominous silence that usually follows one. I shiver at the very thought . . . " The compliment was the expression of her delight at getting *his* letter. At the end she tries a little flirting: "What makes you have hopes? did you guess that I adored letters and wanted another? (Is that fresh or do I really know you well enough to say anything I like . . . You know you were fresh enough to say I did)." As she says in her diary (September 11) her feelings toward Mr. Meigs are very different when she doesn't see him. But Edward must have overreacted to "do I really know you well enough to say anything I like?" for Margaret begins to worry. "What did I say in that postscript?" she asks, and from then on her letters are careful and inconsequential.

July 27, 1903, on board "des Postdampfers Patricia": "I don't want to leave the ship a bit . . . except I do want a Paris hat. Thank goodness I've nearly worn out the cherry hat that I trimmed. Please tell me about Naragansett." He does, at length; he speaks of the overdressed ladies, of their hats and "st-ck-ngs," as he puts it, and their consuming interest in clothes. Tactfully, at the end, he hopes that by this time she has bought her own Paris hat. Hats, as we know from both Mr. Gallatly and Mr. Wheelwright, were subjects in which suitors were supposed to take an interest.

The years go by—1904, 1905—and I am struck by a certain silliness in Margaret's letters; she is having too good a time to think seriously about her answers to Edward. "Do tell me why everyone doesn't think as you do," she says (Edward has sent her one of his articles). "Still if everyone thought the same there wouldn't be much pleasure in life, would there?" The next year, August 23, 1905, Edward writes "Dear Margaret" for the first time and she immediately switches to "Dear Edward." The die is cast, she says in her diary, but there is nothing more—no thrill of excitement, no change in the tone of her letters, which she signs, "I am very sincerely yours, Margaret Wister." Compared to the excitement of Mr. Wheelwright (1905 at Loèche is *his* year) dear Edward seems rather tame. Two days after the die is cast, Margaret writes in her diary, "Had 2 letters from Mr. Wheelwright to-day!! A little much, and the worst is that I haven't been dreaming. He does mean it. My goodness, what am I going to do with the man, I never ought to have taken the charm and the ring. I suppose it must have encouraged him." Really, Margaret! As we know, she plays her cards with such skill that Mr. Wheelwright never proposes but remains a friend, an "angel man." In 1908 he sends her a gold bracelet for Christmas; "rather attractive but awfully light," Margaret remarks in her diary.

As for Edward, he is forbidden in no uncertain terms, during the engagement period, even to send Margaret flowers. March 31, 1910: "As long as I have said that I don't want flowers and that I've taken a strong and particular dislike to them, and that I don't want you to send them to me, that's all I have to say, and of course you are at perfect liberty to do just as you like about the matter." The gracious acceptance of Mr. Wheelwright's gold bracelet, and a flash of the famous temper at Edward, as though he has taken an impermissible liberty! It is a good example of one of Margaret's refusals. Perhaps Mama had sourly remarked, "Edward is spending a lot of money on flowers," or Margaret didn't like the smell, for she was super-sensitive even to the perfume of flowers; at any rate, she was not going to explain. I remember beating on the walls of her refusals to explain and hurting myself in the process.

1902 to 1910—during all these years, Edward waits patiently. Will Margaret believe how much he has enjoyed himself? he wonders in his bread-and-butter letter after the Chester visit. "Such an astute person as you are will easily be able to judge from your own observations whether such an open book as I am was tolerably happy." Yes, an open book, poor Edward, who suffered all his life from his belief in the honesty of others and his subsequent disappointments. What *were* the things about him that Margaret couldn't stand? One of them, I think, was his solemn way of trying to get to the bottom of things; another, that he was a bit of a prig. The word "st-ck-ngs," for instance. Margaret liked a spice of wickedness, a hint of "danger" in her suitors. She frequently says about Edward that he is "so nice." He is so nice that she longs to shake him out of his niceness. "I do my best," she says in her Chester diary, August 17, 1902 after " 'a lovely walk, a lovely talk.' " (She is quoting the Walrus and the Carpenter who are about to invite the oysters to be eaten.) "But every now and then I long for a devilish bit of hard flirtation, as I haven't the heart to flirt with him." As we know, it wasn't "suitable." The unsuitable was identical with what is not done, with bad taste, even with vulgarity. Later Margaret observes that it would not be "a bit in good taste" to elope to avoid the maelstrom of a big wedding. Any lapse from good taste could be measured to the fraction of a millimetre. But what exactly was "a devilish bit of hard flirtation"? For Margaret, whatever it was (her spicy blend of provocation and withdrawal, I would guess) was essential to courtship; she needed it just as a trained dolphin needs to go through its tricks for a reward and languishes without them. Did Edward *ever* flirt? Wasn't flirtation on his list of falsenesses, didn't he believe that falling in love with Margaret (perhaps the one and only real love of his life) was much too serious to allow him to play? I remember his saying once that he disapproved of drinking because it induced a false state of cheerfulness, and perhaps he thought flirting induced a false kind of excitement.

August 22, 1902—Margaret writes in her diary, "Mama says she misses him & I know we all do, but strange to say there is not even a scratch on my susceptible heart." Three days later she gets a letter from Edward—"Imagine my surprise—and I must say my delight." And she will go on this way, thinking and talking about Edward in a special way, anxious to hear from him, glad to see him ("of all perfectly attractive people. It was good to see him") and flirting with the others. As the years go by, her life is so full that she scarcely has time to think about Edward. He is in the background, "perfectly attractive," until, at the end of 1909, he proposes marriage and she accepts. January 1, 1910, Margaret writes in her diary, "I little knew that 1909 was to bring me happiness."

Margaret's diary, 1902

August 6: Had to move Terrie's belongings into my room & moved to Mama's, so as to get Mr. Meigs' room ready for him. My heart has stopped almost several times to-day at the awful prospect of his coming, not that I object to him at all, but as to what to do if we continue to have these horrible foggy days. . . . Several times this evening it gave me a shock to look over & see him sitting there (on my invitation).

August 7: The weather has changed, imagine such a perfect thing. My prayers are answered. It did rain this morning & we sailed over in the pour & went in & rowed home.

August 10: Went over to Lobster Point with Mr. Meigs. That same blue view that has filled my heart for 2 years.

August 14: Well last night I was discouraged, as Commodore Keasbey was going to give the Yacht Club Smoker & we saw no prospect of Mr. Meigs getting to it & it was so mortifying. . . . Mr. Meigs & I went for a walk out by

Stanford's this afternoon. Lovely.

August 15: This has been a frightfully tiring day, but brightened by the fact that Sir Malachi Daly has taken Mr. Meigs to the Yacht Club Smoker . . . I feel in the seventh heaven about it, as it must be tiresome to stick with us all day.

August 19: Tonight to the dance in the boat house at Haman's Island . . . all decorated with flags & spruce boughs & the floor fine . . . & I had a very nice time (Mr. M. stuck with Coralie most of the evening) perhaps that was what made me enjoy myself so, as he wasn't stuck with me!!

August 20: Went out walking with Mr. Meigs round by the Crescent & over the hill & we do get to talking, but I still wonder & am uneasy.

August 21: A walk this evening & we have agreed to know each other well. But not for 9 years do I marry.

August 22: Mr. Meigs & I took a walk before he left very hurriedly by coach. We all miss him awfully, but this afternoon I lay down & had a good sleep. . . .

August 25: Imagine my surprise at finding a letter from Mr. Meigs awaiting me,—& I must say my delight. He finished by saying he dared not ask for an answer, but had hopes. Of course I will.

August 31: Fortunately I am recovering slightly from my attack of always thinking of Mr. Meigs & disappointment of not hearing from him, but as I have the very same symptoms after each parting with a young man, I don't think it's any more serious than usual. I always want to put the personal things at the top of the page, but it seems conceited & selfish not to mention other people first, so I don't & consequently forget them half the time.

September 11: Mr. Meigs came & he & I took a drive & came back to supper. Strange how different my feelings towards him are when I don't see him.

September 20: Dr. Meigs drove Mrs. M., E. and me down to
the Horse Show where it came down in a pour . . . Drove
back to Radnor & took train home. I was petrified at dinner.
It certainly was a family affair as Mrs. Meigs said.

Margaret-Persephone: The Wedding

Imaginary Letter

Dearest Mother,

In the course of rereading the 105 letters you wrote to Edward between January 1st and May 29th, 1910, I have been struck again by your spells of unhappiness. At times you were struggling like an animal caught in a trap; it was the trap of "belonging" to someone else, as you had never belonged to anyone—not to Papa nor Mama nor your sisters. You did not want to belong and you did not want to be conquered. "If anybody dares say that they have conquered me!" you wrote in your diary in 1902, apropos of a letter from a friend's fiancé. "He spoke of himself as the conqueror . . . which I cannot stand for a minute." It was an indirect warning to Edward, who, that very year, had begun his serious courtship. In 1910 the enforced intimacy of marriage from which you would never be able to get away in your life with Edward, loomed with its "rights," above all, the right that Edward took for granted—to get to know you. It scared you terribly, for a privilege of your unmarried freedom was the right to guard your most secret self, which was like the locked room in Bluebeard's castle. Edward was like Bluebeard's wife, who mistakenly thought that marriage gave her the right to explore every nook and cranny of the castle. Oddly enough, it was he who played the female role; he tiptoed around with his bunch of keys, or, like Rapunzel, he let down his hair, and you considered yourself the victim of his curiosity. "It makes me perfectly nervous to have you talking about getting to know each other," you write Edward a month before the wedding. "I feel like a specimen under the microscope, and I hate it. And if you are horrid I certainly don't want to know it." You meant that it would be for you to decide if and when he was horrid, and that it was not a subject for discussion. I can imagine Edward's bewilderment as he tried to explain, and your irritation, for you hated explanations as much as you hated to be known.

In answer to a letter from Edward saying that you don't tell him things, you tell him at length about how you sobbed at the dentist's. You have been tortured by this dentist (Dr. Head!) since you were a child; year after year you write in your diary about painful visits to Dr. Head, and now you are having a nerve killed. "I managed to have self-control enough to stop crying while he kept putting in cocaine, but every time he stopped working I simply shook with sobs . . . And I felt so sorry for the poor man, and tried so hard not to behave badly, because I didn't want him to think he really was hurting me so frightfully." "If you had been here," she adds, "I should have cried on your shoulder." I want to cry myself, partly because of your pain, and partly because of your misguided compassion for Dr. Head. I, too, shook with sobs when I was in the clutches of a dentist who used Dr. Head's antiquated methods, yet I felt not sympathy for him but hate. If Edward had said not only, "Poor Margaret!" but "Why did you feel 'sorry for the poor man'?" you would have turned on him in fury. He might possibly have been after the reason, i.e. women are trained to sympathize even with men who are hurting them, when you simply wanted him to know how hard you had tried to be brave.

Perhaps Edward tried too hard to get at the elusive things that lay beyond immediate explanations. In this respect, your life together was a history of mutual misunderstanding endlessly repeated: his trying to get to know you, or to explain himself, your instant bristling, for you were in as much danger from "getting to know" Edward (or anybody, for that matter) as from his getting to know you. I think this saddened him even though he loved you and needed you, to have truth nipped in the bud over and over again. You two, so much alike in the outward and visible things: class, upbringing, religion, politics—a foundation, one would say, for a solid marriage, were unalike in the inward and invisible things. But how can two people ever stay together except by declaring truces that silence their eloquent inner sense of themselves? Edward's yearning for the truth collided with your hatred for delving and provoked your defensive tactics: ready-made answers, hurt feelings, or silence.

During those months you were exhausted by the conflicting claims of the wedding and of Edward. I will never know what crisis provoked you to say, "no matter how desperately unhappy I might be—not *would* be—with you, I would be a great deal more unhappy without you." Did those storms of dislike for Edward, like white squalls on an inland lake, really come from him or had he unwittingly triggered off a buried fear, an ancient grievance? Didn't your anger come as well from your decimated days and thoughts, from the rules that made trivia important, made you give as much time to adoring your wedding presents, keeping lists and writing thank-you notes, as you gave to the emotional effort of thinking about Edward and answering his letters? And added to all this was the constant meddling by Mama and your sisters, and the necessity to hurt Mama by refusing to live with her. It was a nightmare. But don't go around looking careworn, your sister Sarah warned you when it all seemed too much to bear. March 5, 1910: "The lady in the case," writes Margaret to Edward, "sees about six months stiff work ahead of her . . . the details of which seem absolutely stupid, unnecessary and uninteresting to every man, and yet if all these things weren't done, he would begin to look about him, open his eyes and wonder why." I cannot believe that Edward would have wondered why, unless his mother had wondered for him.

Men hate weddings, you had said in an earlier letter. And women adore them, you might have added; they adore the bride's effulgent blaze before she goes into eclipse as a wife. It is society's most impressive transaction, short of a coronation, and if men do not boycott their own weddings, it is because they perceive that they will be the beneficiaries. And yet Edward must also have perceived himself as a victim bound to a certain kind of life and the social obligations it generated by the shining silver threads of 468 wedding presents. Get us a house suitable for us to live in, they whispered; show us off at tea parties and lunch-eons and dinner parties. And you did, for they seemed to give material life to your own dreams and desires. Your wedding presents sat on the long tables just as they had in a store, like loot brought up at random from a sunken treasure ship. They did not speak to each other until you brought your own order into their lives and decided how each would function in the kingdom of your house. With shining silk thread you embroidered your new initials on every piece of linen, and in the same way you gave some of your essence to the humblest objects—a china tea strainer with pink roses on it, for instance, or the metal duck's head on your desk that held a sheaf of papers in its beak. I see you at the dining-room table pouring tea from a fat little teapot the colour of lapis lazuli with a lacy network of silver clinging to its surface. And just as in the painting by Mary Cassatt in which a young woman drinking tea holds a cup to her lips, just as the white circle of the cup will forever hide her face except for her dark eyes peering over the rim, just as her image is fixed in the painting and hid-den, so you are in my mind's painting, forever holding the chubby dark blue teapot in mid-air, smiling the polite smile that hid your inner world.

Present Poem

May 26, 1910
Where were we in presents, because I shall have to keep you posted. Mr. and Mrs. Sam Motter Dresden basket, Carrie Moffitt, Ice cream spoon, Mrs. McCauley silver & glass plaque, Mr. & Mrs. Megear, silver bread tray, Mrs. McCormick—the Mother of the glass and silver vases,—silver bowl, Miss Martha Brown, silver & glass "relish?" dish, Mr. & Mrs. Sam Lewis silver & glass flower bowl, Mr. & Mrs. Percival Roberts, Ice cream plates with pink edges, Mrs. Lawrence Lewis Jr. silver cold meat fork, Mr. & Mrs. Lewis Wister picture, Mrs. Eugene A. Stout, chocolate pitcher, Martha & Billie Fuller, chair, Mabel Ashhurst Stimson, charm, Mr. & Mrs. John Fox, picture, Mr. & Mrs. Theo Stork, silver sconces, Mrs. Wayne McVeagh, silver cake dish, Mr. & Mrs. Edwin N. Benson Jr., silver salt cellars & spoons, Mr. James Logan Fisher, pr. green cut glass & bronze vases, Mrs.

W. Logan Fox, Silver & glass decanter, Mr. & Mrs. Theo
Starr, silver & glass milk pitcher, Mrs. James Bayard, double
brass candle stick, Mr., Mrs., & Miss Abbot, pie crust table,
Mr. & Mrs. Augustus K. Oliver (my first cousin from
Pittsburgh) lemonade set. Wedding dress going to be lovely,
everything turning out nicely. Best love O O O O O from
Margaret.

(Refrain): One dozen gold & white coffee cups with gold
            monogram
          One dozen gold & white plates
          One dozen painted rose bouillon cups
          Two silver bon bon dishes
          Silver & glass cheese dish
          mahogany drawing room chair
          Large Persian rug (Tree of Life pattern)

Linen poem

April 9, 1910
My linen at Shephard's all marked
With my initials in various sizes
One dozen pillow cases,
one dozen double sheets
a beautiful big table cloth
with a dozen napkins to match
two smaller table cloths
and two dozen napkins
a dozen extra napkins
a dozen small lunch napkins.
If I have enumerated all these articles
before you must forgive me,
because I am so delighted with them.

Metamorphosis

Now it occurs to me that I love the intimacy of circles and spheres: the spherical blue teapot, the winking round Moroccan lamp in my father's study, and the bisected circle of our dining-room table. It took genius to invent one of those old mahogany tables, its parallel underpinnings of wood, cogs and cables which allowed it to expand creakily into a gleaming dark river of wood, or contract into a circle, with its heavy feet clustered under it. Its size reflected family changes: the death of my father, World War II, and the four-year sickness of my mother. Its apotheosis, I suppose, was not as the cozy circle, but when four of five polished leaves were set closely together and covered with a thick, cream-coloured blanket, and then a linen tablecloth as long as a queen's train, soft as satin from years of careful washing. My mother and I set the table together with a shared passion for the arrangement of beautiful objects: the blown glass swans, for instance, each holding a little nosegay of spring flowers, attached by glass chains to a central vase.

A dinner party. And now my mother's wedding presents could serve their ordained purpose, like the desert flowers that burst out after rain. They had been hidden, waiting for their time. Dozens of plates, stacked in cupboards, waiting (unlike the desert flowers) to be seen and admired. But no, not admired, for a rigid etiquette forbade open admiration. It was against the rules for a guest to comment on details; rather she noted in a strange unseeing but extremely precise way (she would discuss it with *him* when they got home) the correctness or incorrectness of her surroundings. In fact, they had all been programmed to obey the social choreography of an upper-class dinner party, with the concentration of ballet dancers, whose eyes have the fixed quality of those who are under hypnosis.

Consider their rigidity from the vantage point of Now, when a hostess bearing a pile of dirty dishes disappears into the kitchen and can be heard rinsing them and putting them in the dishwasher. But at my mother's parties, it was not even acknowledged that the black waitress in uniform who came and went was a human being, and no one, including ourselves, gave a thought to what went on behind the pantry door. Consider the dishes— and no dish-washing machine. There were Crown Derby serving plates, black, rust-red, white and gold, taken away and carefully stacked after the guests were seated, replaced by dinner plates, by salad plates, dessert plates, fruit plates, and finger bowls. Multiply by twelve or fourteen, a minimum of 75 plates and 24 glasses plus 12 coffee cups and a mountain of knives, forks, spoons, serving spoons, crystal bowls, all these piled in the 8' by 10' pantry with its battered sink with separate spigots. Perhaps Amelia was in the laundry room, contemplating another mountain: the twelve foot linen tablecloth, with little stains on it of turkey fat or red wine, and she would have to scrutinize its great length and breadth and remove the stains and wash it and iron it, along with the crumpled linen napkins.

Perhaps at this point she reached for the bottle of whisky she kept hidden and took a little snort, or maybe that was later, when the pile became too huge to bear looking at. . . . Long after the last guest had left. . . . there was still the sound of dish-washing going on in the pantry, a signal, one would think, for one of us to go in and say, "May I help?" But none of us did; upstairs in the library we were discussing the party and agreeing that everybody had had a very good time and that Sarah's (the cook) fig pudding had never been better.

The next morning I would help my mother put away the clean plates until their next flowering. There are still remnants of her treasures dispersed among her children, waiting in cupboards as they used to, to come out on special occasions. The ones I chose, having passed through my mothers hands, have lost their anonymity as wedding presents, and I still think of them as hers.

Married Life

The idea of marrriage is the opiate of the whole world, it seems, with the exception of a few unfortunate dissidents. It is governed by soothing rules like those that decreed frontality in Egyptian painting. If heads look fixedly in one direction, if feet stay forever in a single track, it gives the viewer a feeling of repose and confidence. There is general distress and it is seen as a betrayal of trust if even an unhappy marriage breaks up and Pandora's box lets loose its demons. As for a happy marriage—let a lifelong bachelor speak: "A happy marriage brings more absolute and blissful contentedness than anything else to be reached in our world," says my great-uncle Willy, writing to Edward in 1910 to congratulate him on his engagement. Judging from the childlike sweetness of Uncle Willy's character, bachelorhood, too, was capable of bringing contentedness.But here is an old pro, Horace Jencks, on the subject: January 25, 1910—"I have been through it," he writes Edward, "and I can assure you that there is only one other state that can surpass the period of engagement and that is marriage, when your two lives join into one, when your separate joys and sorrows, successes and failures, become as one, and when above all you have the love and sympathy and encouragement of a good woman. Surely what more can a man want?"

Much has been said lately about the one-sided concept of "the good woman," which in men's view is (or was) the cornerstone of that great edifice, the happy marriage. Horace Jencks goes on to say that his wife is not his better half, but his better nine-tenths, and I have been puzzling ever since over the mathematics of this. The good woman was not only good but was "better" than her husband and the happy marriage required that half of the husband be removed and replaced by his wife's "better half." But here is Horace Jencks who has undergone a more serious operation—the transplant of nine-tenths of his wife's betterness, leaving room for only a tenth of his own. It gives one pause, calling to mind the digestive processes of a starfish, or one of those larvae that lodges inside a wasp and feeds happily until nothing remains but the transparent carapace. Margaret's and Edward's marriage was unlike Mr. and Mrs. Horace Jencks' for the simple reason that neither was a "better half," and that, in spite of all their differences, they were friends, who, when they quarrelled, never tried to destroy or belittle each other. Edward reasoned, Margaret impatiently interrupted his reasoning. Her tactics depressed me when I was a witness and I tended to take my father's side. So it moved me to see how he used letters to state his case in full. "You cannot interrupt before I am through and lead my thoughts into an entirely different channel," he writes on September 10, 1919.

"Here I am with quite a lot of time," he continues, "obsessed with the idea that you are the most desirable creature in the world. So why not try to tell you some of the things that always seem to lead to a row when I try to say them viva voce." Edward does not seem to have realized that his two sentences are at odds with each other and that Margaret's pleasure in the first must have been changed to foreboding by the second. The "thing" that might have led to a row was in this case his unexpressed surprise when Margaret packed a whole chicken with the lunch he was to take on the train. "I had just the slightest inclination to ask, 'How shall I eat it without any knife,' " he says, "but the thought that you were giving me a whole chicken was so overwhelming, that I could express nothing but gratitude." He then goes on to explain that he did not eat the chicken on the train because he was unable to tear it "limb from limb" in front of a fellow passenger, so he ate in a station restaurant. The fact that Edward is so ready to feel guilty speaks volumes about Margaret's power to instill guilt (or make a row) about something trivial. But how could Edward think that she would have scolded him for not eating the chicken on the train, she would have said. In Edward's mind, alas, was always the question, will this make her angry? at the wrong moment, for it wouldn't be something he expected (the chicken) and prepared for, but something unexpected. Lurking anger has this peculiarity: it cunningly feigns indifference, like a lioness looking over a herd of wildebeest, who lets obvious prey go by, and quick as lightning, singles out the weakest calf and runs it down. Edward was a weak calf, fated unwittingly to provoke anger and then suffer from it.

Safe (he thought) in the shelter of his letters, Edward saw Margaret glowing in the light cast by need and homesickness, someone who could be reasoned with and persuaded. Margaret herself had said in her 1902 diary that she liked Edward better when he wasn't there. ("Strange how different my feelings towards him are when I don't see him.") Presence is hard to take, presence in marriage is the enforced reality of two people always together, who have begun by thinking that their differences will be negotiable. Edward kept this illusion alive when he was far from Margaret and wrote the long letters that, in my opinion, saved his marriage and his sanity. And perhaps Margaret saw the ideal Edward, the one who wasn't there "with all my disagreeableness," as he puts it in this same letter. They gave each other breathing-space.

The story of the chicken launches Edward into the real subject of his letter—the "hundreds of little incidents that come up between us and cause quite a violent disturbance in your mind and perhaps less violent but longer lasting one in mine. They are due to the fact that we are different in many ways. My policy would be to try to recognize these differences as clearly as possible, to try to reform ourselves on each other's model when either can see that the other is clearly superior, and, in other cases, to give each other as much freedom for self-expression as possible. God knows that I do not set myself up as at all generally superior to you, my darling, indeed I do not even desire to be or to think that I am. Sometimes I think our differences are conditioned by the very different roles that we have to play in the world, sometimes they seem to me merely differences without any superiority on either side, often and often I recognize that you are far ahead of me. Once you told me that I have the tendency to stop and think when I ought to be acting—I see it and hate myself for it—

and I see a lot of other faults in myself that I have to live with and get along with the best way possible. I try to see too much into the future and get myself all mixed up and fretted with possibilities that are never going to occur, I am subject to the most idiotic alternation of moods, and I am timid and sensitive to a quite unwarranted degree. And you are the greatest help to me, my darling—you send a shaft of your healthy common sense in among my fussy anxieties, and make them vanish 'like to bubbles when the rain peltethe.' If only I could sometimes do the same for you!''

The next day, after one of his alternations of mood, he writes again. ''All day long I have been as happy as I was unhappy yesterday and the day before. What kind of magic glass can it be that passes across one's outlook and changes the color of everything like the spot-light at the theatre? I am sure you have some connection with it, but it must be a very mysterious sort of connection . . . I shall see you next Saturday night. The joys marched in on my stage and drove out the glooms at just about four o'clock yesterday afternoon. Can it possibly be that the thought of eight days without you is unbearable, while the prospect that I shall see you in a week and twenty-three hours fills me with joy?''

Speculating, always speculating on Margaret's reasons for anger, I theorize that Edward's ''fussy anxieties'' were among them. He had turned out to be much more fragile than he seemed when she married him. I recall a somewhat ominous entry in her 1904 diary: ''A letter from EBM saying he didn't get in at this election of the Pa. Hospital directors. It's a dreadful thing in me, but I don't think I could like anybody who wasn't successful.'' Edward was never successful in Margaret's sense of the word, though he was much respected for his scientific research. He was incapable of pushing himself forward, was too modest and vulnerable to fight hard for success. Perhaps Margaret was disappointed by the absence of conventional ''manliness'' in Edward. He had no trace of the unconscious superiority to women that most men project; he had no men cronies; he did not drink or smoke or tell dirty jokes. Margaret was greatly concerned with ''manliness,'' worried when her son Arthur played ''too much with girls,'' determined that he should learn the ''manly'' art of boxing. One would say that she was mortally afraid of homosexuality, like the shadow of a great hawk from which she ran in panic. And yes, she loved success, and if she couldn't have it in Edward, she was going to keep her children's noses to the grindstone and supervise their report cards with a sharp eye.

It must have been a shock to Margaret to discover that Edward was subject to paralyzing depressions, that he could drop from good humour to despair with dizzying speed, and from a feeling of his own importance to a sense of nothingness. November 27, 1920—He is in Chicago at a scientific conference and has read his article at a meeting. It "seemed to excite a fair amount of interest," he writes Margaret, and he has had an "amicable controversy" with two fellow scientists about his "calcium and phosphate balance experiments" with cows. That evening, instead of filling up his time as usual with correspondence and planning for the next day, he decides to do nothing. His mind glides at the whim of the wind—pleasantly—and then it seems to be borne along on a hurricane, or to have been taken over by a daemon who puts out a clawed hand, crushes and shakes simultaneously, and reduces flesh and spirit to something as lightless and dense as a spent star. "For twenty years," he writes, "I have been plaguing myself with the notion that I would confer some vast benefit on the human race and build myself a monument which future generations would look at with tears in their eyes to think that their dear benefactor had disappeared. I have been setting my face so hard toward an imaginary future that I have more than half destroyed for myself the real present. I have been alternating between the excitedly silly delusion that I was getting on pretty well with the monument, the sombre despair of knowing that I wasn't, and the nervous unhappiness of thinking that I might, if only I were doing something different. I am really a very moderately endowed person. I am as stupid as an owl at anything above simple mathematics, I have just the barest taste of a musical faculty, I have no creative imagination, I have practically no social charm, I am ridiculously timid about the most ordinary situations in life, and the least bit of excitement or difficulty makes me so dizzy that the little sense I have got goes flying to the four winds. So with your help, my darling, I am going to make a dead set at being lazier and less ambitious in all directions, and see if I cannot contract my aspirations to a compass better fitted to my abilities."

I imagine Margaret reacting with a mixture of impatience and alarm, and summoning, as she did so often, her "healthy common sense." She would scold him and reassure him, but her comfort could never be enough; he would always be less than he longed to be, would never "confer some vast benefit on the human

Elizabeth (Bessie),
Margaret, and Sarah
Wister with their mother,
c. 1883.

Edward Meigs,
c. 1880.

Margaret Wister,
c. 1893.

Edward, Jack, and Arthur Meigs, May 1892.

MRBM with her sons: Arthur, Edward, and Jack, c. 1891.

Margaret Wister,
c. 1898.

Edward, Jack, and Arthur Meigs, c. 1899.

Margaret and Edward Meigs, June 8, 1910.

Margaret and Edward's wedding party, Belfield, Germantown, June 8, 1910.

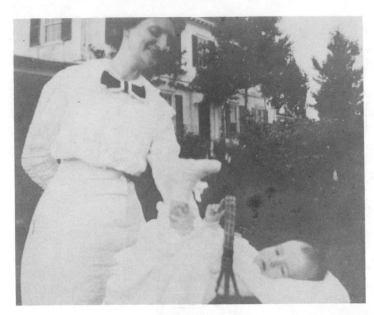

Margaret and Arthur V. Meigs, c. 1912.

Margaret and Arthur V. Meigs, c. 1916.

Margaret Wister Meigs dressed for her volunteer work, 1918.

Edward (EBM) with his children: Wister, Sarah, Arthur, and Mary.

Uncle Willy, with Arthur (AIM) holding Wister, c. 1920.

Portrait of EBM, painted c. 1925.

Visiting Mer de Glace in Switzerland, c. 1923. Left to right: Mary, guide, EBM, Wister, Arthur V., MWM, Miss Balfour, Sarah, guide.

Edward at Woods Hole, c. 1936.

Margaret in Washington, c. 1938.

AIM and EBM at "Landhope," Arthur's country home, c. 1938.

AIM and Mary Meigs at "The Peak," June 1943.

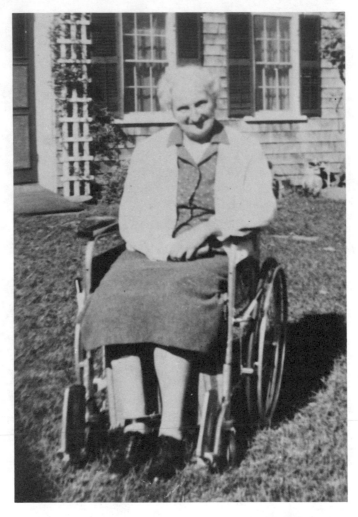

MWM, c. 1957.

race." "Ah, but the reach should exceed the grasp," said Browning, but the distance between reach and grasp mocked at Edward and punished him, even if Margaret insisted that he *was* benefitting the human race. And he had a brilliant mind. Wasn't he first in his class at Medical School? As for "social charm," wasn't that what made her so proud of him at dinner parties when she saw his ability to charm the ladies? What he really meant was that he was incapable of repartee and small talk, of suspending seriousness and talking in aimless circles in order to make conversation. Since he always tried to answer the most frivolous question seriously, he was often silent, turning over the answer in his mind, and the conversation washed over him and he reproached himself for being stupid. Margaret would answer, quick as a wink, without thinking, and this was what he called social charm—her wonderful ability to look interested and to make a quick answer that would keep the conversation bouncing like a ping-pong ball.

The question of social charm was at the heart of their most fundamental difference: that Margaret's social life was her life-blood and Edward was a true solitary, who, here again, did his best to please her. Margaret's "social charm" was a gift and a curse. She was able to suffer torments if she missed a good party even for the best of reasons. Consider her for a moment in Woods Hole in July, 1917. The twins are a little less than three months old. She is invited to her niece's wedding on July 10th. Weddings, funerals for Margaret contained the obligation to go, as if Papa and Mama had spoken through the engraved invitation. But this time the twins, ten weeks old, compete for her attention and make the decision excruciatingly difficult. Edward, who knows the limits of his power, wisely seeks the support of Mama, and uses it as a shield. "I got some very sensible advice from your mother," he writes on July 1st. "The first point is that she thinks you cannot come; and, although I know you will hate the idea of not coming like poison, I do hope you will be able to see it from her point of view. She says none of the family expect you to come, I have been thinking about ways of your doing it, and I cannot think of any way that would not involve a real risk to your health and to that of the twins." He then proposes to do everything he "can to properly represent our branch of the family": he asks about a wedding-present, he asks what to wear. And for two more letters he commiserates with Margaret about her "depression from not being able to go to the wedding," describes the wedding in great detail, and particularly dwells on everything that went wrong: "the surging mass of people," the "steady, ever-increasing downpour of rain," the "confusion and delay at the church." "They were not so lucky in their weather as you and I were, my darling," he says. Now sweetly and tactfully he tries to comfort her and raise her spirits, with what a magical leap of understanding he has put himself in her place!

And Margaret—was she really so unhappy? Terrible, heartbreaking, she writes, not to be able to go to the wedding; she was missing a part of family history, an event that made a new human equation, that fulfilled God's law, not to mention the joy of the great family party afterwards. She could have been there with Edward as a married woman with four children, twins (the pride of answering, how are the twins? Tell me about the twins); like a royal couple, they would have been watched and admired almost as much as the bride and groom. She thought of the radiance of her own wedding seven years earlier, the reception afterwards, the warm June sun, the horses and carriages that drove up to the old stone house, and the ladies, dressed in lacy white, who were handed carefully down from the carriage steps. Margaret felt a dark void in her, as if nothing else mattered as much in the whole world as missing this wedding. "Heartbreaking not to be on hand," she writes. But in the same letter she says, "The babies noticed each other for the first time today—they lay there and smiled and talked to each other!" "Sarah and Mary are too cunning for words," she writes, "as bright as buttons and Sarah holds her head as stiff as a ramrod when she is picked up." Then wedding-regrets surged over her, gloom that "you could cut with an axe," allayed a little by Edward's letters recounting delay, confusion and pouring rain. "Not like our wedding," she thought.

Margaret's sorrow was sacramental because she had missed a holy occasion but it was also composed of pure homesickness for the life she had sacrificed when Edward chose to work in Washington. She felt the strong call of home and the family life she adored, whereas Edward was oppressed by his family and afraid of being caught in the maze of family obligations. For him, Washington was freedom; for Margaret, it was exile. She had to make a new life now without the half of herself that yearned and suffered when fate prevented her from asserting her family oneness. She longed to go back to where her old self lived and say, I belong to you, my family, my friends. I haven't left you! That was why she took the twins to Philadelphia to be born, why she took her children to visit aunts and grandmothers in Philadelphia, why the twins were put through the patriarchal mill of a Philadelphia debut, and why she tried never to miss a family wedding or funeral. All these things helped soothe her sense of loss, and yet she felt her old life slipping from her grasp. Deep in the heart that belonged to Edward lay a hope that a dazzling job-offer would come from Philadelphia. "If you went to the University of Pennsylvania you might be able to develop your cow idea on the side," she says in July, 1921. "If I were you I would do a little quick and deep thinking and you might really not want to spend the rest of your life with the cows." (It has suddenly occurred to me that Margaret looked down on cows, as she looked down on certain people, and considered them unworthy to associate with Edward.) Et tu, Edward must have thought, for Margaret had allied herself with his Ma and his brother Arthur, to get him back to Philadelphia. "A little quick and deep thinking!" But the more Edward thought, the more he dug himself in and could not be pried loose either from Washington or from his cows, for though he was irresolute in small matters, he could resist Margaret's prodding when it concerned his truest life.

The never-ending pain Margaret suffered from her amputated roots was transmuted into a determination to make a life in Washington that resembled the Philadelphia life, in which she flew so effortlessly. Her letters are sprinkled with expressions of triumph or anxiety: "We feel as if we have arrived," "Mighty slow work," "Enlarge my acquaintance," "People who count for something." And Edward flapped along simply to please her. Hadn't she pleased *him* by giving up her life in Philadelphia to come to a city where she knew no one? "Margaret and I keep trying our wings in Washington society," he writes his mother-in-law in 1916, "or perhaps I should say that she already flies very fairly, and I keep flapping and hopping along after her as well as I can."

Edward pokes fun at social life but Margaret is deadly serious. Even in summer she is pursued by social demons: "My problem is to work in and off the many people in Woods Hole . . . Must call on the Richards; it is now 9 a.m. but my sins pursue me." It was a sin not to return a call or an invitation, not to write a thank-you letter. Senseless obligations, designed to clutter women's minds, bringing in their wake guilt and social sorrows that mimic real sorrows of the heart. They are like the weeds that

111

grow among the roots of strawberry plants, that cannot be pulled up without uprooting the plant. Margaret's social self began to be shaped when she was a child; at fourteen she was aleady a little woman. Her models were all around her and the prevailing pattern of womanhood fitted her like a glove. Strange to me—her surpassing interest from an early age in the other sex, her singlemindedness in that respect, and her strategies. February 17, 1904: Margaret (aged twenty-two) describes the social season: "It wasted your ammunition & you have none when the real time of action comes though it makes a display at the time." Obviously, "the real time of action" was the game of catching the man of your choice. It was not like the Margaret of that time to run out of ammunition. "Renounce the devil and all his works," she goes on, "the pomps and vanities of this wicked world simply because there is nothing to go to."

What did Margaret know about "this wicked world"? Nothing, in my opinion, for she thought she was wicked if she wanted her own way, if she went to the men's smoking-room on a ship and drank a glass of beer, if she played cards for money, above all, if she won, "the worst thing I ever did." Her only wickednesses were those she never thought about: the snobbism and racism typical of her class, and her undue admiration for the "pomps and vanities." She was a woman who did not drink, smoke, commit adultery, wear make-up or any perfume but eau de cologne (Roger and Gallet), who was simple, disciplined and chaste in her thoughts, who guarded her children ferociously from knowledge of "this wicked world," and who would have been profoundly shocked by its inner workings. A protective spell enabled both Margaret and Edward to get through life unscathed and ignorant of the most depraved kinds of wickedness; it seemed to be an essential part of their married happiness not to look into the vortex of evil, which would make them sick and dizzy. The marriage contract required the continuation of the state of innocence they shared, bound together like the babes in the wood. Each was really the only good friend the other needed. In January, 1910, Margaret writes Edward a little sharply, "As for being interested in your work of course I am interested in it, far more, doubtless, than you have ever considered being interested in mine." Rapping him over the knuckles as usual—but I am pleasantly surprised by her insistence on equal interest. Equally surprising is the fact that Edward understood what she meant. Their formula for a happy marriage was not like Horace Jencks', by which the "good woman" appears to do most of the work of sympathy and encouragement. Margaret and Edward listened to each other, after the fashion of two people whose minds are shaped so differently that they can never mesh together in total understanding. They had known this about each other from the beginning—that their minds often met in a shower of sparks or a short circuit. But they struggled with the intractable idea of marriage until death parted them.

World War I

Four packages of letters (1917-1918), two from Margaret to Edward, two from Edward to Margaret, reveal their contrasting temperaments: Margaret who throve on the excitement of the War, and Edward, by contrast, "flattened and paralyzed." Margaret spent the summer in Woods Hole, preoccupied by her twins ("the sweetest things you ever saw") and by the two boys, who required "eternal vigilance"—Wister, who was "amusing and pretty bad," and Arthur, full of mischief, and led astray by Bobbie, "a very horrid little boy beside being untruthful." Days were measured by the amount of badness or goodness of the boys and by the wonderful changes in the twins. A month after they were born, Margaret writes ecstatically to Edward that Sarah has gained 10 ounces and Mary 11 ounces. "Did you ever know anything so perfect?" Nor does she ever complain if the twins keep her awake. In 1917 and 1918 she was a true mother, engrossed by her children, bending to their needs, and they took precedence over the War. For a lovely period of permissiveness, she forgot her moral rigour and the line between goodness and badness became relatively blurred. It was sad but inevitable that the sexual threat, in the person of the horrid little Bobbie, should cast a cloud over the bright summer of 1918 and destroy Margaret's peace of mind forever. In 1917 her old social routines were disrupted by the twins, her "two wee ones," who like all babies cried and fussed but even at two and a half months were "bright as buttons." Like Miss Bartholomew, the trained nurse who helped lighten the burdens of motherhood, she was in a state of love which obliterated the fatigue of sleepless nights, days shredded like confetti.

Meanwhile Edward, alone in the house in Washington, lived with the fears born of his brother Arthur's enlistment—even greater because Arthur seemed so casual and fearless. Arthur had taken on himself the task of buoying up his mother and brothers, and this (for Edward) surrounded him "with a sort of heroic, almost sacred atmosphere." He believed that the transformation of Arthur into dramatic hero would last forever, that they would never again quarrel with each other. Arthur's transformation came from the complex joys of wartime: the joy of having proven his manhood, of having become a hero to his family, and, once he had arrived in France, of finding a country that touched his heart. It was typical of Edward to raise his brother to such a plane of sacredness that he humbled himself in the process. Suddenly he could not imagine "in the future treating him familiarly." If he had been more prescient he would have seen Arthur regain his old shape, would have heard the acrimonious sound of new quarrels, or renewed old ones. Arthur had always denied that he was a hero, yet he was seen as one, and the painful change in him from sacred back to profane must have come as something akin to the bends for a diver. A period of noble and generous thoughts and unselfish behaviour is often (always, in my case) followed by an avenging irritability; as we shall see, Arthur could hardly believe after the War that he was the "unsophisticated" young man of his letters from France.

Edward shrank from participation in the war, not because of cowardice but because he had too clear a vision of it. Arthur's view—"even from massacres a good many people escape; so why get excited?"—designed to give comfort to his family, gave them an even greater sense of his heroism and of their own terror. The good soldier thought of those who escaped and the others of those who didn't. Perhaps it was just this concentration on the possibility of escape that kept whole armies from deserting even before going overseas. Edward was torn apart by his conviction of the utter senselessness and crime of war and his obligation to support

115

it. His mind had to be wrenched into a new shape to enable him to hate the Germans, whom he had always loved. His radiant memories of Jena, the university town where he spent the year of 1907, kept intervening, softening his vision of the Enemy, the facless Hun. *His* Germans had faces, and a culture that had become part of his life-forces. He was not a pacifist by principle; his scientific work was the fulfillment of his duty to country and government.

In July, 1918, Edward is offered a commission in the Medical Reserve Corps but decides "not to consider it" for he feels that his ideas, put into effect, "will improve and cheapen the milk supply all over the world." He is in the service of life, not death, and he writes to Margaret in explanation, "I cannot abandon my tree to the birds and storms just before the fruit gets ripe." On September 12th, two months before the end of the War, he registers for service. It took a quiet kind of heroism to tend his tree with war-hysteria raging around him, yet some kind of intolerable pressure must have pushed him to the registry office, a need to break a psychic deadlock, which explains his feeling of relief. "I rather like the feeling of being at least registered for war service," he writes Margaret.

Meanwhile in Woods Hole in the summer of 1918, the War was a tourist attraction. "Everyone rushed in automobiles to see the U-boat shelling the barges at Orleans," writes Margaret July 25th. She herself had run to get her camera when two hydroplanes landed on the beach a week before, and "was grieved a little later when a sailor with a fixed bayonet appeared, and asked for the film!" Can we, who are now hostages of submarines capable of destroying a whole continent, imagine how it was to watch shelling as a spectator sport? Or to feel grieved, not because one has been threatened with a bayonet but because one's film has been confiscated? Either Margaret was absolutely fearless or she knew that she was not in real danger. It was almost like playing at war: the bugle calls, the flag taken down at night. She was making her own patriotic gesture—"patriotic saving," she calls it, by cooking for the household. July 2nd: "To-day I cooked a very good dinner, and have never felt happier or better." And she kept it up, even when Mater bribed her with a cheque to get a cook. Margaret cooked, she worked at the Red Cross, she took care of her vegetable garden. She scarcely had a second to brood about the War as Edward brooded. "There is a peculiar sunny cheerfulness about your letters just like your dear self," he writes her June 26, 1918, when she is launched on her cooking adventure. In 1917, when AIM went off to France, Edward had felt surrounded by heroes and heroines; he was the only person who never "faced anything more terrible than the dentist's chair," he said.

Part of Margaret's sunny cheerfulness came from a determination not to let Edward sink into the depths, but the greater part came from the pride of giving her all to the Uncle Sam who pointed his finger, who looked sternly under his shaggy brows. Your country needs you! She wore the halo of motherhood, she was bringing up two sons. Little did she and millions of other mothers know that their boy-children were being fattened for the next sacrifice, World War II, and that for each succeeding generation there would be, conveniently, a war. Sometimes I am thankful that my parents, who believed that World War I would end war, are not alive to see the creeping sickness—violence, which, carefully cultivated, has become a secret joy. The joy of killing flourishes in torture chambers and in laboratories, in children who flay cats and poke their eyes out, and in the dozens of wars that are slowly torturing whole countries to death. It is too terrible even to have been imagined by my parents, who belonged to a generation (how far away it seems!) still nourished by hope.

Before the War, Margaret and Edward had lived their lives in the context of peace, which, however illusory it was, shed sunlight on their youth and marriage. It was a period when ideals and hopes could be born and have a normal life expectancy and when the mass extinction of hopes was still in the future. Even after the War, when nations were erased from the map and refugees spilled over the new borders, you could focus your attention on a single act of genocide. I remember that once a month our cook prepared a frugal meal which we ate in order to think of "the starving Armenians." Since the food (lentil soup and kasha) was delicious and there was enough for two helpings, I always looked forward to these lunches. If we had fasted, I might have been better able to imagine a starving Armenian and to grasp the fact that at least a million Armenians had been slaughtered in cold blood or driven from their country; perhaps I thought that starving people ate very well if their meals were like ours. My mother, however, put all the earnestness of her soul into this gesture; she totted up the difference in cost between this meal and a normal one and handed over the exact sum for refugee relief.

Margaret made burnt offerings, sometimes to the victims of the gods, sometimes to the gods themselves. In fact, all such offerings beg the gods for protection, they are payments for protection against the Mob, who allow us to "lead our easy sheltered life" as long as we soft-pedal our protest about their atrocities.

Woods Hole in Wartime

MWM to EBM—April 26, 1917 (Philadelphia, the day before the twins are born): We are now living in a palace, you never saw such a wonderful place with everything in it, and you will never know my thankfulness at having arrived safely! Oh, my darling! Do you think our spareroom bed could be as uncomfortable as Sarah's? Mama brought me in this morning with all the bathtubs, etc. and then I went shopping . . . Have communicated with Miss Blacker, who is coming tomorrow to sterilize my things, she is not on a case, am wondering whether I had better have her right away, will ask Dr. Norris tomorrow.

May 15: It seems no one is happy without the twins and Miss Blacker and me staying with them! Mama begs for us and is having a new essential article put in the bathroom! I told you Sarah also longs for us. And I do not want to stay with either of them! I say why the dickens etc., so you see my family are in bad! . . . The trouble is I love you so much I miss you, that is not strongminded of me.

May 15: My darling how I miss you. Mary & Sarah miss you too & wept considerably last night, but were none the worse! . . . You mustn't be cross with Sarah [her sister giving advice] she only means kindness, & I am not going to allow myself to be upset by her or made nervous, as that with me is what would affect the babies. . . . Give my love to cow No. 19. Best love to yourself my darling. Twins is certainly twins.

May 17: Feeding over. The babies are getting along nicely, and I have my corsets on. Excuse such details, but if you had ever worn them you would know what a comfort it is to the

118

back! Harriet was enchanted with the babies, people really seem to be crazy over them.

May 19: What do you think those twin babies gained! Sarah 10 ounces and Mary 11 ounces. I am speechless and breathless. Did you ever know anything so perfect? Last night they fussed for several hours, but they didn't bother me. And I had so much that we had to cut down a little on food!

May 20 (to SBW): Miss Blacker departed Thursday and Miss Bartholomew came, so we are now able to settle down to the routine for the summer. She is lovely with the babies and seems untiring. It is a never ending job. They are the sweetest things you ever saw, and certainly notice things, and sleep well at night, only having to be nursed about 3 a.m.

May 23: Mary and Sarah cried alternately to-day, but slept like tops last night, so that is the result we have been striving for.

May 31: How nice it will be to get all my chickens under my wings again! My two wee ones are a little perturbed by my going yesterday, and have cried pretty steadily, but I shan't do it again . . . Miss Bartholomew reports the children fine and Wister pretty bad but lovely, Arthur good. Miss Bartholomew rushed to her beloved twins, and would spend most of her time here if Miss Blacker like a Gorgon did not warn her off. My it is funny!

May 31: The babies are fine to-day, and I have been lying down before each feeding, although I went out to buy a dress . . . Miss Bartholomew came to go shopping with me and Miss Blacker announced to me that Miss Bar. was very bossy and she hoped, etc. I felt like saying, "the person who never gets a chance to boss around here, is myself!" for Miss Blacker when crossed in the smallest detail, is raging.

July 7: Miss Bartholomew says to tell you the babies noticed each other for the first time to-day. They were too cunning, lay there and smiled and talked to each other.

July 8: This is Sunday weighing day and the babies have each gained 4 ounces. I think that was gained the beginning of the week, as I have been feeling awfully tired for several days . . . Don't worry about me as I am perfectly well and will give Sarah another bottle and see how we get along on that. I am afraid now we will have to increase the bottles according to their capacity which seems large! but I will do it gradually and keep up nursing as long as possible. The bottle agrees well and their bowel movements are beautiful. Really they are too cunning for words, as bright as buttons and Sarah holds her head as stiff as a ramrod when she is picked up. That is enough about babies.

July 23: Let me describe this morning as a fair sample of why I occasionally miss writing. Breakfast, collect 2 pairs of overshoes, 2 sweaters, put them on, nurse one baby, dentist at Falmouth, back at 11.10 to hear that Arthur had got into the Bartow boat and pushed off, then shrieked to get out. He was in his bathing suit with Alma and the boat was tied, but the entire beach was roused, Wister with an enormous bump received from falling. On looking out the window at 12 noon saw Arthur dressed engaged in pushing off same boat and kept him with me while nursing 1 baby. While trying to read Mama's letter between 12.50 and 1 P.M. this occurred. Dinner. "Where is Arthur?" Enter Arthur. "Mother, I took the key out of Mrs. Williams' bathhouse door, and it fell down the crack!" Exit Mother. Enter Mr. Williams and Barratt in bathing suits rattling the bathhouse door!!! Clarence Bartow to the rescue crawls length of bathhouse and rescues key. Forced smiles on faces of the Williams family. Dinner. Sit down to write letter. Since beginning have been out twice to screams and once to bring them back from the clay bank. It is now 2.20 p.m. and I am soon starting to take Arthur to French kindergarten at Mrs. Houston's. He is not as bad as he was, but never obeys Alma at all. In my letters I forget to mention that he is frequently put to bed. The other day he thought he would prefer spanking, it hurt but was soon over. He and I get along pretty well, as no one else can put up with him. Glad to hear you will be along. Twins well. Miss B. says Sarah is so beautiful you won't know her and Mary so smart. In spite of the foregoing account we are fairly happy though it is rather like a life sentence in a treadmill!

July 25: We all feel well to-day, though Arthur's ear is
running, through my fault. I promised him he could go in
bathing and let him go, although it was rather cold . . . I feel
sorry for the child, his latest trick was to use the floor of the
girls' bathhouse instead of the bathroom! Miss B. has mended
the lock and we have hidden the key!

Miss Bartholomew to MWM—July 3 [She had left to be a
nurse in France]: Thank you for writing me about my
babies—Oh, how I'd love to see them just once more. Love
them hard for me & think of yours truly when you have
nothing else to do.

Miss B. to MWM—July 4: We are the first nurses equipped
for overseas in the line of march . . . I'd give a good deal to
see my little babies once more . . . Do love them for me.

MWM to EBM—July 5: Both babies are cutting teeth, so
prefer to scream all night or at least Sarah did, but she seems
perfectly cheerful by day. Unfortunately I have forgotten my
paragoric.

July 5: Our babies are doing nicely, Mary weighs 18 lbs. 12
oz., Sarah 18 lbs. 2 oz. Wister is amusing and pretty bad
except when all alone.

Washington in Wartime: Edward to Margaret

May 29, 1917 (Beltsville, Maryland): I got a rather flattering
invitation from Walker, who used to work with Father on
milk, to work at the U. of Illinois Medical School this
summer. He wants to appoint me on their staff of special
lecturers, with the understanding that I give one or two
lectures on topics of my own selection, and will give me the
services of technicians, typists, artists, or other assistance I
may need. . . .

July 17, 1917: Arthur is as calm and cheerful as possible

about the soldiering business. He has passed his first and second physical examination with flying colors, and seems quite ready for anything that may occur. His attitude is that he cannot go abroad for quite a while; and, when he does go, he may very likely not get in one of the massacres; and even from the massacres a good many people escape; so why get excited? I feel inclined to say just the opposite of the French cynic—Plus je connais les hommes, plus je les admire—and les femmes too, my dearest. It seems to me that I am surrounded by heroes and heroines, and that the only person who spends all his time in stuffy, snuffy chemical experiments and never faces anything more terrible than the dentist's chair is myself.

July 18, 1917: I feel very proud of Arthur. It seems to me that he is acting like a man and a gentleman, and is an honor to the rest of us. I wish we could do something to comfort Mother, for I think she is a great deal upset by it.

July 21st: I am very anxious to hear what you think about Arthur's going into the officers' training camp. I think about it all the time, but can't seem to make myself realize that he may go to France and be exposed to all the horrors that we have been reading about. Still, he has become surrounded for me with a sort of heroic, almost sacred, atmosphere; and I can't imagine myself in the future treating him familiarly or quarrelling with him as I have done in the past. You will laugh and say that lots of other people are doing as much or more than he, and so they are; but it makes a difference when it is one's own brother with whom one has grown up.

1918—June 24: The war news this evening seems so magnificent that it completely occupies my focus of consciousness. 45,000 prisoners for the Italians, and apparently a crushing defeat delivered to Austria just when she is tottering from internal troubles! I must be wise and wait for more and more results, as I try to do about the cows, but I certainly do feel like shouting Hurray and waving a flag.

June 26: What do you think Mother has done? Sent me a

check for $1015 to furnish a cook for the summer, and, I suppose, a butler and a whole retinue of servants. I shall write to her that I am telling you about it, and that the matter is in your hands. I expect you will want to try your experiment for a little while anyway; but, if you find it does not work well, here is cash to provide for meals at the Breakwater, or to entice any cook that you happen to see running wild around Gosnold Road or swimming up out of the Bay. What an easy sheltered life we do lead, how hard it is for us to be self-sacrificing and virtuous, and how ridiculous our attempts at economy are made to appear! Perhaps you will think Mother's methods of persuasion are a little brutal, but I don't think you should. She really thinks that you and the children will get sick if you don't have a cook . . . I was delighted to get your letter from Wister Station this morning. There is a peculiar sunny cheerfulness about your letters just like your dear self. I am afraid, however, that I am going to get some thunder and lightning soon for my fusscattishness about the things left around the bathroom, and I do not dare yet to write at length about the innumerable and enormous roaches that I afterward discovered in the kitchen.

June 29: I was delighted to hear that you got up there (Woods Hole) O.K. with the bairns, and that you are getting on so well with the cooking. Even if you decide to hire a French chef when you hear of Mother's thousand dollars, it will still be satisfactory to think that I have a jewel who can keep the wolf from the door when the pinch comes. . . . Cow #67 seems to be dropping off in her milk as the result of a very moderate cut in the phosphate supplied with her food. If it really turns out that so moderate a lack of phosphate produces so prompt an effect regularly, our fortune is made. Cow #214 is steadily going up, and is now giving something over 56 lbs!!. . . . I got home here about 3 o'clock, and have been having a lovely time. In the first place I interviewed Alberta again: she is now as sweet and pleasant as a May morn. Then I went out in the yard and pumped up my tires and filled the lamps, and put a smoke shield on the exhaust, and got filthy, but did not mind a bit. In the meantime, some of your friends were cutting the caterpillar tents off the fruit trees. Then I came in . . . and polished all my shoes and put new laces in them. So you can see that I have nothing on my mind but my hair.

July 1: I got your Friday letter this morning. After all, the daily letters are a good thing. I love to get yours, and I love to write to you, my dearest, strange as it may seem.

July 9, 1918: Don't you think you will have shown your mettle and that we will have economized enough on the cooking after a week or so more? I do not want you to tire yourself, my darling, and spoil your pleasure in the summer.

July 16, 1918: Mother sent me another letter from Arthur, written in sections. . . . He is working very hard—many nights on trains without much sleep and all that sort of thing—but well, I should judge, and happy, and greatly enjoying his intimate view of France and the French— something quite different from what one gets from travelling and staying comfortably at hotels. Still, his letters make me feel a little sad. I imagine I feel a tenderness in them that comes from being far away from everybody that he knows, and not being absolutely sure that he is going to get back. Well! the war news this morning and to-night has certainly been cheerful. Wouldn't it be wonderful if the Germans could be held right where they are!

July 18: It is extraordinary, but I cannot help my heart yearning over Jena. German or not, it was a dear little town, and those were golden days that I spent there. But that does not prevent me from enormously enjoying the present German check at the Marne. Didn't I tell you that our men would prove better fighters than the Roumanians?

July 25: Please look out for the submarine. It really makes me rather uncomfortable to think of their being as near you as Chatham and Orleans.

July 26: I got a letter from Murlin this morning, asking if I would consider a commission in the Medical Reserve Corps with assignment to the Division of Food and Nutrition . . . I thought at first that I would have to consult you and Rogers and everybody else before deciding; but, the more I thought about it, the more it seemed to me that it would be wise just to decide not to consider it without consulting anybody; and I have just written Murlin to that effect. My darling, I suppose it is all right to say again to you, what you know already, that I hope sometime—perhaps before very long—to make suggestions which will improve and cheapen the milk supply all over the world, wherever they are put into effect.

July 30: It is very nice to hear what you say in the letter I got to-day, that people at Woods Hole are interested in the cow work. I do not think, though, that I need to bring any notes. I imagine that I can sing without notes on that subject enough to satisfy the most enthusiastic. We are all suffering down here a little, I think, from a reaction about the War. . . . So complete a turning of the tables as Foch has accomplished since July 15 gets one up to a pitch of enthusiasm that cannot be sustained very long. . . . Bliss produced a terrible wet blanket last night by speculating about our losses. Of course we don't really know anything except that they must have been fairly heavy.

September 12: Arthur speaks about having been moved to a quiet sector further east. I suspect they were getting him with many more of our army into position for the new drive which started to-day. His letter is dated Aug. 21. He congratulates himself greatly on being again in one of his delightful French houses (that of the cure, this time) and in an undevastated region. . . . I registered to-day, and have my card safely in my pocket. I rather like the feeling of being at least registered for war service. There was a big crowd at the place, and I had to wait in line for about 3/4 of an hour. Things at Beltsville to-day look decidedly more cheerful. No more cows have aborted, and several of our phosphate fed animals have been weighed and seem to be doing very well.

September 18: Your proposition to put rooms in the roof and electric lights in the house at Comtuit [at Woods Hole] was a great surprise. I had no idea that you were thinking of such a thing at present. It is a great comfort to find that you are not flattened out and paralyzed by the War, as I am, and afraid to take a step in any direction. I dare say it will be a very good thing to have done what you propose, and that we shall be able to scrape the money together somehow.

Arthur I.

The ways to be cruel, to inflict pain, are countless;
all have been or will be tried.
                    Journey from the North:
            The Autobiography of Storm Jameson

There are three Arthurs in my family (also three Sarahs and two
Marys): my grandfather, Arthur Vincent Meigs, my older brother
who was his namesake, and my uncle, Arthur Ingersoll Meigs,
referred to as Arthur I. or A.I.M. AVM senior, Edward and Jack,
the middle brother who died in his forties, were all three retiring
and modest, whereas MRBM, AIM and "little Arthur," as he was
called to distinguish him from his uncle, were all cocky. Physically Arthur I. and his Ma didn't resemble each other at all; she
was tiny and he was tall; she had pale blue eyes and he had brown
eyes like his father's, but their combative characters were identical. Edward, who looked like his mother, was as mild and for-
bearing as his father. As for "little Arthur," his character was a
mixture of brashness and humility, of guilt and rebellion, that
appealed to his grandmother, irritated his uncle, and was the
despair of his mother (so much like him in her youth).

127

AIM's decision to go overseas in 1918 invested him, says Edward, "with a sort of heroic, almost sacred atmosphere." The twins were a year old when AIM went through this apotheosis; by the time they were aware of him he had gone back to his old shape, yet I remember having a sense of his hero's ease as he looked down on the twins in their cribs with a kindly, amused smile. He was the only member of the family with an athlete's body. He fitted his perfectly tailored English suits—with narrow pants, with jackets that curved gracefully over his buttocks—as much as they fitted him. I remember his horseman's wide-legged walk and the boots and shoes that appeared outside his bedroom door at night, mutely commanding to be polished. I remember AIM's clothes better than the non-committal brown or grey Brooks Brothers suits that my father and brothers wore. They wore them diffidently, whereas AIM wore his clothes aggressively, as if to say that his body made up for his little brown eyes and pudgy nose, his long, convex upper lip and tight mouth. With time the nose got pudgier, the mouth tighter and the eyes smaller, while the rest of his body stayed the same. Could this man have been the child with long curls, dark, questioning eyes and innocent mouth, wearing a Lord Fauntleroy suit, in a tiny portrait that hung in his living-room? The adorable child turned into a tough, self-righteous man who rode roughshod over people, who had allowed his youthful sensitivity to be smothered.

Photographs of AIM show him changing from the long-haired child to a small boy standing in profile with his brothers, Edward and Jack. Arthur has a vertical forehead and uptilted nose, his jaw is pushed forward with the determined look that he will wear till the end of his days. Even as a boy he seemed to know what he wanted, perhaps not to be pushed around by his handsome older brothers—in whatever costume: a Napoleonic cocked hat or a broad-brimmed sailor hat, or the shiny top hat that goes with his most splendid riding habit. As a young man, he stands again with his brothers but is taller now than Edward. His left thumb is hooked jauntily over his pants pocket and his look says, "Don't tread on me." His feet are planted a foot apart.

In the last photograph I have of AIM he is wearing the full regalia of Master of the Hunt: top hat, long-tailed jacket, white stock, vest and trousers, and high, spurred boots. He stands beside Harriet, his wife, in elegant sports clothes; she smiles at him, he looks at the camera—world-weary and cynical. His arms are hanging loosely, he is holding a pair of white gloves in his right hand. One of his little dogs, his homemade breed of Dandy Dinmont crossed with dachshund, stands near his feet. And just as the young man is different from the lovely child, so the aging huntsman is different from the horseman in a 1920 photograph, in shirt sleeves and rumpled pants and gaiters, whose arms are raised to hold Wister, standing on his shoulders. Wister still has a Dutch haircut and wears a tunic, almost a dress, over his knee-length shorts. AIM is an eager, defiant young man with a proud little smile. There are years of battle of one kind or another between those two photographs, his struggle to be exactly like the people who lived in the beautiful stone houses he built for them, modelled on those he had seen in France during World War I, to keep and ride horses that could win steeplechases and follow the hounds, to drink as hard, to laugh as loudly. When his mother died in 1934, he was free at last to live as he liked, and he began his new life by removing almost every trace of her from The Peak, where they had lived together since he was born.

AIM seemed to have been born with a fully-developed sense of class and pedigree. To him, the word "snobby" was not a pejorative but an adjective descriptive of himself and his peers. "A pretty snobby group," he says of a gathering of Philadelphians at the Century Club after World War I. They had come to listen to a lecture on the politics of Woodrow Wilson, the great war president. Since they were all Republicans, they considered him a villain. AIM disagreed, but the difference was only temporary and in 1938 he joined his friends in drinking a toast to Franklin Roosevelt's sudden death, for they devoutly believed that Roosevelt had "betrayed his class." As a horseman AIM liked to talk about the pedigrees of horses and he wondered if the same breeding techniques shouldn't perhaps be applied to produce perfect ladies and gentlemen. "They say of a stallion that he has the power to stamp his get," he says in 1932 letter to his brother, Edward, "and somehow the Meigses seem somewhat stamped." Even Meigs cousins and aunts and uncles: "Uncle Taylor, Aunt Emily & Charlie Hart & Louisa Green and God knows who all else" had the good fortune to bear the unmistakeable Meigs stamp.

According to AIM, it was essential for the twins to marry (of course they would marry!) men with similar race-lines, preferably from Philadelphia. They would find their proper spouses in the course of their coming-out, he believed, and he found it deplorable that this would be much more difficult because the family had moved to Washington. In his mind he compared the twins to the young Philadelphia women he admired, who all rode to hounds, called him Arty and were the daughters of his closest friends. The twins did not conform to his idea of what young marriageable women should be, they were timid and awkward, and this was because their roots had been plucked up and they had not been exposed to their own kind. At their coming-out parties he sadly observed that they were not popular and he tried to devise ways of mixing them with possible suitors. He chose the image of a sheep-fold: the girls were all to be herded into the centre of the dance floor and the boys would choose them at random. Otherwise, the twins sat on the sidelines, and the boys whispered together, casting glances not at the twins, but at the lovely young women who were already whirling about in the black penguin arms of their partners, with tails flying and snow-white chests puffed out.

Uncle Arthur! When people used to tell me that I looked like him I quivered with indignation, yet I spent my college years, a few miles from The Peak, doing my best to make him like me. The twins had let him down by not finding Philadelphia husbands and by conforming less and less to his ideal of womanhood. Yet I longed to please him and was happy to accept his invitations to dinner at The Peak, to sit with him and Aunt Hattie in their pearly-grey living-room and sip martinis before dinner, to be waited on by the Irish maid and to be served dinner by none other than Percy, who had been my grandparents' butler. Unlike Uncle Arthur, Percy had not changed for fifty years, he was as dour and discreet as ever, and went to his grave with family secrets (if there were any) that I will never know. I laughed when I found mention of him in a 1931 letter from MRBM to EBM, ''I had even asked Percy if he played 'checkers' but somehow that did 'not work', he had an engagement to go *shopping* with Louise [his wife]—and was glad he could not accept my 'invitation'—it would have been too 'irregular' for me to enjoy?'' It was like Percy to put my grandmother in her place and invent a shopping expedition rather than commit the ''irregularity'' of playing checkers with her.

A final photograph: Uncle Arthur and I are sitting on the sunny lawn of The Peak. I'm dressed in my WAVE uniform, hat and all, and he in one of his well-fitting suits. Uncle and niece, and yes, they look alike, each trimly dressed in uniform, I in that of the Navy, and he that of a country gentleman. We are engaged in a pleasant conversation on a sparkling sunny day, meeting on the only ground we could meet on—that of flowers, sheep and geese, Shakespeare and Tolstoy. And war, for he had been an army Captain in World War I, and here I was, ostensibly serving my country even if my unheroic job consisted of sitting safely in Washington in the Bureau of Naval Personnel. I didn't know at the time that he had seen the horrors of trench warfare and had behaved with great courage, or I might have been more humble. The surprise was that at last I had done something to please him and that he was visibly proud of me.

Outwardly, I had to admit, I was like him in the intransigence of my jawline and the smallness of my eyes. And wasn't an artist's soul hidden inside his crusty persona, expressed in the charm and beauty of his houses and gardens and his love for nature and art? Certainly he saw himself both as an artist and as a profound thinker, though (in my opinion) his ideas laboured mightily to get off the ground. Unlike EBM, he was a male chauvinist; unlike EBM he seemed always to be saying, "Look at me!" as he must have done when he was a little boy, showing off to his older brothers. In his letters he gets hold of an idea and rides it with the intent to win, but where are his sensitive horseman's hands to rein it in or make it jump lightly over a five-foot fence? Listen to him on August 21, 1924, in a letter to EBM. He is writing an article about architecture, he says, and has been thinking about a writer's problems. "Writing is *giving out*," he says. " A human being needs certain things in his intellectual or spiritual routine just as your cows have to have certain elements of food in their ration. One has to take in and give out just as we take in food and drink and give it out again. The comparison isn't pretty, but I think could be carried further, for we have to take in a great deal more that we can give out again. . . . Writing is giving out, just as reading is taking in. Talking and listening. Exercise and sleep. Creation and life itself—they are all 'put out and take in.' " Did AIM ever resist the temptation to "carry further" an idea than it wanted to be carried? No, because the sound of his own voice "giving out," as he thought, was dear to him and he was unaware of the listener's unspoken thought, yes, yes, I understood ten minutes ago. It never occurred to him that both talking and writing might be taking, *draining out*, like a pump draining a pond

131

of fresh water. So it was in his "giving-out" sessions with EBM, who emerged pale and depressed and defeated. Compared to AIM's loud and insistent talking voice, the voice of his letters was muted, even sweet and humble at times. "Perhaps we are both like George Washington," he writes his brother, "who, I have always heard, was more at ease and genial on paper than by word of mouth."

AIM had his own reason for never listening to anything I had to say: he believed in the inferiority of women to men. AIM to EBM, August 22, 1932: "As to my interest in your twins: your letter puts it at fever heat, but I must say I regret very much that you have fallen from grace sufficiently far to suppose that the female can in any sense be classed with the male; and can assure you that any little superiority which the twins may show at the present time can be easily overcome later." I was glad to come on firm evidence of what I'd always suspected! In general, AIM believed that young people had to be treated firmly, lest they get uppity ideas. "All youth has to be sat on," he had written to EBM. He believed in preaching humility to young people, he said, adding, "This may seem strange, coming from me." I suppose this ironic humility that popped out now and then was what made people fond of him. In the letter in which he had talked of "giving out," he had wondered "whether I could bring myself to the point of thinking that anything I had to say was in the least degree worth saying. Why say it at all? Why do anything? Those questions asked of oneself simply spell depression, and thank goodness, I've stopped asking them of myself and work away as if I were Will Shakespeare. I don't go very fast and it doesn't all look too awfully good, but I have plenty of time and don't worry a bit. There! I've written a long drool."

There are echoes here of the AIM who lives in the pages of his *Letters Written from France in 1918*—letters to his mother, his brothers, a friend and a cousin. They are sturdily bound in a big tan volume the colour of an army uniform. It was a parenthetical year of his life when he was open and vulnerable, strangely happy, free for once of family and the obligations of life at home. Reading over the letters a year after the war, he wonders at the alter ego who wrote them. "The one thing that stands out to me in almost unbelievable degree," he says in the preface," is the unsophisticated quality, or perhaps it might be described as healthy-mindedness. I felt, one year afterwards, that I was reading something that had been written by a man at least ten years younger." It *is* hard to believe that a hard-boiled man of thirty-six could enter the kingdom of heaven and become an innocent child again. It happened because he fell in love with the French and with France, and everything that he was and did was touched by this love which was like a conversion. He began to see life differently, with new possibilities of human understanding. "We're afraid to talk about what's closest to our hearts because we're afraid of making fools out of ourselves and the danger is very real. The French don't keep silent. They are not afraid to talk about what they're thinking about." In contrast, the Americans saw nothing and showed off, he said. Edward, too, had fallen in love with a people and their culture when he spent the year of 1907 in the German university town, Jena. "You said a pageful when you made the comment that my coming in contact with the French resembled your experiences with the Germans," Arthur writes to Edward.

Arthur did not have Edward's dilemma; there was no penalty for loving the French, and in his state of love he became like his ideal French person—simple, kind, observant. His job in the Military Police was to round up prisoners ("The look in these German prisoners' eyes is enough to break your heart," he writes), and he spent several months scouring the countryside on a motorcycle, or on horseback at the head of his troop of twenty men. He describes himself in several letters as one of the "coffee coolers," those back of the front lines, as opposed to the Infantry. "The Infantry fight the War. They have the hardships and they do the suffering and they are the ones who are regally uncomfortable." He feels guilty until he, too, sees trench warfare and knows the meaning of fear. In August, 1918, he writes, "I haven't even seen anybody killed or wounded but I've seen lots of dead ones, and a great many dead horses, and I've smelt a million smells. I've never had to put my gas mask on except for a minute or two. . . . In fact, I've had a cinch and know it and feel somewhat badly about it." The "cinch" wasn't to last long. In September his unit was attached to the 4th Infantry Division and for almost a month he slept in a dug-out without once taking off his clothes, and became intimately acquainted with the horrors of shellfire. For the first time, he shook with fear. "I amused myself by trying to see if I could stop it with a big mental effort and could succeed for a space of about 30 seconds, and then on she went again till the shelling was over, to recommence when the shelling did."

AIM's life in France is symbolized by a diagram he made in a September 17 letter to his mother and brothers. It shows strips of terrain:

> Beautiful Woods
> Trees, with all their leaves shot away
> The Judgement Day
> Trees with all their leaves shot away
> Beautiful woods.

"The Judgement Day" was No Man's Land where "there's nothing left but stumps, some 6-ft. high and some 20 or 30, and almost all rotten from having stood there for four years. . . . The ground . . . is all upside down. . . . What I'd like to make you feel is how we went Bing! out of the beautiful woods; Bing! into this Horror, and Bing! into the woods again." His own Horror, too, his No Man's Land, was between two beautiful woods: the first when he roamed France and fell in love with it, and the second which begins on Armistice Day with the gladness he shares with "the hundreds of thousands of men, women and children who have infinitely more reason to be glad than I." "Brilliant moonlight last night," he writes to his mother on November 11th, "I went out and took a walk in it. No guns, no artillery, no speculations on how nice a night it is for 'Jerry to come over.' They drop bombs most effectively by moonlight. I tremble lest I give the impression that will make you think, 'Ah, my poor boy. Think of what he must have suffered.' I haven't suffered anything at all. I've had a 'prince' of a time, and I'm riding on top of the wave, but just the same I'm glad it's over." It is mysterious how some men are able to keep the radioactive waste of what they have suffered in war from seeping into their lives.

AIM had in his nature the necessary toughness to be a soldier; he could shut off feeling in order to get through the horrors without going to pieces. Edward could never have toughened himself; he would have gone to pieces. He could not excise his loving memories of Germany any more than Arthur could prevent himself from feeling sorry for the pale undernourished prisoners under his authority. Yet both could speak of the "Huns," the "Bosche," the faceless monster that had to be defeated and deserved to be punished, and Arthur could write, "A lot of the Germans' best men have been killed, which is satisfactory." The best men were faceless like the monstrous war; multiple deaths were "satisfactory." The satisfaction of the body count, once one has assented to the necessity of war, this abstraction in contrast to Arthur's compassion when he looks at his prisoners and sees real men. "A thing happened that embarrassed me awfully," he writes to his cousin, Ed Ingersoll, in July. "One of my sergeants, the nicest man in the world, was taking things out of the prisoners' pockets— they had no arms when we got them—and being a little short on German, commanded—'Out, Down,' making a gesture of taking things out of the pockets and throwing them on the ground. The two poor devils on the end of the line understood only the last part of the gesture and immediately dropped on their knees, in the most abject manner. They looked as if they wouldn't have been in the least surprised if the next command had been to bow their necks preparatory to having their heads cut off. It embarrassed me, and it embarrassed my very nice sergeant."

It is strange that the enemy is transformed into a human being when he becomes a prisoner. He does not feel the change in himself; he is certain that he may still be seen as the enemy and be killed. His life depends on a convention but also on the shock of recognition between captured and captor. Even now, in our merciless time, prisoners are not always killed, and we see them on television, dirty and unshaven, herded behind barbed wire with the kind of heart-breaking look in their eyes that AIM saw. Perhaps the ability to see that look comes from being in the state of love that AIM was in almost continuously in 1918. At the end of the letter about the prisoners, there is a P.S. Arthur had been sitting in the still evening, "smoking my pipe with my back against a fence post." "When, like Lycidas, 'At last I rose and twitched my mantle blue, (brown in this case) a great big moon was sailing up over the shoulder of the hill, and standing in the lane, in the dust, was a funny little French fox, who took a look, and disappeared in the oat field. So you see, it's a land of contrast. A big six inch gun, firing on one side of the hill, and in this particular instance, complete silence between times, and on the other side of the valley, a ripe oat field, a big moon, a small fox and a country lane."

AIM, afraid in his gentlemanly way of giving offence, was always selfconscious on paper. "A half fear that I've said things

135

better left unsaid." The secrets of war: that men and animals wallowed in pools of blood and felt terrible fear, secrets, which if they could be told at all, were for men only. The things that women must not know, and spoken of almost in whispers between gentlemen, were the unspeakable and shameful things that men do to each other. AIM's letter could be shared with his brothers but not with his mother, for "all it would do would be to worry her and do no good." And would it not have worried Edward in the same way? Of course it would have, but Edward could be counted on not to make a fuss even if the knowledge made him sick. A man's letters contained the bloody secrets that women (ladies, at least) were not strong enough to bear. Men have always done their best to hide their crimes from their womenfolk, from the details of lynching to the huge secret of an extermination camp. This thoughtfulness of theirs for the "weaker" sex is based on false assumptions which are too obvious to list, but could be enforced, so to speak, more easily at a time when only newspapers and letters contained the day's news. It worked in the days before dead soldiers, children burnt by napalm, victims of bombing and torture and famine and concentration camps made their incongruous appearance in our living-rooms. Not even MRBM could be protected today from the "worry" of witnessing the world as it really is.

AIM had become a member of the fraternity of death and fear. He must have been glad that he did not have to kill, but glad that at last he was in danger of being killed like the doughboys he admired. That strange pride, the joy of sharing danger, the camaraderie of fear. A support group. "The reason I confess it is, that everybody else does, who's honest at all." A support group for fear, for killing and for being killed. Fear acted as a brake to keep men human, except when they were up in planes or behind long-range guns. An AIM, a George Walker who "shook," the "nice sergeant" who was embarrassed when the German prisoner dropped to his knees, those whose civilian selves have not been eradicated—are they extinct now? Even the doughboys, who had been trained to kill, were different from the killing-machines mass-produced today by systematic brutalization. As children, they learn to practise torture on animals; better to start when they are young. But this is not necessary; a man can be turned into a torturer and a killing-machine in a few short weeks. It used to be a problem—the pity that kept breaking out between one human being and another. It kept men from being really efficient killers. But the problem has been solved by modern psychology. There is no longer a difference between those who are face to face with the "enemy" and those who push buttons or release bombs from a bomb-bay; they are all equally indifferent to human pain, and equally unaware of any human bond.

"He was the most sensitive of the three," said a friend. "Look at his eyes." She was studying my photographs of the three brothers and was struck by the dreamy, yearning expression in AIM's brown eyes. To me this is belied by his belligerent mouth— until I reflect that the eyes, which shrank almost to pin-points in his old age, did indeed register his sensitivity, and the words that came out of his mouth defended him against the observation of his eyes. In the *Letters from France*, all his best qualities coalesce in the terrible adventure of the war. After the Armistice, his brash-ness and sense of humour served to get him out of the Army. He was anxious to get back to his real life, but the Army kept him dallying for several months. "Who is that old man with silvery locks?" he writes of an imaginary Captain—himself—who grows old and dies in a French village because the Army has forgotten him. He tries to escape, and is put into a stockade with other "Casual Officers" awaiting shipment home. In a hilarious letter to his commanding major he describes how he and a certain obnoxious Captain Posner succeeded, by claiming to be friends of the Captain, in getting aboard a ship. "Some members of the A.E.F. will boast," he says in this letter, "of their valorous deeds at the Front, and of what they did to win the War. Not so—I,— though knowing full well how instrumental I have been. I shall boast of how I escaped from the Forces. *That* is what took courage, foresight, intrepidity, constancy, determination,—in a word—all the cardinal virtues. Weak men have no chance. Only does suc-cess come to one who dares all,—who risks all,—and wins. . . .

To think that you commanded such an one.

He! T'is I!"

I try to remember an Uncle Arthur like the high-spirited, funny, compassionate AIM of the war letters and conclude that these qualities came out of a state of happiness and well-being that he never felt again.

Letter to Leonard Beale, from Bethelainville, France,
October 21, 1918

Dear Leono:

 . . . Now then, about the War . . . I don't know if I'm
going to say anything disgusting in this letter or not, but if I
do, I don't want it repeated or read to Mother, because all it
would do would be to worry her and do no good. . . .

 Perhaps I have made too light of the Military Police.
Certainly, a burnt child, etc.—and I've been "burnt" more
this last time than I ever was before. In fact, shell fire is a
very serious matter. Not when you're out of it, but when
you're in it. Now don't suppose I've been hit, or am sick or
anything, for I never was better in my life, but I have
undoubtedly had the experience of feeling a complete and
real fear. All this bellyache is merely a 'leading-up' to a
description of what it feels like to be in town that 'jerry'
(that's the Germans) shells. The reason I confess it is, that
everybody else does, who's honest at all. Besides which,
there's something inside you that tells you just about how
much scared you are and how much scared the other fellow
is, but believe me 20 minutes or half an hour's shelling of the
town you happen to be living in, can very effectively 'spoil
your pleasure for the whole day.'

 It's having your own men get hit and seeing it happen, that
raises Hell with your nervous system. One day just after
dinner, Jerry began dropping them over. About two minutes
afterwards, along come the Frogs, carrying three of their men
on stretchers to the hospital immediately next to which we
were camped, and saying, with that rotten look in their eyes
which one soon gets to know too well (it's the 'scared
look'—I don't mean in the least a 'coward' look—there's a big
difference, of course) 'Camarade', meaning that some of our
men had been hit. We ran over, Walker and I—he was the lt.
with me,—and some of the men, and there they
lay. . . . They had both been asleep under a hedge, and a
shell had lit about six feet from where their heads were.
Hoban was half out of his mind. He'd been shot through the
leg—not seriously—and was wriggling about and bleating that
he didn't want 'them' to amputate it. But Johnson. My God,

he was a nice looking sight. He was lying pretty still, but moving a little, and perfectly conscious. Hit in the leg and in the neck as I afterwards learned—but his head! The shrapnel splinter had hit him right in the eye and closed it or put it out—I don't know which. (Later learned it was put out) There was a great lump there on his cheek bone and another above his forehead—but his whole face and hair was just solid blood—just bright red.

We picked him up and carried him over to the Hospital tent which was near by, and he kept mumbling and moaning about his nose—poor devil—which I suppose was the least thing the matter with him. They operated on him and they evacuated him and I saw him again before he was out of the ether. The Doctor held out very little hope and I've never been able to learn authoritatively yet, whether he lived or died. (He lived)

That night Walker and I slept in the shelter tents—and we weren't dug in at all—we had the laughing and courageous idea that when you got under the shelter tent you felt safe even if you weren't. We were wrong. Jerry commenced about midnight and shelled two or three times, I'm not sure which, but it was a good deal, and there was plenty of it and we didn't enjoy it at all. They lit pretty deminition close, too—one about 20 ft. from the picket line, without touching a horse, and lots of others plenty close enough. Of course, you've often heard the sound described. Those that light far from you make a lovely long whistle and then explode,—but if one has you in mind, there's mighty little whistle. The best description I can give you of it is that it felt, in the dark there (and we're all afraid of the dark, just like children) as if some rotten dirty Octopus or Tentacle, or whatever you call those beasts that Wells describes, was reaching out his dirty ugly talons in the dark and trying to get hold of me. He put one in the Hospital, about 100 yards away, and killed two men operating, and the noise of the scufflings and movings when people get hit and get carried away somewhere—that didn't add to the pleasure of the occasion either.

Next morning I said to Walker, "George, were you scared?" He was about ten feet away from me in another tent. . . . He said 'I shook'; and that was what I wanted him to say, so that I could tell him how much I shook. . . . There's no place you can go. At least, you can go anywhere you like, but it isn't going to do much good. We moved into dug-outs the next day. That is, the Officers did. It seems pretty bad, I know, but there are enough of these dug-outs—there were in Cuisy, anyway—to take the Officers and some of the men, but not near enough to take all of them. . . .

The Major and I were riding into town one afternoon, and just as we reached the top of the hill, Jerry opened up. He was shooting them in salvos this particular time, and he had the range to a hair's breadth. There were four lit all at one time, just about on the four points in the town that we had posts on. That wasn't nice. And then, by golly, he plumped one in right in the middle of our Camp with the men in line getting their supper. It gives you a sinking feeling to see them scatter and run, and we could see the whole rotten performance just as if we'd been up in a balloon. You could see they'd got the traffic and it was blocked in a line running back over the sky line. When I got down to Camp, all it had done was to knock the tongue out of the limber of the Water Cart and hit two men, neither of them seriously—one in the leg, who could still walk, and one in the leg, who couldn't.

The posts in town had fared worse. One man, out of the five, just got bumped by a spent fragment, but could still stay on his post. One didn't get hit at all. One got badly hit, in the head, I think, but it was dark in the dressing station and I couldn't find out exactly. The other two were standing in a group, with our Adjutant, Lt. Smith. Smitty was in the middle and wasn't touched. Cpl. Alexander was hit hard in the head, right through his helmet, and the other man, Short, got it through the chest. Again, I don't know whether they are alive or dead, but they were hit hard. The same shells got two mules in one team and three horses in another, all of which were wallowing round in pools of blood, and were shot by the Major. The next night they dropped a shell that exploded the gas tank on the car right in front of Headquarters and burnt it to a crisp. . . .

In reading this over, I see that there's one impression I gave that I want to change. I said 'there is nothing you can do.' That is wrong. There is a thing you can do, and that is, crawl in your dug out, and the longer your community stays

there, the more it gets addicted to that said habit. Also, I
called Cuisy a town. There was just one roof left in the town
and that was full of holes. Some other towns nearby you
could hardly tell when you got into the town. I remember
one bleak rainy afternoon with an eager wind that Walker
and I rode down into Bethincourt. There wasn't any town.
Just rock piles. You see they've been hammering these places
for four years. The country is as bare and waste as the downs
of England and this town was backgrounded by a marsh in
which stood the gaunt stumps of what had once been a
wood.

All this has been just a word on behalf of the M.P.'s and all
the other so-called coffee coolers. . . .

Heigho! . . . I've written of life and death and hope and
fear. All rather large subjects to tackle, as you'll no doubt
admit. I'd rather like you to send this letter to Eddie Meigs
and show it to Eddie Ingersoll . . . but I look upon it rather
in the nature of a man's letter and have a half fear that I've
said things better left unsaid. You wanted to know and I've
tried to tell you. If my memory serves, I wrote a series
expressing a species of bucolic bliss that I experienced in a
charming country in a back area in Aug. I can't remember
exactly what all I said, but this one sets out to maintain the
'balance.' You should see the mud here. It's a lovely sight.
And you must also remember that we're now on our way to
another back area, but I'm convinced now that I like summer
better than winter.
Adios. See you soon,
A.I.M.

MRBM

December 20, 1919—AIM writes to his mother from Paris: "The sun was half out, for a wonder, though the streets were shining wet. I wandered through the Luxembourg Gardens and past Foyots and I thought of you a great deal. Do you remember how we used to go over there? And I went and looked up the Espalier trees that you were so interested in, over in the corner, to see what they were like in Winter. The water was out of the basin and the leaves were off the trees and the grass was quite green and there were only very few children playing about and it all looked very different and deserted—but just as nice as ever. What excited me the most was a coach and pair on the Pont Neuf on the way back. Two enormous, coal-black, French coach horses, with long fluffy shiny tails, and a coachman in blue livery, with white gloves and a tri-color cockade, and a beautiful carriage body that looked like a sitz bathtub, swung way up in the air on C-springs (there must be a flight of steps to get in and out by) and iron tires, and wheels that dished out, and a crest on the panel and an old party (I couldn't tell whether it was male or female) bundled up in the inside. It was most exciting and made me think of Thackeray who I'm reading."

This is Ma's son, wandering with alert senses and seeing the very things that would appeal to Ma. They both loved the tranquil world of trees, flowers, and animals, particularly the landscape of The Peak, the family place, to which, after the War, AIM added elements of Norman architecture: stuccoed brick walls capped with red tiles, little towers, wrought-iron gates, a Sunset Tower with a winding staircase and a conical roof, a Burning Pit which wafted blue smoke and a delicious perfume of burning leaves and brush. Some of the animals—cows, chickens and horses—had always been there; AIM added sheep, geese, ducks and a donkey. The sheep streamed from their shed down to the pasture in the early morning, the line of ducks and geese wobbled over the uneven ground to their dirty pond, whanking and quacking the entire way. The Sicilian donkey Thérèse, with her big, furry head, always stood close to her special chum, a white horse with a convex nose and drooping lip that spoke of extreme old age. One of his back hooves was always lifted so that the edge of it just touched the ground; this ordinary stance of a horse at rest fixes him in my memory. Many years later I worked for a long time on a big painting of my grandmother in a field with the old white horse beside her, and became so angry when it failed to convey what I meant (i.e. some message about death) that I took a knife and ripped the canvas from top to bottom.

The lives and tastes of AIM and MRBM were so entangled at the Peak that they could not be separated. Or so I thought until Ma died and it became clear that for years AIM had suppressed the wish to make over the house in his own image. Consider the fact that he lived with his Ma for fifty-one years—fifty-one years of her fussing and supervision and helpful advice. No wonder he bought an old farmhouse 100 miles away and that Ma lost him, not to a wife (he married after her death) but to horses and a new world of horsy friends. Still, he kept his headquarters at the Peak, and mother and son stuck together until she died in 1933. Sometimes I see AIM as an irascible saint, worn down by his efforts to be patient with his Ma, bottling up his rage and letting it out in spurts of furious impatience, not with his Ma, but with everybody else. He *loved* his Ma. Otherwise he would have left her, wouldn't he, like any other son? But I suddenly imagine a scene in which Pa, on his deathbed (he died in 1912) says to Arthur, "Take care of your Mother," and Arthur promises to. Ma of course has every reason in the world to want her unmarried son to stay with her, just as an unmarried daughter would be expected to.

143

So we will suppose that Arthur was so tightly bound by his promise to his father and in the web of his mother's irrefutable arguments that he could not leave even if he wanted to. He beat his wings violently; he bought his farm 100 miles away, but Ma kept hold of him.

"It won't do much good to try to stop Mother from doing what she wants," Arthur writes to Edward in 1918. "She has the habit." "Mother makes such a row," writes Edward to Margaret, "when she has to do what she doesn't want that I do not oppose her as much as I ought when you are not near to support me." MRBM, Mater, Ma, Mo, Mummy-wum, "the mother"—all these combined in the woman just over five feet tall whose will was the fulcrum Archimedes needed to move the earth. Her voice in conversation was loud and good-humoured; I see her at the end of the dining-room table, see her jutting nose, big, yellowish teeth; her faded blue eyes are alight because she has set off a heated argument between her sons. Margaret and the four children are, as usual, silent. Once when my brother, Arthur, was little (he told me), she had tried to make him finish his dinner. "Adults know what children like to eat," she said. "Do you know what *worms* like to eat?" asked Edward in a voice that trembled with anger. The scene is caught in a spotlight; I see Edward's flashing blue eyes, the sudden pallor of his face, MRBM's mouth open in surprise, and the little boy who is restrained from laughing by his father's terrifying seriousness. He understands that Edward has put himself in his place, and more than that, that they are both worms. But Edward is a worm with a ferociously-kept secret, his very own, i.e. what he likes to eat. His mother had never been able to pry it out of him, though she knew what worms *ought* to eat. Clearly, she did not understand in this instance why he brought up the subject of worms, when she had only been acting for the child's good. So she went on saying, "Eat!" to the end of her days. Eat! My ideas, my advice—and if you didn't eat you had refused to share in the sacrament of her little know-it-all body and proper Philadelphian blood.

And yet (for there is always an "and yet"), the same grandson who did not want to eat had a unique relationship with MRBM, magical almost, for he was fearless, and thus was the only one of us who could not be bullied. She bullied Edward, who was too high-strung, too easily shattered to oppose her; she tried to bully Margaret, who, as a daughter-in-law, was vulnerable, but who

144

was strengthened by Edward's weakness. As for the twins, they were mortally afraid of all grown-ups and curled into the innermost recesses of their shells when MRBM tried to draw them out. But Arthur was not afraid of grown-ups, at least, of older women. I remember his seductive power over even very old women, and the amazing fact that people I dimly perceived as old kooks, and shrank from, were his real friends. They loved him because of his courtly charm, his perfect gentlemanliness even as a boy, and his wonderful interest in every word they uttered. Even his brashness, which offended AIM and made him wish to dress his nephew down ("All youth has to be sat on," he said in this connection) was a passkey to MRBM's heart. He wasn't hopelessly shy like the twins or elusive like Wister (known as the Man of Mystery); he was full of crazy enthusiasm and chatter like MRBM herself. And how nice he was to look at, with his brown eyes, slightly pouting, sensual mouth, and straight dark hair, how different from the mousy twins, and Wister, an awkward adolescent.

In this period (1930-1932), the two Arthurs (AIM and AVM) make frequent appearances in MRBM's letters to Edward—the first, completely "dominated" by "horses, architecture, telephoning, building and rushing up to his farm" ("rushing affairs," MRBM calls them), so that his Ma never has time to talk to him, and AVM, an undergraduate at Princeton, who comes to the "Peak" to see his grandmother and recover from parties. She is a better mother to him than Margaret, who worries ceaselessly over potential moral lapses, the dangers of drink, etc. MRBM, on the contrary, is struck by the kind of wonder only grandmothers can feel, at one remove from the obligation to scold. "Arthur is very difficult to follow even in imagination," she writes Edward, November 27, 1931, "he is like 'Puck' in A Midsummer Night's Dream, here there and everywhere—but I hope he will be more deliberate at Christmas."

He had first dazzled her "when he was a child of 12, and went with me several times to sessions of Congress, both houses," she writes Edward in 1930, just after Arthur has won second prize in the Current Events Contest of the *New York Times*. "It is *glorious*," she says. In 1924 she had been "amazed at his intense attention and interest, and his mastery of the names and faces of the various members who spoke, and his understanding of what it was all about,—and this has never cooled down in the interval of five or six years since!?" (Not a glimmer of this ardour for

145

politics could be found in the twins or Wister, who kept their enthusiasms—if they had any—hidden from sight.)

Arthur delighted MRBM; even his "mad career of parties" delighted her. Here, too, she was impressed by his successes, for he was the only one of her grandchildren who was as spontaneously gregarious as she was. "I had so much wanted to write you about Arthur and his mad career of parties," she says to Edward, " . . . he was so pleased with them all, and although so sleepy in his *daylight* hours that he was half asleep when he was 'standing up'—with it all, he had quite a talent for 'going where he went' and getting what he wanted, when he got there;— I was amused to hear him tell that among his dancing partners he had danced with quite a number of the girls' *mothers* . . . and I said, why you dear thing, that was very diplomatic on your part and very flattering to them . . . for *one* of them drove him *home* twice from these balls, and was only too glad to have the chance. The day after the Newbolds' dance Nannie Morton Smith . . . told me that Nanny Beale had told her, that when *A. V.* asked her to dance with him she said, 'Well, you are the first Meigs who ever asked me to dance with him,' which was a hidden criticism of his uncle A.I.!!"

The secret of Arthur's fearlessness lay in his license to be himself with MRBM, to know that the very things that would have provoked his mother's wrath or her dire suspicions, would be treated with good humour by his grandmother. January 22, 1932: "Arthur V. seemed to enjoy *Rigoletto* immensely and it is a real pleasure to have him here,—I am trying to 'train' him to be more punctual, and to be more provident about having more money in his pocket when he travels, on the whole I think he ought to have more the idea of spending more *time* to carry out his engagements, but the money-point of view requires a good deal more study.—?" February 9, 1932: "I enjoy seeing Arthur once a week lately when he comes for the opera—when he suggested 'Susie' I was a bit flustered, never having seen her, but on the whole, I thought it would be better not to be too enthusiastic, he seems so young to be so fond, and I am not sure whether he will bring her or not,—in any case I felt I had better tell Margaret, for after all he seems like a son to me, but he *is yours* to command, or rather for me to consult his Pa and Ma."

"He *is yours* to command," or perhaps hers, too, but only after consultation with "his Pa and Ma." Theirs to command.

Grandparents (MRBM was the only one left), aunts and uncles, do not, like parents, carry the burden of the "right" to command. "I wish you were our mummy," said one of my nieces to me when she was little. "But if she was our mummy she'd be just like Mummy," said her sister with a child's amazing wisdom. This same child had accurately guessed the number of beans in a big jar, an intuitive feat of the same order as knowing that parents and aunts are acting out prescribed roles. Even MRBM, who loved to command, fell into the comfortable role of grandmother to Arthur, knowing that she could spoil him with impunity. More than that they could be friends, a subtle bond between an old woman not far from her death and a boy, a bond that could not exist between the two Arthurs. MRBM tried tactfully to "train" Arthur; AIM wanted to sit on him. He itched to exercise the parents' right to command. No doubt this had something to do with the stern bond between man and man and his regret that his nephew was not made in his own image. At any rate, he behaved more like a surrogate father than an uncle—to all of us. I remember his sharp appraising eyes which took in the woeful inadequacy of our entire beings (though, to be fair, he wrote to Edward that he had "wonderful kids"). Love for both AIM and his Ma was so indistinguishable from criticism that both were capable of making other people's lives miserable. And this made MRBM's disinterested love for her grandson all the more remarkable. For, given the right to command, her love could be like an iron fist, and everything unlikable about her—her possessiveness, her arrogance and irascibility—could be used in the service of this right. Impossible to know if she questioned herself and her rights; both she and AIM seemed to be as supremely comfortable in their characters as porcupines in their quills.

How vulnerable Edward and Margaret seem in comparison, more *real*, somehow, for they could be hurt, could bleed, were black and blue, with little unhealed wounds all over them, inflicted by MRBM and AIM with their indefatigable suggestions about the best way to live. MRBM and AIM were perfectly satisfied with their lives; they did not compare themselves to others less fortunate, as Edward did when he wrote to Margaret, "What an easy sheltered life we do live." Edward alone, I think, has a sickening vision of the time when the gates of the garden would be torn down and an epidemic of pure evil would sweep over the world. Pure evil, as insatiable as desire, was remote from the garden, one learned about it at second-hand, or not at all. MRBM's poles were "good" conduct and "bad" conduct, what is done and what isn't done, what is permitted by the Bible and what is forbidden, the speakable and unspeakable. In the absence of real evil, "bad" took its place, the word that covered vulgarity of all kinds, all lapses from good taste or good manners. AIM was bad when he accepted two invitations for the same evening and then tried to wriggle out of the first one. Pa and Ma had to reason with him all day long until he wrote "an excruciating letter of apology." They were able to see breaches of etiquette as if they had been fitted with special lenses, but they could not see the evil in their own careless phrases, such as: "The theatre was *packed*—almost all 'Christians' which was also very gratifying to both of us." Remarks of this kind can be found sprinkled through family letters, including those of Edward and Margaret. Anti-Semitism was part of the vocabulary of the Christian upper classes, and crept even into children's books. "Good people, I mean Christians," says twelve-year-old Jack in Mrs. Molesworth's *The Girls and I*. Mrs. Molesworth, one of the most popular writers for children of her time, dropped this into her readers' little ears without being aware that she was infecting them with the virus of evil, that she was one of the unconscious carriers of an evil that became epidemic.

When I think about MRBM, I divide her in pieces like a pie: a big slice of conformity, which observed upper-class routines like one of her pedigreed carriage horses, a slice of spoiled child crying, "I want! I want!", and a slice of originality bursting to get out of the little body, of energy that had to be spent running her friends and relations when it could have run thousands. I imagine her on a ridge with her generals, dressed in her hat like an upside-down kettle, her long linen coat and ground-length skirt, her big nose held high, her pale blue eyes lit by the joy of authority; she raises her right arm and the battle begins. I see her walking briskly around the battlefield looking at the bodies of dead men and horses and, like Napoleon, remarking that it would make a splendid painting. Little grandmother! Would I be as frightened of you, as submissive now if you suddenly appeared before me? Or would I respond to your spirit of fun, and laugh at your imperiousness? Weren't you like one of the puppies you loved so much: "so human, so quick, so madly excitable and destructive"? Wasn't your playful and autocratic girl's character fixed forever when you married the mild, sweet-tempered "Pa" and found that "I want" would work just as well as with a self-effacing husband, three sons and a daughter-in-law?

June 20, 1928—Margaret in her diary: "They are here, Edward as if he had been through the wars, his mother perfectly cheerful, straight from Budapest. Edward says he feels twenty years older, he is in a highly nervous gloomy state such as I have never imagined. I am doing my best to quiet him down & cheer him up but can make no impression." At the top of the page, there is a note in parentheses written in 1934: "After this experience Edward had nervous prostration which lasted about 4 years." She does not add that in October, 1928, an X-ray examination showed "infiltration, fibrosis and one large cavity in the apex of the left lung. The appearance is that of an old tuberculous process in the right apex." In other words, a death sentence, for though Edward spent most of 1929 in a sanitorium, he was never cured and died in 1940 just before the discovery of aureomycin.

Obviously, MRBM had exacerbated the depression and nervousness that were both part of the disease and part of Edward's character. He had the overstrung sensibility that made him a perfect victim, without the power really to fight even if it had been possible to win. He knew too well that he could neither win the battle against his mother nor defeat the disease that was slowly killing him. He had not wanted to go on the trip with his mother in the first place, had embarked in a state of furious irritation, and had forced himself to be calm by writing long humorous letters to Margaret. He strode around the promenade deck, several miles a day, says MRBM admiringly. "Edward is a Viking." Both wrote happily from Spain; MRBM was a good sport about the inconveniences of travelling and both were enchanted by Moorish architecture, by the gardens and cathedrals and museums. My own memories of MRBM in Europe are of a self-important person who insisted on loudly speaking the wrong language, with a terrible accent and a sense of indignation when she was not understood. She embarrassed me, as she must have embarrassed Edward. But she must also have tortured him in other ways, have shot poisoned arrows into his Achilles heel: his disloyalty to family roots, proven by his leaving Philadelphia. I imagine her grilling and accusing, talking of the brilliant career he might have had as a professor, asking him why he had to bury himself in the Bureau of Dairy Industry, even if he was chief of his division.

She must have rattled on about "the twins" who would never find Philadelphians to marry, who cared not a hoot for their family roots. "They must come out in Philadelphia," I hear her saying, though we were only eleven years old in 1928. She must have blackmailed Edward with the accusation that his decision to work in Washington had deprived both Margaret and the children of their real home. She had Edward at her mercy at last (and this was exactly what he had feared); she must have nagged at him until he wanted to cover his ears and flee from her. He was incapable of answering back; his answer had always been flight, but this time she had done her destructive work so skillfully that even Margaret could not help him to mend.

Yes, MRBM was like the puppy who jumped on her back and took hold of her ear without using its sharp little teeth. She was frolicsome and gregarious, could not bear to be left behind, dogged people's heels or rushed ahead of them, barking excitedly. "How would it do for us all to go together to Japan?" she writes to Edward in 1910. . . . "You know how I always *love* to have you with us." To have you with us, not to be with you. But Edward and Margaret went alone to the Orient, far away where they could be out of reach of Mother-Mater. It was the third link in the chain of Edward's rebellions; the first was his year spent in Jena in 1907, the happiest of his life. The second was the time he spent as instructor of physiology at Harvard Medical School in 1908-09, though his "loving Ma" kept him on the leading-rein of her letters. The fourth and final one was when he pulled up his roots and went to work in Washington. But MRBM countered by buying a summer house in Woods Hole down the road from Edward's and Margaret's house, and there she was again, free to interfere in everybody's lives. "It will be nice for you to have Mo nearby," AIM wrote Edward with unwitting irony.

Mo had arrived with her big, open Packard and her chauffeur, James, and went out for daily drives at 35 miles per hour with some sacrificial family lamb, all too often one of the twins. AIM wrote his Mo in 1927, "Please have a lovely summer and be sure to remember how much you are loved by your AIM." He had always written lovingly to her and never more so than during World War I when he was in France. "Apropos of all you say about my birthday and how much you miss me, and how nobody understands you as well as I—it makes my heart very full and warm, to think that I have such a mother." It was a case of a successful chemical reaction between mother and son. She was his "mummy-wum" and he was her "sonny-wax," words that make me smile when I think of the reality—a thirty-six year-old man and his sixty-seven year-old mother, both as pugnacious as Pekineses. It must have pleased MRBM to have turned out this son in her own image; it must have disturbed her to see Edward slipping away from her influence. For she couldn't have helped seeing that even if he had behaved like a loving son, she had the immediate power to irritate him, to set off all his puzzling refusals. It had been going on since they were boys—AIM's moulding and Edward's refusals, as we see in a letter from AIM to Edward in June, 1924. "I was telling Mother last night," he says, "that I feel a deep sense of gratefulness now to her and Father for the many things they made us do that I hated at the time. They didn't make us do things all the time that we hated. In fact they shaped their whole lives round what seemed to them to be our best interests. . . . You say it made you feel gloomy."

It is obvious that Ma held the reins of power and was the standard bearer for proper behaviour, and that Pa went along with her, just as Edward accepted Margaret's judgement of "what is done." Wives who had been shaped by patriarchal rules became mistresses in the art of shaping. The words they spoke had been whispered by the great Ventriloquist, and they took His voice as seriously as Pythia, the priestess of Apollo, took the voice of the Delphic oracle. The oracle told them that children had to be made to do many things they hated, just as they had to be made to eat things they hated. Pa knew better than to try to override "Mother's" decisions in the household domain. Even when his portrait was being painted by William Merritt Chase, he trusted her to give the painter advice. "Mother is to come in to criticize," he says in a letter to Edward in 1910. "She manages with him wonderfully and he often puts in the very dabs of paint that she suggests, and I am sure she has been in many ways helpful and has done no single wrong thing to the picture." It was surprising that Chase, "a strange little man, very human . . . with an immense idea of his importance," as Pa says in another letter, accepted "Mother's" suggestions. In the same way, she was helping to paint the life-portraits of her sons, and had the responsibility of "doing no single wrong thing to the picture." But human beings are less tractable than paint, and Edward, at least, grew tired of being dabbed at.

I should like to know which of MRBM's suggested dabs affected Chase's conception of Pa. There is no trace of severity or impatience in the face, only the gentleness Edward describes in his 1914 memoir of his father, "which made it difficult for him to bear the sight or even the thought of suffering." Edward ends his memoir with a glowing tribute to Pa as paterfamilias: "He was the centre of a family life of which no adequate picture can be given, but to which all its members will look back as to the foundation for their belief in the possibility of human happiness." This was the family life touched with love for the father who had died two years earlier and untouched by his private recollections of occasional feelings of gloom. Edward was so like his father in his "passion for the truth . . . gentleness . . . strong sense of justice, intense conservatism, hatred of display," that I wonder what his father could have demanded of him to make him feel gloomy. "Many things," says AIM. And I conclude that Edward felt that even if he was like his father, his father did not always know what his "best interests" were. They were certainly not identical to those of his mother, whose altruism (as AIM perceived it) was really a device to bind her children with hoops of iron, as Blake put it. Edward felt the gloom one feels if a parent says, "I'm punishing you for your own good," or "it hurts me more that it hurts you."

AIM would faithfully repeat the lessons he had learned from his Ma, about the importance of family and roots and breeding. He believed, as we have seen, that human beings, like horses, could "stamp their get." It was a pity that he could not put his theories to the test, for he had no children. But he stamped his horses in his own way; their names all began with M: Miltiades, Menelaus, Mephistopheles, Madrigal. As for MRBM, her initials, intricately twined, were all over the place: on the door of the big Packard, just below a band of simulated wicker caning; on the black door (in cadmium yellow) of the town-car, on the velvet ribbon she always wore around her neck, a circular plaque with a silver monogram inlaid with tiny diamonds. No other letter in the alphabet could convey the absolute respectability of the Meigses as well as this good, solid, symmetrical M; Margaret's maiden initials—MW—incomplete (though they were unique, for they could be turned upside down and still remain the same) without the final M, the two M's embracing the modest W (a palindrome), like two upright hands with thumbs touching. For the

152

rest of her life, she signed her whole name, Margaret Wister Meigs (except at the end of her life when she laboured over the writing of "Margaret"); she had not lost her name, she was saying, merely stood under the wing of another equally powerful.

It is a pity that people have so little time now to write letters, for they can often hold the best of a person, and a correspondence is a lifeline between two best selves. AIM had stated a great truth when he wrote to Edward about the difference between their written communications and their face-to-face meetings, when they fell to "calling each other nincompoops." Exceptionally, the letter-writer is the flesh and blood person, slow to anger and stridency like Edward, but even Edward, when he clashed with AIM, became excited and anxious; his voice rose, his eyes widened. ("It seems that most of our energies go into controversies," AIM writes EBM, June 23, 1924.) But Edward was never unreasonable and bullying as his brother was, stripped of the sanctuary of his letters where the ego feels as cozy as a caterpillar in a cocoon. More important, a letter provides a place from which one can reach out to others and gives evidence of love which a person face to face with another cannot or will not give. Thus MRBM, the indefatigable letter-writer, discloses a gentle self, who goes far beyond the nagger she was in person. Her letters to Edward, her thanks to him for his, show a continuous relationship of need, one for the other that lasted until she died. At a distance, her meddling was diluted to the proper dose of kindness and interest, and we see her as the relaxed alter ego of the MRBM who was as fussy as a bantam hen. And aren't the lovable, vulnerable people in the letters as authentic as the uncle and grandmother I knew, for whom my love was so grudging, whose jostling, hustling egos seemed to take up so much room? Now (in 1987), where are the letter-writers whose alter egos are set free by the written word to romp like colts in a field? There are not many left. In her old age, MRBM's aggressive handwriting became a compact, orderly script written with the finest of pens, a medium for her most delicate feelings. Her last letter to Edward speaks what she could not have said directly to him: "Let me tell you, the present you gave me . . . of a carnelian owl . . . is one of the most precious bibelots I possess—because *you* gave it to me and *I like it*." Two months later she was dead. Edward took back the carnelian owl, and after his death it sat on its ebony perch in Margaret's room until she, too, died, and it was claimed by her son Arthur. "The darling little carnelian owl," as MRBM called it, has always sent me a mute message of continuity and now it speaks through MRBM's letters; it has become the symbol of her tie to Edward, the thing that mattered most to her.

MRBM: Some Letters to Edward

October 29, 1909: Pa and I are dining tonight with the awful Scotts of Brookstone—I try to forget it as much as I can if we could only have been asked somewhere else, enough to have declined, but failing that, Pa's tenderness for the "old place" and his general kind-heartedness for bores—there seemed no way but to "accept with pleasure." . . . Pa and I would like to know how much your "furnishing" has cost you, for we are going to send you a check for the amount—I hope you will not consider this acquiescence in your being away from home for I am looking at it only as a college outfit, and want you at home as much as ever. You can imagine I want to hear how you are settled, the sort of place and the people, I *do* think it is far better than the other horrid suburb of the Med. School. . . .

September 27, 1909: Your letters are of the very *very* best, so pleasant in the telling and so satisfactory in the consideration you are receiving on all sides . . . I am very much amused at your meetings and goings with Ellis Robins—I think he is a "straw" which shows the blowing of the wind, for to like to be with you when he is so accustomed to "celebrities" both literary and social seems to express his appreciation of you by some subtle quality of his own, which has carried him quite a distance, so far, it must be granted . . . Sally and her Ma, and your father and all the oculists in sight have been having a "circus", all because of Sally's "young man," it seems she met a certain *Morgan Jopling* out at Marquette where she has been visiting a school-friend for the last two months, and arranged to her own satisfaction to marry this young man . . . without consulting her father or mother—even having thought of the lot to build on, and the kind of house to her mind . . . Nothing remains but the shock-in-waiting for her father on his return at the thought of losing his daughter in such a remote place as Michigan. The young man is 26, a graduate of Harvard and with a good financial outlook from a rich or probably rich grandfather! . . .

October 23, 1909: On Thursday we did the Dick C. wedding, I thought the bridal party far from handsome and quite lacking in that "beauté du diable" for *thirty* was a young average for bridesmaids and ushers,—there was a crowd at the church and the groom's relatives were quite the more distinguished in appearance. As for the Roebling house, it was very big, very rich, and very tasteless but J. Holland provided the food so no one grumbled. It seems the girl has no money but what "Pa" gives her and it is said at the Princeton Club this is $10,000 a year, which is rich for poverty but poor for "yellow rich."

March 12, 1910: This afternoon Margaret came in after the *last* Phila. Orch. Conc. to have a cup of tea with me and a sort of Good-bye for Germantown. Pa is so pleased with his prospective daughter that he took up quite a large part of the visit, and showed her your miniature & Great Grandfathers and all the other "Meigsiana" collection of family portraits.

March 30, 1910: . . . I also observed for the first time in my life VERY critically the *Oakley groom* . . . who was a "swell show" and Margaret was in "conniptions" over his attire, and has handed you over to me for your wedding-costume,— Arthur I. says he is the authority on style, will you submit to our combined opinions?

April 30, 1910: We are very much pleased with Pa's portrait, it really is a work of art, and I think Chase has been trying hard to make it so. I have asked him out to the Peak on May 7th to stay over night and see the May Pole Dance and Revels of Bryn Mawr College which he seemed to have a fancy for—I asked Dr. and Mrs. Weir Mitchell too but I could not catch them. I was delighted to get your note about your "croak" having cleared, and your safe arrival in Boston,—do take it easy, long *sleep*-hours for "il faut reculer pour mieux sauter," later on!

155

December 4, 1929: . . . I feel as if I had not seen you for a year—and I have such an intense desire to talk things over,—Arthur is so immensely occupied with riding and horses, and has so many "boards" and meetings, and although he is not so very busy at architecture, he does not find that altogether an enjoyable holiday . . . No melting of the snow which is over 3 inches deep over the whole countryside . . . and the temp. for the last two days, 22° from early morning till dark and lower still in the morning,—this afternoon I took a drive with James in the closed Packard to Valley Forge, and I have never seen such a spotless white. . . . The lunch of 22 on Thanksgiving went off very gaily, Sally Jopling and Morgan and Jane were all staying with us . . . Jane is a very modern girl, quiet in her conversation but quite able to go everywhere by herself, goes to balls always with an "escort" as her boy-friends are called and motors in his car without any other companion or chauffeur, smokes many cigarettes and has cherry-colored lips, very *dark cherry*; on the other hand, I think she is a great joy to her parents, and they give her "her own way" with entire approval, as there is no other way for the modern girl, they believe . . . Dr. Owne Toland . . . told me at the wedding reception of Bernice McIlhenny, where he was an usher, being a classmate of the groom . . . who was the smallest man I ever saw married, much shorter than myself, and whom Dr. T. told me, was a "bit tight" I was not very favorably impressed . . . I went to two weddings on Sat . . . one at, or on, the Lincoln Drive in the East Park, the other, Ellie's niece, Emily McFadden at Rosemont, to Mr. Randolph Harrison of New York—a very desirable party, Ellie tells me & has but one drawback, he *must* live in N.Y.

February 1, 1930: About the "Punch" subscription, —I entirely agree with you about your preference to subscribe to it yourself—I have had two long talks with *Miss Donnelly* (quite a friend of mine) of the Dept. of *Magazines* at Wanamaker's, and she tells me that she is crediting me with *three subscriptions* on my *Feb.* bill, *one* for *Punch*, *one* for the *Nature Magazine* and *one* for the *American Boy*, the last two were sent for "Xmas" presents from *Eliz.* to your children and charged by mistake to me, —and *Margaret* has subscribed

156

for your "Punch" since last *Nov.*—as you write me, so this is
all straightened out, —and I have discontinued all these
"*copies*" & had them cancelled, which were sent to
Washington as I did not know about Elizabeth's subscriptions
for your children, and I dare say, she may have told me—but
it is much simpler for all of us, to do as I suggest for the
present—— . . . I have but one criticism to make on
anything you ever write me, —and that is the *color of your
ink*, it has an ancient and a "brownish" cast, which might
suggest it had passed several seasons in its bottle, —I find
"Waterman's blue black" writing fluid in a "*10 ct. bottle*" is
much more convenient than the pint at a time I used to
buy—which spills on my fingers and gets thick, but I buy
several ten cent bottles at a time which, —one of them, —fills
an ordinary inkstand, and leaves two unopened for future
use?

May 19, 1930: It has been very difficult for me to settle
down, and know how to begin, with all this rushing about of
Arthur's, he has been completely absorbed with four or five
different "rushing affairs"—first *horses*, next architecture,
telephoning, building and rushing up to his farm, which is a
motor trip of about 100 miles . . . he has now bought 4
farm-horses . . . but at present there is no good stabling for
his many riding horses, which number, counting the gray
mare and the brood-mares 8 more . . . and he has countless
meetings of all kinds, both financial and racing, . . . and
indefinite dining with the horsey-set as well as his old
cronies, etc. etc. etc. !!!

January 25, 1931: I have not yet put away all my "Xmas"
presents! Everything has been so *rushed*, but I have the
darling little "carnelian owl" on my bureau and I love to see
it there when I go to bed, it looks so "sleepy."

May 4, 1931: Even *now*, when I want to write *you* a letter I
have nothing to begin with but ink, all pens are *rusted* in the
penholders, —no writing paper in the desk so I have to make
out with a tablet, —no time for gardening or the country life
with almost sublime weather and lovely blossoms and Jap.
cherries and budding lilacs and wisteria ready to burst with

delight . . . I cannot give you an idea of how I fuss and fiddle, and only *just stand still*, like Alice when she tried to run faster and faster with the Red Queen.

May 18, 1931: —The wisteria, the lilacs, my grand *flame-color* azalea, which is at least 6 ft. high and twelve feet in circumference, —are superb; to say nothing of the "Tulip rainbow" at the end of the bowling-green, and the splendid paeonies now at their best, are wonderful; by actual measurement, the blooms are 26 in. in circumference, and 10″ in diameter, this would seem inaccurate geometrically, but it is a *fact*, which you might be able to prove by seeing them, but I have just carefully measured them with a tape measure!? they are the bloom of the *woody* variety of paeony, a lovely rosy pink, and almost crimson center . . . It is a great satisfaction to win a prize, and I congratulate you and Margaret and the Twins on the blue ribbons—but horses to me are an "embarras" for with the overwhelming interest which Arthur has in them, and the vast number he is showing at Devon, they *dominate* and control.

December 16, 1931: I loved your account of your dancing at the Marine Ball, I hope it was more graceful than the modern back & forth shuffle of the party at Arthur's ball with the frightful oriental "Tom-Tom" music of the saxophone and no-rest-variety, —with the hideous noise, and all as an accompaniment to the monotonous shuffling scuffling slow movements of the dancing no grace, no rhythm, no swing to even remind you of *dancing*?!

January 22, 1932: . . . Arthur I. is if possible even more interested in his farm and horses,—he had a horrid raid of two police dogs, who came two nights in succession, and killed *eight* of his sheep. Roy was provided with a gun the second night, Arthur took photographs of the massacre, Roy did not kill a dog but he must have hit him . . . I have been absurdly busy going and coming to meetings and lunches and dinners, which I half like and half growl about like the "Irish Member" described in *Punch* years ago,—"and there's the 'Irish Member,' devil take him, for there's no doing with him or without him."

Mother-love

"There's no doing with him or without him"; that was MRBM.
As I think about her I see that she was one of the dominating
influences of my childhood; from her I inherited a love for beautiful landscapes and beautiful houses, for flowers, animals and
birds. I inherited her aesthetic sense, her gift for painting and her
sharp tongue. My letters are more like hers than like those of anyone else in the family except my brother Arthur's. His handwriting, too, though more barbed and tangled, is modelled on hers
and I have letters of my own which show that I once imitated
her aggressive style. It is strange that I did not feel a special kinship with her but a paralyzed antagonism that prevented me from
mourning her death in a heartfelt way in 1933. It was the same
year that our governess, Miss Balfour, left after eleven years with
our family. To me, MRBM, AIM, my mother and Miss Balfour
all exercised the same kind of power over children—the power
of watching for us to do something wrong, the power of instant
disapproval. In this respect, MRBM was certainly the most benign,
though her well-intentioned insistence was a form of tyranny, and
I find it hard to explain now why she made me feel so shy that
my thoughts scuttled about like frightened mice. I think that for
the period of Miss Balfour I was virtually incapable of feeling real

159

love (i.e. the kind that is confident and relaxed) for any member of the family.

It was a revelation to read Margaret's letters to Edward just after the twins were born and to discover mother-love, like buried treasure, her happiness in us, the twins. It made me want to dance with joy! The letters told of a heavenly time when the planets revolved around us and Margaret was so full of love that it pours out of the little blue envelopes, love for Edward, love for *us* ("my dearest, my sweetheart, I love you so," "my two wee ones," "Sarah so beautiful you won't know her and Mary so smart." "Everybody wants the twins," "the beloved twins.") I scarcely knew of the existence of this loving mother and it explains my own capacity for love, which finally bubbled up after its long life underground. What made it possible but the sense of having been cherished and spoiled when we were infants, hungrily feeding at her breasts—with plenty for each, Margaret shyly told Edward. The feeling of being drowsy with sated hunger, warmed by the tenderness of her smile as she looked down at her almost bald twins. Seven months exactly before we were born, "a little squeamish this morning," she wrote to Edward. We were making her feel squeamish, though she didn't know about me, who arrived without warning, ten minutes after Sarah. "Oh my darling, how I love you," she wrote. By then she was a seasoned mother with her two boys, aged five and two. "The children are well and pretty bad," she wrote. Now, suddenly, I remember the time before the time of real badness, of freedom without any prohibitions except to prevent us from falling and hurting ourselves.

Even Bessie, who appears in Margaret's letters and diaries like a wicked older sister in a fairy story, fell for the twins. May 6, 1917, Margaret to Edward: "Bessie and Mary [Bessie's daughter] appeared tonight and were enchanted with the babies. They said they had never been as excited as when you told them there were twins! Mary brought them lovely bibs and Bessie a cheque of $12.50 for each, a bank account for each." No doubt twelve dollars then was the minimum sum required to start a savings account, and the parsimonious Bessie . . . but it just occurred to me that she had divided her customary baby-gift in half, for, like many other people, she thought of the twins as a single entity. I was glad to learn that Bessie and Mary were among our hordes of fans, even if I know that the sight of twin babies sets off an excessive, almost hysterical reaction in every female breast.

Dearest Mother, without the testimony of your letters I'd felt deprived of mother-love; I'd forgotten the age of innocence before Miss Balfour. After I read them I had a dream; I was lying face down on a slope with Greta Garbo, who was going to make a film about the twins and their first years. I felt the warmth of her body next to mine and was filled with a winged feeling of bliss, lighter than air, and woke up happy. Garbo was going to make a film about the reality of our threesome, you and the twins, one at each breast! I look at the little pieces of blue-green paper, five words on each line in your unchanging handwriting. You are patient and understanding, too happy to scold. "Arthur hammers all day long, putting a deck on your boat, and removing it, but I don't believe the boat can be hurt, and the children [the boys] have such a wonderful time and play so long and happily that I don't interfere." Dimly, very dimly I seem to remember this permissive time, the time, too, of our nurse, Peggy Malloy. "You always seemed to me sweet and sunny," Arthur writes me, March 6, 1986. "Old Peggy Malloy felt the same way. She sang a song about your heart . . . the punch lines were, 'Hi Mary, ho Mary, listen, love, to me! Bigger than a sweet potato down in Tennessee!' "

My heart was bigger than a sweet potato before Miss Balfour, when naughtiness was still imprecise. "She's very positive, Mum," said Peggy Malloy about Sarah. "She threw two cups of milk upon the floor." When Miss Balfour came, we became acquainted with all kinds of badness, particularly those relating to little girls. Eleven years later your twins emerged "repressed" (said Uncle Arthur), "suppressed" (said Aunt Sarah), ignorant of life and almost pathologically shy. For years my heart would beat like a kettle drum if I had to speak to a grown-up. We were not at all in your image, the saucy, irrepressible Margaret I know from your letters and diaries. We were the "white rabbits." How I hated your friend who called us that; she swooped on us, laughing (she herself looked like the March Hare) and we panicked.

You had only one irritating Mama to rebel against; all mother-power was concentrated in her, and after Papa's death, father-power as well. Sometimes I wonder—did your direct relationship to Mama stamp the idea of fidelity on your heart? For Mama and Papa were faithful to each other, and the reality of two: Mama and Papa, Mama and you, you and Edward, became your deepest belief. Your faithfulness unto death is what I admire most in you, and I think it came from the certainty of never having been aban-

161

doned. Your heart was always intact. One of your twins inherited an intact heart with its lifelong fidelity, and the other one (me) lived her childhood and adolescence with a heart like a slippery and elusive nut. Wasn't this because we had a double-mother, you and Miss Balfour, neither one of you real or completely trustworthy, in league with each other (for our good, you thought) and against us, for each of you cancelled out the mother-power of the other?

July 10, 1986: Last night I dreamt that I was walking side by side with you, holding you close to me, with my arm around your waist. I said, "There's something I've been wanting to ask you for a long time. Did you ever have any regrets about Miss Balfour?" And you said, after a tiny hesitation, "No, no regrets." I woke up wanting to cry, for I had wanted you to answer, "It was the biggest mistake of my whole life." But you had forbidden your mind to harbour any regrets and even in *my* dream I could not make you betray yourself, just as someone under hypnosis refuses to do what she would not do in a waking state. The dream brings back my frustration when, no matter how hard I tried, I failed to pry out of you something you didn't want to talk about. In the case of Miss Balfour, it was the unbearable knowledge that you had forfeited eleven crucial years of our growing-up (age 5-16), had handed over your mother-power to Miss Balfour. The development of your twins' hearts was slowed because we were separated from our real mother by the presence and authority of Miss Balfour, and we took it out on both. In my dream you seem to be saying, "Now that we love each other, we don't need to hash over the past." Or am I saying it to myself? Uselessly, for I go on hashing, still seeking answers to the unsolved mystery: of you, Father, Miss Balfour; you, Miss Balfour and each twin; Miss Balfour, Sarah and Mary—triangles overlapping triangles. All those early triangles were kill-loves; they set the pattern for endless repetitions of the equation that first protects, then wounds and destroys.

"No, no regrets." And I imagine that if I had really asked the question, you would have closed the subject by saying, "You're like your father. You think too much."

Miss Balfour

Miss Balfour (Sheila Marjory Goldie Balfour was her full name) was preceded by another Norland Nurse, Miss Lugar, whom I must have loved because I spent the whole day of Miss Balfour's arrival in tears. "Why are you crying?" she asked kindly, but I could not tell her—or myself. Miss Lugar, according to AIM, had suffered from "defects of character." In 1924 he writes to Edward to ask if perhaps Miss Balfour knows of another governess with her own ideal qualities. He has spoken to a friend whose Swiss governess is proving "less and less satisfactory," about "what a nice woman Miss Balfour was." "My own bachelor notion of this thing," he says, "gleaned entirely from observation—is, that the principal requisite in a governess . . . is a pleasant disposition and a kind heart, and it seems to me that brains become a lesser consideration." In a subsequent letter, he speaks again of his friends, now in Europe. "The maid they have with them," he says, "is by this time utterly fed up with Europe and wishes herself back in Phila. Again, the superiority of the incomparable Miss Balfour!"

It is clear from AIM's observations that the perfect governess is one whose relationship is perfect not with the children, but with their parents, one who is capable of walking the tightrope of being in charge but not taking over, of enthusiasm without passion, of emotions under continuous control, who shows a continuous readiness to help, and a discretion and delicacy of mind equal to the parents'. If the governess seems perfect to the parents, there is no need to ask the children if she seems perfect to them. Besides, in our peculiar way, we "loved" Miss Balfour, and I remember the horrible shame of times when I didn't love her. "I hate you! I hate you!" I shouted at her once. Silence followed, as if the sky were about to fall. It didn't need to fall; guilt struck in its place. Perhaps it was at that moment that Miss B. observed that sticks and stones could break her bones but words couldn't hurt her. (But words could hurt, for she washed out my mouth with soap when I said on another occasion that Arthur was a "damn fool.")

The "incomparable" Miss Balfour would have gone to the stake sooner than admit that she was "utterly fed up" with anything. Perhaps it was because she was perfect that she did not gather us into her arms and tell us stories about her childhood, perhaps it was against the rules for a Norlander to become too fond of her charges. Perhaps, if she seemed severe to the twins, she was seen as just exactly *severe enough* by their parents. Girls required a special severity. Wasn't she as gay as a lark when she organized games and parties at Woods Hole for "the boys": treasure hunts that led breathlessly around the house and garden, games of Spin the Platter and charades and amateur theatricals? The twins were said to be too young for these parties for which Miss Balfour exercised all her ingenuity and enthusiasm.

Perhaps Miss Lugar had been unable to walk the tightrope and had asserted her *self*, and had been seen as subversive, too loving? Not severe enough? Was she "utterly fed up" with something? Miss Balfour must have prayed nightly never to be seen in any way as threatening to our mother, her friend and potential enemy, never to be seen except as the "perfect governess." The governess, as Charlotte and Anne Brontë discovered long ago, is oppressed per se. For even if we were the nicest family in the world, even if my parents treated Miss Balfour like a friend, wasn't she inevitably a subordinate, didn't she lose eleven years of her youth and her enormous energies and talents in a relationship that is humanly destructive by its very nature? Didn't she give too much of herself away, lose too much of herself by attrition, and finally, suffer the fate of every governess—to discover that she is not really a member of the family but has become obsolete?

She had walked the tightrope with such total selflessness that it was unthinkable to ask her to leave. We were sixteen and I know that my mother was brooding over the regrets that she refused to acknowledge in my dream. Did she and Edward agree that it was time for Miss Balfour to go? Edward, if he wanted her to stay, would not have risked saying so to Margaret. Miss Balfour, despite her perfection as a governess, her indispensable qualities as a housekeeper, was a woman. I am convinced that my mother, dazzled by Miss Balfour's perfection, had forbidden herself for years to think, "Miss Balfour is another woman," convinced that Miss B. never once stepped over the line. Except when she allowed Arthur to kiss her goodnight (in 1928)—that little pleasure stamped on by Margaret like a scorpion! Perhaps that was the first time that an alarm bell rang in Margaret's mind. In 1925, she had not been in the least afraid of going off to Jamaica with her friend, Dorothy Riggs, leaving Edward, Miss Balfour and the four children in the house in Washington.

March 1, 1925—Edward to Margaret in Jamaica: "I have got a little more accustomed to your absence than I was at first, but things do not seem to be just right even yet. Miss Balfour and I discuss the question whether it is natural for you to miss all the charming members of this household or not. She seems to take it for granted that you will, but I have a disturbing suspicion that Dorothy and Jamaica will be so delightful that you will never think of us at all, except as of a noise happily left in the distance. I should not like that; but on the other hand, I should not like you to miss us so much as to make yourself very unhappy and perhaps blame it on Dorothy. Please be careful and miss us just the right amount . . . Mother arrived yesterday evening . . . and is very sweet and dear as she always is. I am leaving her to the mercy of all four children . . . I hear all kinds of noises and tremble for her safety . . . but hold resolutely to my desk."

Miss Balfour and I! Miss Balfour and I! Reading this letter I considered these possibilities for the first time in my life: 1) that my father and Miss Balfour were often alone together; 2) that in their state of perfect friendliness and ease they could discuss whether it was natural for my mother to miss "the charming members of this household." Didn't Margaret's heart give a little thump of fright when she read this? Edward and Miss B. discussing *her* feelings! Edward and Miss B. in league, not, of course, against her, but engaged in discussing her, and how she hated to be discussed!

165

And it was in the present, that "discuss," i.e. more than once. Edward, innocent as a babe, had written with his usual candour, "Please be careful and miss us just the right amount." If he had tried to think of ways of making Margaret think of him, he could not have chosen a more subtle one. What are "Miss Balfour and I" discussing today, she must have wondered, while a little cloud cast a shadow over her mind. Not that there was anything really to worry about, for in the same letter Edward announces the arrival of his mother. "Sweet and dear as she always is." More food for thought!

Edward, "a bit of a blab," as he says of himself, would not have babbled in this way if he had had anything to hide. Nothing precise is needed, however, to plant a germ of suspicion—merely the sudden vision of camaraderie ("Miss Balfour and I") which might have tipped the precarious balance from governess into woman. But I have no evidence whatever that my mother's view of Miss Balfour changed then; on the contrary, for on April 13th, just after she gets back from Jamaica, she writes to Edward at the Agricultural Station in Durham, N.H.—a letter exactly like all the others, and, if anything, more serene. It was a day, minus Miss Balfour, with the children, "well and geting along like peaches and cream. Yesterday Arthur and I went to church early, then I took all four to the cemetery, then I tried to discover an old man in the Soldier's Home, whose daughter was one of my Girls' Friendly in Germantown. He was out. All of us lunched at the Allies' Inn and then the Children's Service. In the evening I went to the Chapel of the Holy Comforter to the G.F.S. Admission Service, and spoke, my first experience of doing so in a church!" A typical MWM day, followed by two more, full of "shoes for the little girls," Spanish, Ladies' Day at the Brass Tack Club (the little house "the boys" had built in the back yard), Girls' Day, "and on, ad infinitum!"

Busy, cheerful days without Miss Balfour, unlike the summer before when Miss B. had gone to Nantucket with her sister, and, says Margaret to Edward, "all four children are fighting like anything." "Wister is as easy to take care of as an eel and with Miss B. in Nantucket I am distracted. I can't leave any two together. Sarah . . . is the best of the lot." The presence of Miss Balfour saved my mother from becoming "distracted," in other words, going crazy. Distraction, the occupational disease of mothers without governesses, maids or cooks. My mother did not realize that Miss Balfour was herself a "distraction," or a distracter, a

more dangerous and long-lasting one than "all four children fighting like anything."

February 27, 1928—an entry in a little mottled blue and black
diary with the dedication: "Mary R. Meigs for *my namesake* from
her loving Valentine." Her Valentine was her grandmother,
MRBM. It was a typical winter in Washington under the rule of
Miss Balfour. First entry: "Feb. 18: Cool. Drawing in the morning just sew, sew, sew in the afternoon, found a darning needle
after ages of search." February 20: "School as usual, walk after
school French after that supper and then bed." The same on
February 27th, except for the following in pencil crossed out: "a
very impressing speech made by Miss Balfour at the Elipse (sic)
made us both cry." We had been naughty, rude, fresh? Oh, poor
Miss Balfour! What a life for a young woman, her days as strictly
divided as ours, clockwork days. "Nothing new," repeated day
after day in the little diary. "Nothing new" repeated twenty-eight
times. Dittoes. Then, "Broke a window got a knife" and the next
day, "just the same except we didn't break a window again." I
have to keep my mind on the fact that if we were hustled and
hassled, so was Miss Balfour, by her ideal of perfect children who
would not be a bother to their parents, a thankless task day after
day, to insist on what was unnatural—to turn two children into
creatures of discipline (still obsessed by time after sixty years).

It was not Miss Balfour's fault if I was able to see "nothing new"
for twenty-eight days; it was mine. I was no more awake to life
than a doormouse. There were two exceptions noted in the diary:
the knife and the *The Three Musketeers*: "It was beautiful peachy.
Dennis King D'Artagnan, ice cream Willard supper bed." The blue
diary doesn't come to life until the family sails to Europe on the
"Arabic," Miss Balfour takes to her bunk with sea-sickness, and
I begin to look around me. But I remember free times even in
winter, lived in the spaces between hustling and hassling, hours
up in the "nursery" drawing, reading, making things (I loved to
make boxes and flew into a rage when the pieces wouldn't fit
together). There was no television, no radio, we were not allowed
to go to the movies, and very few friends came to the house. The
twins had each other and closed up like sea anemones against the
adult world. We saw Miss Balfour all too often as someone who
cut short our innocent joys. "Mary, your face is as red as a beet.
You'd better stop." We are racing an express wagon around and
around on the cement floor of the Poikile, MRBM's open Greek

167

temple, with childish shrieks. A sudden vision of Miss Balfour who put up with noise for what seemed to her like an eternity, but who was always seen as the killer of joy.

I have a memory that I cling to. The twins have been put to bed at the Peak up on the third floor, reached by stairs covered with a sweet-smelling grass carpet. I am waked by flaming light, filling the west window, and begin to bawl with fear. The house is on fire! Miss Balfour comes in, to scold me, I think, but she comforts me like a mother, a real mother. It's just the sunset, she says. Miss Balfour, my foster-mother, that memory erases your severity, when you were doing your duty as a perfect governess, and my sulkiness because I was in your power, and I remember that we forgave each other many years ago.

One would think that with Miss Balfour's departure, our mother would have felt free to mother us. What an irony when, alone with her twins at last, she was suddenly the victim of our concentrated hostility. "I disliked Miss Balfour until the day she left and then I loved her," said my sister recently. "Don't you remember how we would go and see Miss Balfour and complain to her about Mother?" We had been kept in a state of childish naïveté for so long that we had no social graces whatsoever, and now our mother was fiercely determined to turn her ugly ducklings into marriageable swans. And how we fought her, longing for the lesser fussing (it seemed) of Miss Balfour. "You've hurt my feelings," she used to say when we refused to follow her program for our improvement. My sister tells me that she swore never to use this punitive phrase with her own children, not knowing that our mother had learned it from her own Mama. "I hurt Mama's feelings terribly," Margaret says in her diary April 9, 1897. Mama has evidently complained about her hurt feelings (Margaret was fighting with her sister Sarah) and Margaret (unlike my sister) has taken it to heart. And because she understood what Mama meant, she expects her daughters to understand her and to be sorry. It shows something about the twins' relationship to their mother that her hurt feelings are a matter of complete indifference to them. Mama could get at Margaret but Margaret, repeating the formula, merely stirred up the twins' resentment, which almost cried aloud, "How about *our* feelings!"

It is strange that the reconciliation with Miss Balfour was so simple and immediate, unpolluted by the poison that ran through the post-Miss Balfour years with our mother. The explanation lies as always in the nature of relationships and the nature of letting-go. For years Miss Balfour and I wrote each other and I continued to visit her, even when she moved to England. It was the same period when, locked into the mother-daughter relationship, I was doomed to make my mother unhappy without any hope of real reconciliation until a few years before her death. It is strange, too, that old age made her and Miss Balfour so much alike, removing all bitterness and leaving the sweet and patient beings who had been kept in check by the fear of not being the perfect mother, the perfect governess. Each could relax at last into what she might have been if she had been able to view her imposed role less sternly.

Summer Memories: Woods Hole

Washington to Woods Hole—the passage from the constraining disciplines of winter to a heaven of freedom—via a long train trip and two paddle-wheeled steamboats (and how marvellous the great wheel was, half-hidden, its flukes rhythmically beating the water before they disappeared!). Waiting for the boat to dock we could hear the paddle-wheel churning and grumbling as it manoeuvred us broadside to the dock, a sighing sound when the boat leaned its length against the rope bumpers; then silence and stillness under our feet. The door to the gangplank was opened and we stepped out into the dazzling sunshine, dressed in our city clothes: hats, long-sleeved dresses, leather-soled shoes and knee socks.

And then the metamorphosis—into middy blouses and bloomers, and to sneakers, light as air! We flew off on winged feet, all of us, like flying Bodhisattvas. Our sneakers (Keds) were brown but I remember Miss Balfour, our mother and her friends, in white sneakers or brown and white loafers, taking off on slender legs and white-flashing feet. I remember the whitening of generations of shoes, the opening of the bottle with its crusted rim, the calcimine smell of whitening that spread over my mother's loafers like make-up on a clown's face, their stiffness when they dried, the faint grey-blue of telltale shadows under the whiteness.

Memories as fragile as sea-shells wash up, memories of pure joy, carried in with the rising tide and gently scattered above the tide-line. Woods Hole sounds: a song sparrow singing in the morning stillness, a bird running over the roof without insulation, the sighs and groans of the house itself in a storm. The house breathed fog and the perfume of rosa rugosa and bay bushes; its ears were open to the faint slapping of little waves below it or their sudden roar when a northeast gale struck it broadside. Then it rocked and creaked like an unwieldy galleon and my mother marshalled her troops: her children, Miss Balfour, and Addie, the cook, stationing us and herself at our posts with towels, mops and pails. I remember my exhilaration when the cold northeast wind entered the house; it kept us in a state of excitement and fear until it veered to northwest and laughed its way out in glittering sunshine.

The house transmitted sounds: conversation downstairs in the living-room (the twins eavesdropped), whispering, snoring, the flushing of the toilet, the tread of Addie's feet in her room under the roof, a loud pattering sound when she sat down on the chamberpot, the creaking of her bed with its ancient springs. Arthur slept in the cold bedroom on the north side where the windows were dimmed with salt spray; the twins were in the room next to him, Wister and Miss Balfour in rooms opposite each other across the hall. Our parents had moved over to the Annex, which almost touched Comtuit; it had been designed by AIM with a deep sloping roof like a huge hat, with small-paned windows from which one peered in frustration at the water 100 feet away. Miss Balfour's inexorable schedule woke us at 7:15 and got us down to breakfast after a cyclone of impatient shouting, for there was one bathroom and no two people could ever be there together. When we got downstairs, our parents were already seated at the oval oak table, Father in his perennial thick brown tweed suit and knickerbockers and Mother in her long Russian linen smock with a blaze of red roses embroidered down the front.

On fine days the prevailing southwest wind woke lazily in the late morning, heralded by a soft inward billowing of the gauzy curtains at the living-room windows. In the harbour, ruffles of wind sped over the calm water until the moored sailboats and dinghies, which had been heading in all directions, spun around to face the wind. Farther out you could see a black cone-shaped buoy pushed over at a sharp angle by the current that is the pride

171

of Woods Hole. Even the steamboats, coming through the Hole against it, when the channel buoys, ringed with foam, were almost lying on their sides, seemed to strain and spin in the whirlpools. Our great terror, in a small sailboat, was to find ourselves suddenly borne backwards, with the sail flapping crazily, and to be carried toward sharp rocks which lay just below the surface on the wrong side of the buoy. When the current was with you, the boat rushed through with such speed that the sail hung limp and the water gurgled around the rudder. Then the boat slowed and the sail filled, and you knew that you were stuck on the far side of the Hole until the tide changed. Five years ago, on the broad-beamed ferry which carries people and horses (but no automobiles) to the islands, I felt the swift water of the Hole turning indolently under us, as though we were riding on the back of an enormous Manta ray, and I was filled with the concentrated joy of old memories.

Memory magnifies, gathers light from tiny sources as the eyes of birds and insects do; it sees a thousand times more sharply than the human eye. From the distance of more than half a century it picks out something insignificant that is suddenly full of meaning: the wicker basket over my mother's desk, shaped like an oriole's nest, with its rusty tin container in which the water gathered the putrid smell of decaying leaves, greenish-brown water with little circles floating like colourless oil. The heads of the zinnias kept their splendor while their leaves drooped and turned brown so imperceptibly that you hardly knew they were in the process of dying. Before her stroke my mother went out every day to pick fresh flowers, and arranged them in the pantry where there was a sink lined with battered zinc exclusively for the flower ceremony, where on shelves above it stood a disparate army of tall, short, round, square, glass, copper or crockery vases and bowls and lead flower holders. I see my mother's concentration on her choice of flowers, her hands arranging. Her hands were beautiful; sometimes she would hold them both up, and gaze at her graceful fingers, the moons in her oval nails, as though they belonged to someone else, as though it was safe to admire a part of herself she could hold at a distance.

I have a tiny photograph of my mother wearing her Russian smock, standing in the disorder of her garden. It was like her modest soul—a confusion of old-fashioned fragrances—of heliotrope, mignonette, rose geranium and lemon verbena.

Mignonette—with a lacy pink-brown domed head and a gentle powdery smell, less sweet than heliotrope but with an elusive fascination. I close my eyes and bring back those summer smells, subtle and sweet, the sharp smell of marigolds and the robust smell of the huge bunches of zinnias we brought back every year from the church fair. The zinnias, with their stiff, gaudy petals, leathery leaves and scratchy stems, imperceptibly dying, exhaled the worst stench of decay.

Decay—a little hint of paradise slipping away. And then an epidemic of theft and vandalism; the house is robbed, the Japanese prints and paintings are stolen, a fire is lit on the living-room floor, coke is sniffed, an arm pushes open a screen door, reaches in and plucks a radio off a table. Blue flashing lights, sirens drowning the lovely sound of the foghorn at Nobska Light. An exponential leap. Once, when Margaret and Edward were young, there was a conspiracy of happiness and of pure scientific purpose in Woods Hole. What delighted greetings there were between friends who trotted to Louie's vegetable store in the cool bright morning! The drawbridge that cut the village in two would almost certainly go up as you pursued your way to the post office or the fish market; the mast of a boat would glide by your head, and friends shouted cheerfully to each other across the gap. Now when the bridge goes up, there are herds of people, strangers to each other, who wait in glum silence, and long lines of impatient drivers, enraged by the idea of losing five minutes of their precious time.

Picture me sixty years ago, dressed in my green bloomers, middy blouse and tie, and brown sneakers. I cross the drawbridge, turn left on School Street, and left again down the grassy driveway to Mr. Swift's hardware store, an old clapboard shed painted white. Inside there is an enchanted clutter of pails, boathooks, rope, oarlocks and oars, fish-hooks, lead weights, bailers, grappling-hooks, paint brushes and paint cans, yellow slickers and black hip boots. The air is sweet with the redolent, tarry smell of oakum. The shelves are piled high with small labelled cardboard boxes that contain every kind of nail, screw, bolt, screw-eye, hook, hasp, tack, hinge and pulley in existence. Oh faraway time before prescribed amounts of hardware were packaged in plastic bags and hung up on a pegboard! Now there is no one like Mr. Swift with his neatly trimmed white beard, who will emerge from a fairyland forest, and peer over his glasses with surprise and delight. He has all the time in the world to pull out the cardboard boxes, to potter and putter until he has found exactly what you have come for, for time was different then. My sister has reminded me that he would sometimes show us the paper currency he had washed and ironed, and that he lived to be 100 years old.

The knowledge of time is almost as fatal to happiness as the knowledge of good and evil. Yet it wasn't only when I was a child that time seemed different in Woods Hole. There was a turning-point, like the changing of the tide in the Hole, at which time was jostled from outside and our summer pace changed. Woods Hole had begun to race in time with the racing world. First there was a cosmic warning—the great hurricane of 1938, which smashed through the village, wrecking boats, flooding houses and leaving six people dead. We waded out of Comtuit, where the wicker furniture was afloat, in time to reach a house on higher ground, and from there watched the harbour water raging over the causeway into our bay, swirling past the legs of a man clinging to a tele-phone pole. We could dimly see the men who tried to throw a rope to him against the wind, and one with the rope tied to him who fought his way into the flood. In an instant he was swept past the pole and had to be hauled to land, and the man on the pole lost his grip and was carried away. I remember my shame-ful feeling of relief because we were all safe.

Woods Hole and the dream of safety. Some of the eccentric, kindly folk who lived there, like Mr. Swift, were old by the time of the hurricane and World War II. The best part of their lives was lived before time and the pouring in of the world, like the raging flood in 1938, changed Woods Hole forever. Miss Tinkham, a small person with silvery hair and skin, and eyes the colour of blue chicory, was one of many frail and innocent souls whom my mother warmed with her kindness; she used to have Sunday lunch with us, dressed in pale blue or lavender, with white stockings and shoes. For her shyness and sensitivity, the twins, heartless brats that we were at age ten or so, had no pity, and we used to mock at her behind her back. I am sorry to say that we called her Misstinkham, with the mistaken idea that she smelled of the goats she kept in her tan-gled garden, along with at least a dozen cats. Sometimes one of the goats would cross the road and put her head through the open win-dow of Mrs. Osterhaus's house. Mrs. Osterhaus was a Japanese-American lady, the village matchmaker, who much later embar-rassed me more than once by stopping me in the street and saying loudly, "I have A MAN FOR YOU!"

174

Miss Tinkham's calvary began with the hurricane. She had managed to get the cats and goats to high ground but suddenly remembered a kitten stranded in the garage. She started back to her house at dusk in the rapidly rising water, found the kitten and clutched it under one arm. With the other arm she tried to keep herself afloat, for the water was up to her neck and her head was bumping against the garage roof. It was just at this moment that Wister and Lawrie, his brother-in-law, came by in a rowboat, and hauled her out with the kitten still alive. The next morning, returning to her house in the bright sunshine, she saw a thick layer of stinking mud and the dead bodies of enormous sea-worms lying over everything. Her beautiful garden was ruined, her furniture had been swept out of the house and flung far and wide.

Three years later, during the War, a sailor climbed into the living-room where Miss Tinkham was sitting with a cat in her lap. He tried to rape her, she screamed, the cat leapt at him and he fled. He was tracked down, and incriminating cat-hairs were found on his uniform. The near-rape precipitated Miss Tinkham into her private domain of gentle absence, alone with her family of cats and goats, but my mother persuaded her to come to Sunday lunch once more. My mother had had her first stroke, had a nurse by her side and spoke with difficulty. "Too much," she said, when Miss Tinkham praised the flowers. She looked surprised; it was not at all what she had meant to say. Miss Tinkham's eyes widened with fear and she made a quick getaway after lunch. Her family called her; they took all her time, she told my sister, and between her family duties she fell asleep, sometimes with her head in her dinner plate. She had been dead for three days when she was found by Louie, the grocer, who wondered why she had not come to do her shopping. The goats were complaining, the sixteen cats were all crying to be fed. The cats had made a shambles of the house and the smell was awful.

Plant Life of Woods Hole, from a notebook done at the Children's School of Science by Mary Meigs, 1926.
   "A little marsh-plant yellow-green
   And tipped at lip with tender red,
   Tread close, and either way you tread,
   Some faint, black water jets between
   Lest you should bruise its curious head

You call it sundew, how it grows,
If with its color it have breath,
If life taste sweet to it, if death
Pain its soft petals, no man knows,
Man has no sight or sense that saith."
(Author unknown)

Flowers found on July 23, 1926
White clover, queen ann's lace, white yarrow, pink yarrow,
daisy, peppergrass, roundleaved plantain, lanced leaved
plantain, rabbit's foot clover, butter-and-egg, shepherd's purse,
red clover, St. John's wort, mustard, pink clover, butter-cup,
blue grass, chickweed, thistle, head all, cranberry, fern,
bindweed, wild grape, rose, bayberry, sedge, iris, bittersweet,
blackberry, pigweed, hackweed, aster.

Anti-Semitism

Perhaps a great niece, playing in the sand at the foot of the sea-wall at Woods Hole or hopping up and down in the little waves, feels the same ecstasy that we felt. The beach is the same; the rocks we named are in their places: Turtle Rock, Table Rock, Elephant Rock. A few feet away on the public beach there is absolute bedlam. The difference lies in the explosion of people and in the amount of noise they make—a gain in the sense of community and a loss of peace of mind. There is no time for peace of mind, not the kind, long-drawn out as molasses candy, that we had. Seventy-five years ago Margaret and Edward built the house which for a long time held a tranquil peace. Even if Margaret could write to Edward from Woods Hole, "My sins pursue me," her life there meant a suspension of the driving seriousness of Washington. Even if there were forms of summer seriousness, and her social schedule was breathless, it was impossible not to fall under the Woods Hole spell which commanded happiness.

Margaret's "sins" were social sins; she hadn't returned all the calls she owed or written all her thank-you notes. Her real sins, and Edward's, which we shared as children, were habits of mind that they had learned from their parents and that they perpetuated even in the happy atmosphere of Woods Hole. They were lies that had been transformed into counterfeit beliefs: the racism and anti-Semitism practised by many white Christians in Woods Hole before World War II.

January 25, 1987: I had a dream in which a rat suddenly and painfully bit me on my left hand. I succeeded in jerking its teeth loose with my right hand and held it away by gripping it just behind the head. It was dark and silky smooth and looked at me fixedly with very bright eyes. I was afraid of getting rabies from the bite and went with some other people to a place where a campfire was burning. If I could shake off the rat I was going to throw it on the fire, but I woke up before I could do this. The dream seems to me to be about my struggle with the subject of anti-Semitism in my family, wanting to shake it off and not being able to. No one would be the wiser if I decided not to quote directly the four or five passages from letters, the excerpts from diaries, in which Margaret or Edward or AIM or MRBM carelessly let fall anti-Semitic remarks, sure (if they thought at all) of not being rebuked. To quote them is to commit a kind of disloyalty to my family and to expose them to retroactive accusations. Their only defence would be the same one that is used so often to defend the indefensible, that is, that they were victims of their culture and their class, and had been indoctrinated just as all their peers had, they and their children. I wish that they had wondered where their ideas came from and had asked themselves how they were made to believe (they who were Christians) falsehoods that were the opposite of Christian teaching.

"What really surprises me," said a friend who had just read the first draft of this chapter, "is their vulgarity." She was talking about the language of their anti-Semitism and the paradox that "ladies" and "gentlemen" could commit such offences against "good taste or refined feelings" (Webster). Webster defines "vulgarity" as, among other things, "coarseness of speech," which was what my parents prided themselves on never speaking—they who never said "tomayto," or used swear words stronger than "gosh" or "darn." There is even a list in Margaret's 1904 diary of "vulgar" speech. (Examples: "residential homes," "retired to bed," "in the middle of *Tannhauser*, 'Say, ain't there thirty-one days in this month?' ") Unfortunately, the computer in Margaret's head that recognized superficial vulgarity, i.e. Webster's variety, and flashed the message "vulgar!" or "common!" was not programmed to recognize genuine offences against good taste and refined feelings. These were an accepted part of a class vocabulary; unlike "tomayto," they were not signs of *not*-belonging, but of belonging.

When I first came to these contemptuous little phrases, like maggots, in the family letters, I wanted to hide them, not mention them in my book; I was ashamed and angry. Yet I already had clear memories of anti-Semitism when we were growing up: we belonged to the Chevy Chase Club in Washington at a time when it excluded Jews, and I remembered, too, concerted efforts by my parents and their friends in Woods Hole to discourage Jews from buying property there. The direct shock of words, every one of them nakedly anti-Semitic, hurt more than my memories, and where before I had wanted to find reasons I now wanted to confront my parents accusingly. But what right had I to feel angry and accusing when I myself lived in a moral fog until I was shaken out of it by events outside of me, and by people who saw more clearly that I did? To what extent were my parents responsible for the moral fog? Hadn't their own parents raised them in it? It almost seems that in the course of time they had developed special gills in order to breathe the fog of "refined feelings" without suffocating. For no one in my family tried to get out of it, until, in our generation, we were shocked out of it. If I haven't the right to be angry with them, I can be angry at the social and educational and religious systems that permitted and perpetuated racism of all kinds. But since their schools and churches were endowed by *them* and were staffed by people of like mind (i.e. those with "good taste and refined feelings"), the ideas that held them together circulated like goldfish in an aquarium, and there was no way for them to get out even if they had wanted to. This closed system, which included racism and anti-Semitism, was so much taken for granted that it did not even need to be discussed. The vocabulary was a kind of shorthand, by which a single derogatory word served to denote a whole race. But proper Philadelphians spoke these words so lightly that they did not notice their heavy burden of contempt.

They had no sense, as one has when the conscience begins to wake up, of "What am I saying?" What they were saying was as natural to them as their belief in the intrinsic merit of their names. Both could be used in lieu of currency, passed around and exchanged. Somehow or other, a mechanism in their heads had switched off the power to hear meanings—*these* meanings. Or to feel feelings. For they did not feel boiling anger, hate, or the desire for revenge, as people do who have suffered from crimes committed against them. Mostly they felt a remote, comfortable disdain, which on occasion could turn to fear.

The fear became more precise after thousands of Jewish refugees from the Russian pogrom in 1881 settled into an area in South Philadelphia a few blocks from "Philadelphia's Victorian gentry," as E. Digby Balzell calls them in *Philadelphia Gentleman*. "Because of a prejudicial stereotype derived from the behavior of lower-class immigrants," says Balzell, the cultivated Jews who lived north of the Victorian gentry were then discriminated against by this same gentry. "Quite naturally, this produced an all-too-human resentment and anti-Semitism within the Jewish community itself." Mr. Balzell seems to be saying that if *even* members of the Jewish community harboured the "prejudicial stereotype derived from the behavior of lower-class immigrants," then it was understandable if the Victorian gentry shared their view. It was "all-too-human." My own view, based on family letters, is that the Victorian gentry were already anti-Semitic before 1881 and that the arrival of the immigrants merely gave them an excuse to be more so. By 1885, according to Balzell, the people who lived north of Market Street, i.e. "everybody" for the Jewish upper class, were "nobody" for the Christian upper class. Nobody. What a horrible word! "A person of no influence, standing, etc.," says the ever-snobbish Webster. "Not *anybody*." Anybodies in those days all lived south of Market Street and north of South Philadelphia. Anybodies took their status with them wherever they went; their first concern when they left home was to find other anybodies, who were as snobbish, anti-Semitic and racist as they were. Even on shipboard.

On board the S.S. Pennsylvania, September 18, 1903, Margaret writes in her diary, "The girl I was positive I had met somewhere in Phila . . . turned out to be Miss Maule, her Father, Mother and sister, which is some light breaking over this ship's company." Of another passenger, "Miss Goodrich from Chicago," Margaret says, "Her grandfather lived in Chicago and was one of the early settlers. Nobody's great-grandfather lived there!!!" (Margaret's exclamation points.) She means, of course, that Miss Goodrich's great-grandfather pre-dated the settlement of Chicago, and yet her surprise is pregnant with meaning. In Philadelphia, unlike Chicago, "everybody" had a great-grandfather who had lived there, and "nobody" was someone who didn't. On September 15th

Margaret had written, "The people on this boat are hopeless. All German-American Jews. Not a redeeming man. I sit next to the dull limit." September 16: "Mama . . . sits in the Ladies Saloon—hears the most killing conversations which she details to us. The people are too hopeless. I couldn't imagine anything worse." Margaret and Mama were sorely tried, even if Mama managed to eavesdrop on "killing conversations." But it was they who were doing the killing. "As for the man next to me at table," Margaret says, "he is the most hopelessly unresponsive person I ever ran across. I told him as much last night."

Margaret had lost patience with "the dull limit" the moment she perceived that he was a German-American Jew. In the judgement of proper Philadelphians it did not matter where Jews came from, or even whether they were rich or poor; the "prejudicial stereotype" was instantly applied. The poor were lower on the scale of "nobodies" but the rich were also those whom they did not want to know. In 1907, three years before my parents' marriage, Edward writes to Margaret from Karlsbad, where he has gone with Pa and Ma to take the cure. "This place is chiefly inhabited by New York Jews," he says. "There are a few Christians and Austrians, but the beaks are so prominent that one does not notice anything else. I daresay they [Ma and Pa] will like it better after they have got settled and found out who are here that they know." These three sentences contain a noxious essence like the base of an expensive perfume which in itself is a horrible smell but in combination produces "refinement." Everything detestable about the Philadelphia (or any?) upper class is concentrated here; their complacent snobbishness, their anti-Semitism, their herding instinct, their total inability to see and judge these aspects of themselves. Three years before his marriage, Edward (I disavow any relationship to the man who wrote that letter!) could write Margaret with the cozy certainty that she would understand and sympathize with the family ennui at Karlsbad. Even if her own beak was so enormous that, as she said, she could not eat corn on the cob; even if both families were full of beaks (MRBM, for instance), she would agree that "the beaks" could only be Jewish, and did not recognize it as a truly vulgar stereotype. In three years, Edward and Margaret would be joined in holy matrimony. Anti-Semitism was not among the differences they were going to thrash out; it was part of their shared inheritance, along with all the other prejudices of their class.

Edward's 1907 letter isn't the last instance of anti-Semitism in the box closet; there are two others, in 1922 and 1928, both from Woods Hole. We had brought the baggage of racism and anti-Semitism even to paradise, from the belief that black people belonged to a servant-class, fear of the "R.C.'s," alertness to the possibility of being cheated by the "Gees," i.e. the Portuguese, to the smouldering anti-Semitism, which flared up in summer in a particularly direct and nasty way. Woods Hole, August 2, 1922, Margaret to Edward: "So glad my mind is relieved about Kolman. When you see the Jews here you won't wonder." Obviously, Kolman had wanted to go, in some capacity, to Woods Hole, and had decided not to, to Margaret's unseemly relief. Perhaps he was a scientific colleague of Edward's who had asked for advice about buying a house. When a distiguished Jewish couple were arranging to buy the house across the street from us, Margaret and Edward and their friends met to discuss the threat to their way of life. This couple and another down the road, whose coming had also provoked a secret flurry of opposition, became the cultural leaders of the community, and Margaret was pleased when she was invited to their tea-parties. The daughter of one of her friends fell in love with the nephew of the distinguished couple, a writer. They married, were unhappy, and divorced, a cautionary tale to add to the collection. Anti-Semitism thrives on chance misfortunes and does not go away even when individual Jews are remarkable; they are merely viewed as people who have overcome their handicap.

Woods Hole, June 2, 1928, Edward to Margaret: "By the way, Mrs. Loeb wants to sell Mother the lot between 'Windy' and the Hughes place for $6000, which seems to me pretty Palestinian, but Mother insisted on offering $5000 for it." Mrs. Loeb was the sister-in-law of Jacques Loeb, one of the most brilliant of all the scientific stars in Woods Hole. She was a neighbour and a friend; her husband, also a scientist, was one of Edward's colleagues. And yet—fast as light—Edward's reaction—"pretty Palestinian," which had been lying in wait to make the stereotypical association. MRBM succeeded in getting the property for $5000, which, of course, in Edward's mind wasn't "Palestinian" but shrewd. And I think, addressing my parents directly, what about you? Didn't the penny-pinching Protestants in the Meigs and Wister family fit your own stereotype of the Jews? A brand-new derogatory word is needed to encapsulate the anxiety of rich people about spending minuscule amounts of money. Consider Uncle Arthur, for instance, worrying about the price of a can of turtle soup. "It costs 40 cents per person. Whew!" he said, after interrogating Aunt Harriet at dinner.

I think about the family to which I belong. My grandfather was a physician, my father a physician turned scientist. They were honourable, kind men. Members of the "helping" professions. The whole family went faithfully to church every Sunday and listened to sermons about loving one's neighbour as oneself. Even as a child Margaret had noted down texts and the subjects of sermons. "He says that nobody gives anything to the Jew," she wrote, aged fifteen, about a sermon by a missionary. Undoubtedly, he was talking about money, not love, and about his cause, conversion. Episcopal ministers were not likely to preach against anti-Semitism. People of all races, classes and nations live with the contradictions between their goodness of heart and their prejudices. It makes me think that there is a shameful need in every human being to think ill of other human beings, for why do racist ideas take root in us if there is not already a receptive soil that makes them sprout and flower?

The damage that racism does to others is obvious, but what about the damage that people who are racist do to themselves? Each member of my family had built a prison inside her/himself, in which whole populations were locked: Jews, Roman Catholics, lower-class immigrants, "common" people, homosexuals and many others. They thought (if they thought) that their prejudices came from an outside threat, but they were inside; they cut off their hearts' blood and the air they needed to breathe freely. They did not talk about these secret dungeons; I do not remember ever hearing racism or anti-Semitism discussed. I feel now that I lost the years of childhood and adolescence in a state of passive, silent acceptance. Eventually, each of us four children "peeled off" like planes in formation, and each began to take an erratic course out of the opaque silence that had been undisturbed by the questions: is it right? Is it just? Or for that matter, is it Christian? If our parents had lived longer they would have seen a granddaughter and a grandson marry Jews, and a great-granddaughter being brought up in the Jewish faith. I ask myself, not quite sure of the answer, wouldn't they have changed by this time, wouldn't they have moved much closer to the acknowledgement that everybody is "everybody"?

Silences and Secrets

During my childhood sex was present only as something invisible, an anti-matter; it was like molten magma deep under water which stirred in the lightless depths, glowed red and was extinguished. My parents had four children but the nature of the sexual encounters that produced us, pleasurable or not, is veiled in mystery. In all the letters that I have read, even between brother and brother, even between man and wife, there is not a single mention of sex, the word *sex* or the act. Hints in the course of a flirtation: Frank Wheelwright who writes to Margaret, "I remember when I provoked you one evening, I was often provoked to spoil a Platonic friendship . . . that I reddened slightly and unknowingly to your glance but also *pleasingly to you.*" Undoubtedly Margaret was pleased both by his breach of etiquette and by his blushing for it. "You possess a naïveté which is charming," says Frank. Her naïveté consisted of not seeming to realize that in a man's mind one thing led to another, that her gift for attention and welcoming could be misconstrued. Sex for her meant only one thing—the sacred secret between man and wife. There was no difference between her view and that of the Roman Catholics whom she feared and disliked, except that it had been learned from Mama and the Episcopal church. Perhaps some of her squeamishness about Roman Catholicism came from the fact that a man in the confessional could extract a woman's most intimate secrets.

If Margaret knew some of the unmentionable words for sins of the flesh, she had locked them in a place of solitary confinement. Now and then one would break out and leer at her—the flesh of her flesh! In the summer of 1920, when my brother Arthur was eight years old, Margaret wrote to Edward from Woods Hole: "Do you remember what I told you of Arthur and Bobby two years ago? Dorothy discovered that it has started again, Arthur having taught Lawrie. I am nearly crazy. Alfred also. I am keeping Arthur on the place. What are we going to do? If anything like that happened at school it would be terrible. Naturally, I have not mentioned this to Grandmother or Miss B." It (what exactly was it?) was running like wildfire through the band of eight-year-old boys: Bobby, Arthur, Lawrie, Alfred. Two more letters on the subject of It: September 1st: "The boys have been good lately. I have kept them at home alone and sincerely hope the trouble will not crop up, as nobody would have them around to say nothing of worse results." September 2nd: "As far as I know, nothing of the kind has occurred since with the children . . . When we get home perhaps you will talk to the children [Wister, aged five, as well?] and try to impress upon them the unpleasant consequences of such things." So she had succeeded in scaring them, or perhaps in driving them underground? Certainly, her efforts to instill in her children disgust for sex and shame of their bodies reflected her own disgust. Was there some unacknowledged trauma in her childhood, something she had seen or heard or read, or was it simply the old Christian lesson learned by heart—that sex for women is only permissible in marriage, and that it is more a duty than a pleasure?

As for Edward, I have searched for and not found any mention of sex; kisses, yes, which he sends in the form of circles with dots in the centre, one for each member of the family, each one smaller until two tiny circles denote kisses for the twins. In his letters, he misses Margaret, longs to be with her, loves her, yearns to see her, but he does not say he "wants" her. I remember that sometimes in a burst of high spirits he put his arms around her, bowed over her awkwardly, for she did not melt into his embrace but stood stiffly, smiling shyly. "Isn't your father sweet?" she would say. Margaret never lost her air of virginal innocence. I believe

185

that the happiest years of her life were those before her marriage when her relationships with men were a delightfully dangerous game. Like a lady lion-tamer she kept her suitors from stepping over the invisible line; it was known both by the lions and the lady that they could jump on her and devour her, but they sat back respectfully on their haunches, baring their teeth from time to time (like Frank Wheelwright) while she stepped lightly around them, calling them to order with little flicks of the whip. Even when I was growing up this worked; the belief in ladies and gentlemen was still alive; "gentlemen" did not take sex for granted, and "ladies" could still say no.

My whole family had hidden bodies, each with its own secrets. None of us was ever naked except in our bedrooms or the bathroom (never together there!) and even when the weather was sweltering, we kept our doors closed all night long. There seemed to emanate from every one of us a prayer—"forgive me my body!" I see the three men of the family wearing their two-piece bathing suits, without a trace of the animal pride that men on beaches now take in their bodies—the strutting gait, the manly poses, the bursts of friskiness like horses playing in a field. And even when men began to bare their torsos, theirs remained selfconsciously pale. I remember my unease at the sight of them, as though a guilty secret had come out in full view. We all behaved as though we had something to hide. Our bodies were like the pit ponies that became blind working in the darkness of the old coal mines. Margaret would always be frightened by this light that hurt her eyes, while her children struggled to get over their infirmity.

Letters, of course, are self-censored or later destroyed in the interests of discretion. And yet one can learn something from the omissions, one can read between the lines or in the artless revelations that get by the censor. In one of Uncle Arthur's letters from France in World War I, he recounts his adventure with two sisters, Antoinette and Augustine, in the company of three other officers. One evening Antoinette sat in his lap "for a considerable time to the undying envy and admiration of the rest of the company, who said again and again, 'I didn't think the old Captain had it in him.' . . . The Major, he wanted to get her away. He tried to pull her away but No! No! she liked me best, and she clung to me in a manner most touching and amidst the shouts of laughter of the others. Finally she relented and allowed the Major to kiss her." Arthur, too, kisses her, kisses both the girls

186

goodnight every night and "goodbye very affectionately when I parted from them yesterday." "Now, what is the moral of the tale?" he asks his brother Eddy. "Those girls, as far as I know, were perfectly good girls. It would be a great disappointment to me to find out otherwise . . . They were the daughters of a stone-mason but they were perfectly lady-like. You could introduce them to your wife or our Mother." A good example of the artless and unconscious sexism and snobbery so typical of Arthur while he is patting himself on the back for his discernment. "Augustine showed lots of signs of breeding," he goes on. "A well shaped body, good hips, very good neck and head and good hair. She fell down in an important place, though. She had pretty coarse hands, and the big joint back of the big toe on her foot—right on the inside of the ball of the foot, stuck out, the way it shouldn't. This was pretty apparent through the slippers that they all wear round the house and in the streets, too, . . . when it isn't raining." He couldn't get over the paradox—that village women who tended the cows, cut wood, and even "dallied with the manure," who had work-worn hands and bunions, were perfectly ladylike, that they could "go to church on a Sunday, dressed with a taste, a res-traint and a refinement that makes you gasp." They were "per-fectly good girls," "you could introduce them to your wife or our Mother," and this idea in Arthur's eyes of their perfect goodness protects them as "ladies" were protected then. To Eddy, he had to apologize for kissing Antoinette and Augustine. "Why isn't it infinitely easier and simpler to become intimately acquainted 'si vite,' and dispense with this burden of formality we all carry around? . . . No fear, of course, in our chaste country, but it makes a reason for coming to France." Did he really believe what he was saying?

Years later, writing his preface to the *Letters*, Arthur says, "the views expressed on the morals of the Magnotte family are more significant for the freshness of the point of view than for any manifestation of clearmindedness, but it would be refreshing to recapture such a mood." Perhaps it had come to the ears of "the old Captain" that Augustine and Antoinette were less perfectly "lady-like" than he believed them to be. How he wanted to believe! For he writes again to Eddy two days later, still obsessed by the subject of the two girls and the importance of their being able to combine ladylikeness with French informality. He com-pares them to X and Y—friends at home whom he considers "both very charming ladies." "You see," he says, "it has long been a notion of mine that it is only by reason of the fact of Y . . . being an extra fine lady, and possessing the qualities of ladylikeness in a higher degree than others, that she can be 'sprightly' as she sometimes is, and still remain just as much of a lady as she was before . . . It is difficult to do, and I think the French can accomplish it without effort, whereas with us it is very rare."

Clearly, the ideal woman for Arthur was the equivalent of a geisha, her function to charm but not to excite uncontrollable desire. Gentlemen of his time had been taught that ladies did not excite uncontrollable desire (or feel it either) and this resulted in the chivalrous equilibrium that permitted both sexes to flirt within iron-clad boundaries. Finally, at age fifty-four, Arthur found his ideal in the hospital where they were both recovering from minor operations. It was as though she had been born for the sole purpose of being his wife, of managing and giving grace to his house. She was beautiful, with an oval face like Botticelli's Venus, intelligent enough to bone up on architecture, horses and gardening and to know when not to argue with him. They loved each other; she must have confirmed all his views about woman's place. A little cloud of sensuality hung over them; somehow the manliness of Arthur and the womanliness of Harriet combined to emanate an aura without their so much as touching or looking at each other. I compare this to the chaste distance between Margaret and Edward, compare Arthur's view of his wife as satellite and Edward's view of Margaret as his complement or, sometimes, as he says, his superior.

September 18, 1924—Margaret to Edward: "We went to a very lurid movie . . . called 'Sinners in Heaven,' mostly played by a girl and man on a desert island. I find movies of that kind pretty unpleasant and common, but what is to be done, keep the children away as much as possible, I should say." It was easy to keep the twins away from any suggestion of sex; they were not allowed to go to movies and even some books were banned. I have a memory of my sister and me sitting with our mother in wicker chairs on the back porch at Woods Hole, on a sweet summer day with the sound of children playing on the beach below, and little waves lapping. We were fifteen or sixteen. Our mother was reading aloud from Cellini's *Autobiography* and I saw her eyes travel rapidly over the page while there was an almost imperceptible pause. She was skipping, would not read aloud a passage that offended her sense of propriety. The absurdity of this lay in the fact that the book was mine and that I could look up the offensive passage at any time. I thought it absurd then, but now her censorship touches me, for it came from a lifetime of discipline, of automatically spreading her wings to protect us from "commonness," and perhaps to keep herself from thinking about it? For she was troubled to her very depths, sickened even by hints that something dreadful was out there in the "common" world, like a gigantic penis always erect. "Keep them away as much as possible." She had kept herself and us away and I do not blame her, though I would like to tell her that those who have been too protected find themselves defenceless and strangely lonely in the real world.

"Don't look, Mary! Come along!" cries Miss Balfour when I stop, transfixed by the sight in a park of two copulating dogs. "What are they doing?" I ask. Don't look. Keep them away. "I have kept them at home alone," a prescription for further experimentation, one would think. But wasn't my mother as heroic in her way as the little boy who held his finger in the dike, or as firm as Canute bidding the tide to stop short of his feet? Day and night, she and Miss Balfour paced the length of the dike, on the lookout for tiny holes, ready to plug them up to keep the world out, to keep us in. Sometimes my mother peered over the edge of the dike with a delicious kind of vertigo and caught a secret and held it fast. Wasn't one of her dearest most respected friends the daughter of Emily Dickinson's brother's mistress? One thinks of Austen Dickinson and Mabel Loomis Todd and their illicit embrace, excited, alive, entering the mausoleum of my mother's faithfully-kept secrets. Yet that ability of hers, which had the power to madden me—to lock up any secret including the secret of sex, and throw away the key—was another sign of her trustworthy character. I remember how I would prepare an assault on one of her secrets—a meeting with the Secretary of State during the War, for instance, a social occasion when he had remarked that whatever he might say was "off the record." My mother held her ground while I goaded her. I wanted her to confirm my view that there was nothing *really* off the record, i.e. top secret, or the Secretary would not have said it to the tea-drinking ladies. But my mother would not even be trapped into a discussion of what off the record meant. Of course the Secretary, in his kindly way, was trying to make the ladies feel important and special, and this worked perfectly with my mother who had the honour of having been entrusted with a secret (whether it was one or not) and the double honour of keeping it.

For my mother every secret had the same weight and carried the same responsibility—to keep it, and the house in Washington with its closed bedroom doors echoed her discretion. Sex was neither audible nor visible there; it was not even imagined. During the War it seeped into the house like the summer dust. It was generated in the frenetic atmosphere of wartime Washington, and I, who as a WAVE had encountered a new world, unwisely brought my world into the house. The house and I knew of the time when I had made hasty love with my WAVE friend in the four-poster in the guest room, in the afternoon—a time of danger. The bed had a lace canopy stretched on its beautiful slim posts, a thin mattress over slats, heavy creamy linen sheets and lace-trimmed pillow cases. The room was furnished with a nineteenth-century highboy with dainty feet and slender legs like a cheetah's, a Chippendale bureau and a ladder-backed chair from my great-grandmother's house. In this room there were mute messages from the past about house parties when four or five innocent girls spent the night in the big bed. Virtue, virtue, it whispered while the wooden slats creaked in protest and I tried to suppress a groan of pleasure. Startled by a voice, "Mary! Mary!" I threw on my uniform and rushed downstairs. "Telephone," said my brother, looking curiously at my flushed face and bright eyes. "You look peculiar," he said after I'd hung up. "What have you been doing?" "Nothing," I said crossly.

It was the first and last time that I shattered the unwritten law that the house kept in my mother's name. In fact, the house had already provided me with a symbolic warning—a knife on the stairs. It was there when I came home late one night, halfway up between the first and second stories, propped against the tread, not a big murderous knife, a middle-sized kitchen knife with a wooden handle and a sharpened edge. I was alone in the big shadowy house where a murderer could be hiding in any one of a hundred dark corners and closets, in the attic, the basement, the dumbwaiter, the wood elevator. I left the knife on the stairs and tiptoed up to my room, where I spent a sleepless night, rigid with terror. I never learned how it had got there and decided that the resident poltergeist wanted to teach me a lesson, for the knife was both a sex-symbol and a symbol of the warfare between my mother and me, of my wounding hardness of heart, running full tilt into her unassailable virtue. Her great fear for her children's moral welfare, her manning of the sex-dike, was part of her truth, and she felt compelled to be fiercely protective of a vulnerable part of herself.

Imaginary Letter

Dearest Mother,

Ten years ago, when I was writing my first book, I tackled the subject of sex in our lives, put it to rest (I thought) and gave it a decent burial. And here it is confronting me again, having risen from its grave and put on flesh, as lively as Salome dancing in front of Herod. Except that, unlike Salome, it is invisible; it sends out messages as fugitive as dream-images. What good does it do to pounce on these dream-images in your diaries and letters if I can't make them answer my questions? I have to try to get at the answers by indirection, leap backward in time and think of how you were with *us*, your children. You were angry and fierce, you were repeatedly alarmed. Yet before your marriage you were fascinated by sex—no, not by It, but by men; you wanted to get as close to the fire as possible without getting singed. It excited you to be close to "danger." Danger was the threat of sex; it was also men's violence, expressed in war and in civil disorder. In 1919, Edward writes you from Washington about the race riots, "I am glad that you are not here, for you would probably insist on going downtown after dark to see the excitement." You would have gone wearing the magic cloak of the lady tourist, which protected you from violence both in art and in life, though there are many entries in which you express shock ("too much kissing," you say about a play in 1909). But an entry in your 1905 diary took me by surprise, made me more curious about those two people: Margaret Wister and Mrs. Edward Meigs. November 30, 1905: "Have started *The House of Mirth*, Aunt Betty asked me what I thought of Lily Bart's going to that man's rooms to tea & I foolishly spoke the truth. I would have done the same thing. Only give me the chance & that's the kind of thing I long for!" No doubt Aunt Betty was scandalized by this glimpse into Margaret's soul. And yet Lily Bart was not seduced by the gentlemanly Lawrence Selden, nor by her other men friends. Her misfortune was always to be seen just as she was leaving their houses and to be perceived as guilty by Mr. and Mrs. Big Brother who have spies everywhere, who, like oafish children pulling the wings off a butterfly, reduce Lily to a torn and trembling nakedness. *The House of Mirth* is a study of rich New York society, the obsequious pursuit of names and money, the hypocrisy of marriage. Lily Bart longs to share this life; she goes after a series of rich men, only to let them go because her deepest self—the one with delicate scruples—hangs back. "That man," with whom she has tea, is a kindred spirit of Lily's deepest self. He belongs to a fraternity of percipient upper-class bachelors in both Wharton and James who mingle with the grossly rich but are not corrupted by them. He is the only character in the book who resembles anyone in your life; his integrity is something like Edward's. You must have hoped until the end of the book that Lily and Selden would acknowledge their love for each other and marry. I, too, hoped it, having been hypnotized by Edith Wharton and brought up on a diet of highborn romance. But Edith Wharton did not permit them to marry, for she had to show that Lily, a flower grown in a greenhouse, cannot live in ordinary soil. She is so fastidious that she literally starves to death (abetted by sleeping pills), deprived of all the nutrients her species needs to flourish.

What did Philadelphia society have in common with the rich New Yorkers in *The House of Mirth*? Your immediate world was much less rich, much more serious about the purpose of life, yet the same, as all societies are the same, in which blood is drained from the veins of every female born and replaced with patriarchal plasma. Sometimes it felt to you like champagne bubbling away in your veins, directing your pleasure into attracting men. "That's the kind of thing I long for!" You were always under the rule of Big Brother, who makes the laws, and of Mrs. Big Brother, who enforces them for him. You and Lily Bart looked at marriage differently, to be sure; for Lily, marriage to a rich man meant freedom, including freedom to love other men, for you, marriage was a pledge of love and fidelity, as well as a new life. But once married, why were you so fierce about sex? Didn't you sometimes feel the anger born of sexual frustration, which spends itself in moral rage or guilt, passion turned in on itself like a snake biting its own tail? Even before your marriage you were full of anger ("As for my temper. Beware, take care," you write in your diary in 1900). You seem, like many people, to be almost proud of your anger like a willywaw, the Aleutian storm that comes out of a clear sky. Your willywaws were touched off by the merest hint that sex had entered your children's heads or would enter them until the "proper" time, i.e. marriage. No wonder the equation: sex = anger, disgust, silence was branded on our childish minds.

Could you have become only one married woman, the one you became as Mrs. Meigs? Would you have been different as Mrs. Gallatly, Mrs. Wheelwright, or Mrs. Yeoman—more relaxed with Mr. Gallatly, grimmer with Mr. Wheelwright, more like the unmarried Margaret with Ritchie? Your marriage was not dreary, like Aunt Sarah's to Uncle Jim; you and Edward did not resemble the couples I see everywhere, man and wife yoked together like a couple of oxen, plodding along in gloomy silence or to the sound of a monologue, hers or his. In many ways you adapted perfectly to your new being, to your new harness hung with tassels and polished brass, suitable for drawing the royal coach (how you used to love royal couples, princes of Wales, presidents and their wives—all those who take part in society's great processions!). But didn't you sometimes think with nostalgia of the old flirtatious Margaret? Margaret went further than Lily Bart, for wouldn't Lily have been "compromised" by going moonlight sailing with a gentleman, wouldn't Mrs. Big Sister have been standing on the dock with pursed lips when Selden and Lily came back? But we have to remember that *everything*, all your fun, all your "hard flirting" was under surveillance and that innocent pre-marriage games were a preparation (like bundling in colonial America) for marriage. By the time you were fourteen, your socialization was complete, and a child's vague thought had coalesced in your mind—marriage. From then on you had only to learn how to "handle" men, how to win one, how to change the chemistry of your being so that you had a single priority—marriage, which, like a cuckoo nestling, shoves the rightful offspring out of the nest.

Sometimes the obligations of a married woman toward the ideal of marriage seem unspeakably dreary, calculated to kill all spontaneity. Suddenly to lose the sense of one's single self, one's right to make decisions, suddenly to have to submit every wish not only to a husband but also to a whole Board of Censors, male and female judges by the millions! You are accountable to them as a wife; you will be accountable to them as a mother. You have forfeited forever your right to be selfish. But your long training—to enjoy the things *allowed*, to be thankful as a prisoner who is allowed exercise—it stood you in good stead.

As for sex—the excitement, the floating and rocking of Margaret were protected for Mrs. Meigs, by an archangel with a big sword. No more playing with fire! either for you or for those representatives of your virtue, your children. Even at the age of five, you thought, a child was in danger from the pleasure of discovering his own body. Well, it is high time for me to bury my old bone and concentrate on the successful welding of a man and a woman, like two trees planted close to each other. "When your two lives join into one, when your separate joys and sorrows, successes and failures, become as one," wrote Horace Jencks to Edward on the eve of his marriage. Since I was not a witness to Horace Jencks' married life, I can't pronounce judgement on its oneness. Wasn't there a predominant *one*, namely Horace? I have my suspicions. Thank goodness, *you* kept your shape and became a Mrs. Meigs quite distinct from Dr. Meigs. As for love, sympathy and encouragement, you gave it in abundance to Edward. You had enough physical energy for the two of you and as Edward's strength waned, yours grew. Your intimate life together will always be hidden; there is no way now to know more, no more letters to be read or to be opened in the year 2000. You have closed the door as you did when (I was very small) I saw you sitting on Edward's lap on the chaise longue in your bedroom. Closed doors! This one had been partly open but you jumped up to close it, and I still remember my uneasy shame at having witnessed something forbidden, and a vague disgust at the vision of a man and a woman (my parents!) embracing. Even fully-clothed as you were, it suggested an intimacy between you that was utterly unfamiliar to me. Or had I simply not wanted to notice, trained already to a keen awareness of the signs that said No Trespassing? More than anybody I have ever known, you were law-abiding and thus, inflexible. If the law of the land told you not to drink alcohol, you did not drink a drop; if, when the USA went off the gold standard, you were told to turn over your gold currency to Uncle Sam, you not only did it but you also required your children to yield up their little hoards of Christmas five- and ten-dollar gold pieces. How meekly we went along with this patriotic gesture, and I think now of those lovely little coins of the '20s with keen regret. Finally, if the moral and religious law of your time prescribed marriage as such-and-such, you cheerfully vowed to obey it to the letter. You were among the very few, I believe, who did.

The House in Washington:
World War II

Dearest Mother,

When I think of the house in Washington, I'm immediately warmed by the sun pouring through the window next to your desk, scarcely wider than a grandfather clock, piled with a chaos of bills, letters, cards, bits of paper you have saved to write notes on, envelopes with a corner missing where you've torn out the stamp. At your left elbow was a little table stained by white water-marks, on which stood your family of plants: a big parent begonia with flowers that glowed ruby-red in the sunlight and its unpromising offspring in little pots, a vine attached by string to the window frame, with a single heart-shaped leaf, perhaps one of many bowls of narcissus which had emerged from the dark like Persephone and were now in flower all over the house.

The house in Washington was your outer garment, as much a part of you as a bird's feathers. Father seemed to occupy only small areas of it: his study, his place at the end of the dining-room table, the big wing chair in the library. Sometime on November 6th, 1940, your life together stopped and only the letters in the attic held your voices talking and talking to each other. I wish I had tried to communicate with Father's sweet, uncomplaining ghost when I lived in the house (entirely yours after his death), during World War II. It was a time when everything that I was living was in conflict with the house's spirit (yours) and our secrets clashed. As for the box closet, it was a closet within the closet of your house, which held me captive then and still exerts its backward-pulling power.

So the dialogue spills over time's boundaries. You died twenty-nine years ago, and the house was demolished, but I still search it for memories of you. Not long ago I asked Sarah if I was ever nice to you during the War. "I don't remember your ever being *not*-nice," she answered. Is it true that I was never *not*-nice? You had opened your house to a small army of young women and supervised the running of it. You had lived through World War I and had lost Edward a year before this one began. You must have had a sense of life as unending tragedy and a sense of our levity in the face of it. We scarcely thought about the seriousness of the Cause, but flew about like bees in a marvellous garden. But now I know that you, too, during World War I, had felt a giddy joy. You had your twin babies and you were serving Uncle Sam.

We, too, were serving Uncle Sam. We all had wartime jobs by day or by night, so that we appeared and disappeared like Cheshire cats. Some found houses of their own but four of us stayed under your watchful eye: Sarah, Annsie, Riqui, and myself. The four of us were divided, not just by our unpredictable hours but by our relation to you, the guardian of the house. Annsie and Sarah found favour in your eyes; both were engaged to irreproachable men who were serving their country, they could talk to you, they were understood and loved by you. Annsie looked like Gretel, with flaxen pigtails and clear blue eyes. She was not sure that she was in love with Jack but you persuaded her to marry him, and I know now that you were thinking of yourself and Edward and the doubts you'd had. Riqui had been one of our classmates at college. I asked her recently to tell me what she remembered about you during the War. "Do you remember how perceptive your mother was about Annsie's pre-nuptial doubts?" she wrote in reply. "We were *so* wrong. Annsie wanted to cry off, but wailed that she couldn't because the cake had been ordered. We tried to persuade her that was no impediment, that she ought not to be forced into matrimony because of a cake. She just sobbed more. Later she implied . . . that we had tried to come between her and Jack. So much for our good intentions."

197

Ours was a small sin against the holy ideal of matrimony, but to you it was, no doubt, a straw in the wind. You had a sixth sense, moral antennae as sharp as a dog's hearing, that recognized wrong even when it was invisible. It was a little like Miss Balfour, who knew when we had stopped on the way home from school to eat an ice-cream cone at the Peoples' Drugstore. "I can tell from your voices," she said. You had this same uncanny power to read signs, and Riqui and I, who were suspicious of marriage and hid the details of our lives, spoke the sign-language of wrong. Even when you were away, you had the feeling that horrors might be going on in your house. You suspected Riqui of illicit love-making, not in the house, but somewhere, and accused her of having "loose morals." Yet forty-one years later Riqui says in her letter, "Your mother put up with me reluctantly but with a characteristically stiff upper lip . . . We sparred but never drew blood, and bless her, she never intruded on my privacy. I hadn't the wit, later, to tell her how much I appreciated her forbearance; perhaps stupid pride forbade my admitting that she had had much to tolerate from me."

You had much more to tolerate from *me*; all that I tried to hide from you about my life, my love for another WAVE, my dubious friends, the drunken WAVE who threw up in the wash basin, the WAVE who lived in the house for a while like a stray cat, had orgies of eating and then throwing up. Finally, when she confessed that she felt compelled to raid the refrigerator and devour whole loaves of bread, you were kind to her because it was the result of an unhappy love affair. You sympathized with all genuine heterosexual travail: the WAVE's, Annsie's, Sarah's. Thornie was in the South Pacific (I knew where because my job was to keep a classified list of naval units' mailing addresses). He worked to save wounded and dying men in a Marine hospital on Bougainville. Thousands of Marines were fighting in the jungle, were being killed, some were tortured by the Japanese; they tortured the Japanese in turn and blew them out of their caves with dynamite. Now and then a censored letter would come from Thornie, and when I saw Sarah reading the letter, I was filled with the wish to be unpleasant. It came from helpless envy; she had a heroic fiancé, who did not kill but saved human lives. She could weep for him, she could talk about him, she was part of the immense loyalty to the War and to the idea, thousands of years old, that men go to war and women weep and wait for them. You, too, were part of this; when Arthur was exempted from military service because he was deaf in one ear, you felt a complex bitterness. Part of the mass brain-washing of wartime is to insinuate into mothers' heads the willingness to send their sons to war. Underneath there must be a molten core of pain and unwillingness, yet mothers are able to feel a strange stab of disappointment if their sons are exempt or if they decide to be conscientious objectors. There were also reasons closer to home for your regret: you wanted Arthur to be separated from his work in his secular-religious movement, Moral Rearmament, by Country, the unarguable authority. You hoped that he would find a nice girl to marry—a WAVE or a WAC officer, a woman who had no ties with the people you feared. You wanted him to come back and resume his life as a lawyer. Instead, he married a beautiful dark-eyed girl in the movement and became, at last, a persona grata, for the non-marriage of your children was a worse anxiety than their choice of vocation.

What did it do to Sarah to think about her man out there? What did it do to him to see the worst that men can do to each other? Sarah had a real connection with the War; she cracked Japanese codes, which helped to end it sooner. Thornton came back from hell as kind as ever, with no visible bitterness or trauma; they married during the War and the marriage was happy, like Annsie's and Jack's, like Arthur's, like Wister's. Your deepest joys were the successful and happy marriages of your children and their friends, uncomplicated by pre-marital sex. How simple and beautiful it would have been to be part of your universe, to deny the imperious selfishness of my whole being, which was pushing me in another direction!

"One Sunday," says Riqui, "you and your mother and I went to Montrose Park for a picnic. As soon as we had consumed our lunch you and I were ready to move on, but your M. felt rushed and complained at being at her children's mercy. It was the first time I had thought about a parent's point of view . . . about offspring . . . Monstrous self-absorption! But even in those days I appreciated some of your mother's rigid self-discipline & uncompromising views. How lovely not to be submerged, nay drowned in oceans of doubt." I read this and wondered, did I think about your point of view, even in the elementary matter of whether to linger in a peaceful picnic spot? Monstrous self-absorption. My world of inchoate rebellions shut out all of your certitudes, and failed to recognize your heroism. My secrets, my failures, my unreal connection with the War, my inability to make a good job of a bad job or even of a good one. Or to feel the necessary loyalty to the Leviathan super-ego. All these things festered in me, poisoned my blood-stream and erupted in a bad case of adolescent acne, which flared with a kind of punitive violence whenever I fell in love. And I fell in love continuously, or rather simultaneously, for at one time I was in love with two WAVE lieutenants, with Fred, the most beguiling of the artists in my unit, and with Gil, the rightful object of your misgivings.

Gil had a pale, disdainful face, red-orange eyes and thick, wavy hair the same colour, a straight back, a determined walk. She had a deep whisky-tenor voice and a fake English accent. She would look sidewise down her long nose and hold out a hand, as limp as a dead fish, to be shaken. You did not shake it; you stiffened, gave Gil a black look, and tuned away without a word. With your astute eye, you had seen nothing to like about Gil; you must have guessed that she was a Lesbian and had what you saw as a dangerous hold over me. You could not guess my shame when you met—of Gil's loftiness, her false accent, her eyelids drooping like her hand, and her heavy attempts at witty repartee. I could not talk to you about Gil nor explain that she could also be natural and tender and crack deadpan jokes that were really funny. Gil's power over me came from an alternation of tenderness and vulgarity sparked with inexplicable rage. Her anger was like a switch-blade; no doubt it came from a hoard of resentments, hardships; anyway, it was a weapon that served instead of reason or politeness. For the first time in my life I had come in contact with someone who was a witch's brew of all the things calculated to appal you. *This* was the real world, I thought. For Gil drank like a fish, made scenes in restaurants, became maudlin and incoherent, had to be dragged home and put to bed. She had a love affair with one sailor and was married (briefly) to another. She was a far cry from being a lady; she mocked at ladies, and the false accent, the airs she put on, were perhaps her little joke at your expense— and at mine.

Against a background of continuous horror—the War—you and I were fighting our mother-daughter battle. "How lovely not to be submerged in oceans of doubt," says Riqui in her letter. "Ours not to reason why. Ours but to do and die!" chanted one of my fellow-WAVES in Bu-Comm (the Bureau of Communications) when I complained about a sudden flurry of cables just before quitting time. Not to doubt; above all, to forget oneself and one's paltry concerns! Finally my ineptitude resulted in my transfer to the outer office, where I was assigned to classifying mail. I wept bitterly for a whole day; it seemed to hark back to my school days, and how could I explain to you? Or explain the wording of my first fitness report: "Ensign Meigs is not stupid, but lacks personality"? I thought arrogantly that it was the Commander's fault if he could not see my personality; it was invisible to people like him, whom I feared and despised. Now, forty years later, I see what he meant. Personality meant the glad performance of duty. It was another thing which separated me from you, for you wouldn't have lacked personality; you would have done the job I had cheerfully and efficiently. You would have said, "Ours not to reason why," and meant it.

Later when I was given a new job in an artists' unit in BuPers (the Bureau of Personnel) I discovered people like myself, ex-civilians who were full of doubts. They mocked at everything with cynical gaiety: at the War, at their jobs, at me, and at my relation with you. I still have a series of drawings made by Ted Roscoe, the most cynical and jolliest of them, showing me successively as a stripper, a prostitute, an apache dancer, a gambler, and a painter of burlesque posters. In one with the title *Miss Meigs dining at the Murray Hill*, I am wearing an outlandish ruffled dress, seated with a slingshot aimed at the balls suspended on the jet of a little fountain. On the wall is a reproduction of Bonheur's "The Horse Fair." "Who's Victorian?" says the caption. Today the messages contained in this drawing seem obvious to me; then I merely saw that my artist friend was encouraging a reckless alter ego, "Stripwoman Hyde," he called her, who was kept in check by my Victorian upbringing and by you, who guarded the house (the Murray—Mary Hill). My cynical friends mocked at you, just as Gil had, because they had caught their tone from me. And now something is shaking me and saying, "Listen to me! Your mother was always true to herself, and you were false both to yourself and to her because you shut away love. Stripwoman Hyde wasn't a free spirit but was the person you became in your mother's house." The more I look on your integrity with sympathy and sorrow, the less I like Stripwoman Hyde with her sulky rebellion and closed heart.

You did not need to swear an oath of loyalty to the Stars and

Stripes (as I had); your commitment was already clear and unassailable. We all had the same obligation—to suspend criticism and to swallow our sick sense of horror. Millions on millions of people were killing each other; the good news was about death, deserts and islands strewn with enemy dead, cities of dead enemies, and the bad news was about *our* dead. We began to take mass murder for granted; bombing saved lives, we were told. Hiroshima and Nagasaki were "justified" by the need to "win" the war. Mass murder was slipping imperceptibly into genocide. But in World War II, we thought smugly, only the Germans practised genocide. The Holocaust—wasn't it worse than anything the Allies had done or could do? My beetle-browed Commander in BuPers pinned a photograph of stacked naked corpses from Buchenwald on the office wall to drive home the point—that the War was about the moral difference between the Enemy and us.

Fortunately, the Japanese understood the readiness of the powers-that-were to kill them all, if "necessary." Since then, the fate of the whole world has rested on the words "readiness" and "necessary," defined by those same powers, grown a million times more powerful, and the terror waked by Hiroshima gnaws dully and continuously at our lives. You would think that the two atomic bombs would have restored our ability during the War to feel *appropriately*. They didn't. A terrible new world had been born but we didn't wail No! or lose our sanity; we were anaesthetized. In my state of wartime anaesthesia I had taken a trip to New York (before Hiroshima) to visit an aircraft carrier, which had just come back from the battle of the Coral Sea. I was revising a cookbook for enlisted men on carriers and wanted to see the galley at first hand. What I saw was a huge hole in the ship's side; the galley had been blown away and hundreds of men killed. Now I ask myself, why didn't they pitch her overboard—the trim WAVE in her piqué uniform who asked to talk to the cook? The cook was dead, unable to tell her how many eggs went into an omelette for 1100 men. But they did not throw her overboard; an officer invited her to lunch in the officers' mess, where wine was served and the conversation was polite and cheerful. It seemed almost a conspiracy to guide her thoughts away from the gaping hole, which they were too gentlemanly to talk about. "Something in the nature of men's talk," as AIM put it, would have been the terrible details of the battle. No, we didn't lose our sanity; we felt the joy of being young, of the swirling excitement of hundreds of new friends, of parties on parties. My sister and I both remember sitting at our desks with our heads in our hands, taking little naps after a late night.

In 1942, when your twins began their war work, you (Mother) were sixty and we were twenty-five. Could you see your old self in our "monstrous self-absorption"? Did you ever "feel light-hearted enough to giggle and laugh and be silly," as you did before your marriage? You who loved to giggle and be silly had to do exercises in seriousness, in hardness of heart, like a soldier in training. You became a soldier during the War, much more than I did, in my WAVE uniform. You didn't reason why. "Et puis! Pour ce qui est de l'avenir!" Frank Wheelwright had written you back in 1906, when you were twenty-four. When will you be serious about life, he implied. He did not know how hard you would practise, how sobering marriage would be, and how Edward's death and then the War would erode your natural cheerfulness. "When I get cheerful a balloon is nothing to me," you had written Edward in 1910. I do my own exercise, recall your two faces, severe and happy, see you even during the War when you were helpless with giggles, just as we were, defying the forces that dragged us down. I think of your patience and good temper in the face of our unpredictable wartime comings and goings. I think of your narcissus bulbs bursting into flower after their sojourn in the dark.

Margaret's "Isms"

June 5, 1902—Margaret Wister's Diary: "Adorable book at the Library, 'The Lady Paramount', such a comfort to get a book where everybody is well-bred & doesn't deal with the passions of the lower classes." July 17, 1904—Loèche-les-Bains: "Mr. Gallatly's uncle is Marshall in Marshall & Snellgrove . . . I am almost snob enough to wish his uncle weren't, for he is one of the nicest fellows I ever met." To me, this paradoxical statement must mean that Margaret would consider Mr. Gallatly an even nicer fellow if his uncle weren't in "trade." Her "almost snob enough" is either a proof of her self-delusion or it has come from her artless pride in really being "snob enough." She has already observed that Mr. Gallatly is "rather nice, though of course upper middle class" and I took this to mean that she did not consider herself upper middle class but in a still higher realm, perhaps on a level with the "aristocratic people" in *The Lady Paramount*. And this is confirmed by a single diary entry in 1920, about a reception at Corcoran House in Washington. "All aristocratic Washington there," she says.

It was strange that Margaret "almost" wished that Mr. Gallatly didn't have an uncle who ran a business of some kind, in view of the fact that her own father ran the family iron works in

Duncannon, a little town on the Susquehanna River. He had been selected from a troop of brothers by his mother, the kindly and formidable Quaker lady who thought nothing of inviting fifty family members to lunch at Belfield. His brothers went to college; he did not. Margaret's family moved to Belfield when her grandmother died, but perhaps her determined classism had something to do with her childhood in Duncannon. It was sad that her great gift for friendship and her real interest in people were sometimes hobbled by her belief in the social hierarchy. February 5, 1916: "Am still marvelling over the Great American people whom we saw last night," she says in her diary the day after a White House reception. "The looks do seem confined to the upper classes. Knew all the Cabinet ladies." On January first, she had written, "Must start with my diary as we are living in Washington. Edward & I paid Cabinet calls . . . E. found it lonely not knowing people." In a month's time she had reached two of her goals: to know the Cabinet ladies, and to be invited to the White House. She was launched in the giddy excitement of Washington society.

I take comfort in the fact that Edward always lagged behind; in fact, my heart bleeds for him. He hated to pay calls; he felt lonely among the Cabinet ladies and the military gentlemen in full-dress uniforms. "Ed. generally eludes me when it comes to a ball," says Margaret, January 27, 1916. Edward was saved from the excesses of snobbishness by his dislike of social life and his need for solitude. "Edward prefers sitting at home to doing anything," says Margaret, who this time wanted to go sleighing. In a very real sense, it was not Edward who determined Margaret's life, but the contrary. The size of the wedding had generated a flood of wedding presents, the wedding presents had required a house big enough to hold and display them, the house had required a staff of servants to take care of it, and the combined reality of house, wedding presents and servants had required dinner parties and luncheons. Margaret was a willing cog in this perpetual-motion machine, and Edward, the absolutely necessary husband, could slow it a little but he couldn't disentangle himself. Wives are socialized (I say as a feminist) but how they adore their socialization when it runs as smoothly as the engine-room of a great ocean liner!

The perpetual-motion machine was oiled by "isms": class prejudices, snobbery, anti-Semitism, racism. Both Margaret and

Edward had been been brought up to believe in their right to feel superior; everybody around them seemed to affirm this right, and their ease depended on the general assent to class hierarchies. The so-called servant class and the working-class appeared to agree that they had their "place." Our servants also had their place in the house—plainly furnished little rooms in the attic or the basement, with (in Woods Hole, at least) a wash-basin and a big pitcher, and a chamber-pot under the bed. As children we neither made our beds, nor cleaned our rooms, nor washed our own clothes, nor cooked a meal except on the maid's night out.

The sense of class depends on not looking at the possibility of bitterness and rebellion brewing in the "lower" classes, or, having looked, not caring. Too much sympathy had its dangers, and empathy was almost impossible. "I dare say I am unsympathetic but it is a bore when you want to have a little company and have a gloomy cook," Margaret wrote to Edward from Woods Hole. Bertha, the cook, had complained about her rheumatism. Margaret exercised a kind of occupational toughness that depended on a person's place in the hierarchy of helpers. "You can bet I made her walk," she wrote to Edward, indignant because when it began to snow one day, Bertha asked her to send her home in a taxi. She would certainly not have made a nurse or a governess walk; she herself would have proposed a taxi. (Apropos of this, her letter to Edward May 17, 1917: "Your mother did not ingratiate herself by making Miss Bartholomew [the twins' nurse] walk to the trolley after 7 p.m. carrying her bag.") She seemed to accept the myth of those times that hardship was less hard as one went down in the social scale, particularly if one was black. Bertha walked home in the snow and history doesn't record what shoes she was wearing (I hope Margaret lent her some galoshes!) or how deep the snow was, or how far she had to walk. Only that she came back to work seemingly without rancour, owing to the peculiar pact between mistress and servant that sometimes flew in the face of justice.

The pact had been made in the spirit of mutual need and was sustained by money, as little as possible, passing from employer to servant. There was also an understanding between friends about the amount to be paid. "Mrs. R. L. is the one who has upset Woods Hole completely, by paying the colored woman $3.00 per day," Margaret writes to Edward in July, 1918. "She only workd one day for her, but it has raised all the prices, so that nobody is satisfied." "Nobody" does not include the people who benefit-ted from Mrs. R. L.'s largesse; it means "somebody," i.e. Margaret and her friends. The ladies of Woods Hole groaned in unison if their servants demanded higher wages, and were indignant if working people such as the Portuguese who helped with their gardens, asked "too much." After World War I, Margaret remarks that since times are bad people should be willing to work for less and wages should come down.

Except in the case of Mrs. R. L., class hard-heartedness, which Margaret would have seen as shrewdness about money, was the norm. Even five years before her marriage, Margaret was concerned about the "problem" of servants, i.e. their ready availability for low wages, and their staying power. For here is Mr. Gallatly writing in 1905: "I neglected to say that my sympathies are entirely with you on the subjects of marriage and servants, which you so fittingly class together as the two main worries." Mr. Gallatly, the light-hearted Oxford undergraduate, was speaking the language of Margaret's worries, just as he spoke the language of her hats. But Margaret was serious. It was not conceivable then for people of her class to live without servants, and the availability of servants perpetuated their employers' sense of class difference and their inability to think of their servants as human beings like themselves. This inability made it almost impossible to put oneself in the servant's place when one *needed* her. "Alberta is still at home sick, tiresome toad," Margaret writes Edward during the flu epidemic. True, she was hard-pressed, with all four children sick, and she ended by doing all the nursing and cooking herself. Incidentally, "tiresome toad" was an epithet she used impartially when something provoked her. "What tiresome toads the lawmakers are," she said in another letter. We were all tiresome toads at one time or another, but in Alberta's case, it conveys the unmistakeable impression that she was being sick on purpose.

It is all very well for me to pick out examples of Margaret's isms from her letters and diaries; she is defenceless and cannot answer back. If she could she might say that it is unfair to use selective material of a very private kind to judge overall behaviour. She might say that as children, we lived a comfortable life because of her class attitudes, and that we shared them with her. She might say that actions speak louder than words. It is true. Her words were sometimes petty—and who doesn't say petty things behind people's backs? (I do) but her actions, in her context, were exemplary. I, too, have taken advantage of low wages—in Guatemala, for instance, in 1949, delighted to find that nine dollars a month for a cook was considered generous. I had no pangs of conscience about exploiting people apparently willing to be exploited. It is only when apparent willing turns to determined non-willing that the exploiter wakes with a start, and a guilty conscience. The exercise of imagination that requires the exploiter to see non-willing before it is visible, is very rare. It is hard to make connections. I remember my mother's pride when she told a story about her Quaker grandmother who was a link on the underground railway at the time of the infamous Fugitive Slave Law. She had hidden a runaway slave in a safe place, and when a mounted soldier came to look for him she was standing outside her front door looking into the distance. "He went that way," she said, pointing down the road, and he galloped off in pursuit. Margaret would have done the same. She had a quick sympathy for people in distress and she would have tackled the devil himself in defence of one of her principles. It was not that she stopped having principles when it was a question of class self-interest, but that they were made to fit the situation. According to the code of honour of her time she was rigorously kind and fair. Her servants loved her, and it was a real love, a response to her essentially simple and friendly nature. When they were in need she helped them, she paid their hospital bills and gave them pensions. Perhaps her stint of cooking during the summer of 1917 made her more understanding. She called it her "mad career" and felt "proud of having cooked a complete set of meals and still feeling extremely cheerful." After about a month of cooking for seven people, she wrote Edward that she had come to have "a wholesome respect for cooks, as it takes me all day to get through the three meals."

There is no longer a mutual understanding to assure the existence of a servant class. People cannot be made to feel like servants even if they are willing to work as servants, and money can no longer guarantee a feeling of class superiority. As I say this, I know that it isn't true but that it should be true, that the should be, which was not acknowledged in my parents' time, is acknowledged now. My mother understood how the walls had come tumbling down in her physically helpless years before she died. I have already told how Amelia punished her by not coming to see her and how when she finally did my mother said,

"Never leave me," and wept. She had said the same to me when I was taking care of her, had clutched my hand and said, "Don't leave me." Every difference fell away in the presence of her need—for a true friend in Amelia, for a daughter in me, the need to love and to be loved.

Letter to my Father

Dearest Father,

Today (January 4, 1987) I went straight to a forgotten file of my own letters and found one to Arthur written in 1938, two years before you died. You, Mother, Wister and I are doing a picture puzzle of a coaching scene; Sarah is reading *The Idiot*. "I'm having the greatest success with these horses' feet," you say. "Look at all the feet I've got." Pause. "There's the horse's nose." "It's bad enough reading *The Idiot*," says Sarah, "without having Father go crazy right next to me." A scene of family life—life before television—when we were together, as unselfconscious as children. We were united by mindless games; we prattled over our picture puzzles, like hens searching for grain. Games filled the spaces between us with something as warm and light as goose down. Conversations as disjointed as the puzzles, senseless laughter, and the crazy release of giggling, pure laughter like a baby's laugh, which must be one of those clouds of glory that we trail, detached from original sin.

This pure laughter came to save us from unbearable tension after your funeral, gathered in the library again. "Who was the extra pallbearer?" someone asked. Yes, a stranger in shabby clothes who joined the pallbearers on the street and helped to carry the casket. Each thought that he had been asked to be there; perhaps he was a scientific colleague of yours, someone too deep in thought to care about appearances. And putting forward various hypotheses, we all began to laugh immoderately. Perhaps, someone said, he had lingered at the side-doors of churches for years, waiting for his moment of glory, to be part of a big funeral in a fashionable church. But how did he get out without being noticed? It made us wonder whether, in fact, he had been there at all, or whether he wasn't a ghost. Yes, I think now, he was a messenger from another world who had come to say, Death makes me your brother.

Your death took your children by surprise. The day before you died I wrote you a long letter from Bryn Mawr about a speech I'd made there at a forum on Responsibility in Freedom. My only memory of this speech is of my paralyzing terror and the loudness of my slow, flat voice. I wanted you to know that to my surprise it had been a success, wanted you to be pleased, but you never read my letter. The next day, as I was driving people to the polls to vote, someone caught up with me to say that you had died.

You had faded away so quietly that in our self-centred way we scarcely noticed that you were dying. I still have a photograph of you sitting next to Uncle Arthur at Wister's wedding in August, 1940. You are wearing a navy blue jacket and creamy flannel pants that hang on your skinny legs, your face is flushed, your eyes are very blue. You have a haggard and desperate expression—a clear warning to us. But there seemed to be an unspoken agreement among us not to notice, for it was clear that you *wanted* to fade away, and to die, alone with Margaret, in your own house. "I may come down this weekend," I write you from Bryn Mawr the day before you died.

In imagination, I try to go back to the time when the house in Washington was throbbing with the rhythm of seven people all in a state of high seriousness, engaged in observing their schedules, when you were sitting at your desk in your sacred domain, your study. It was a little room near the front door, like one of those rooms in certain early Italian paintings, where Saint Jerome sits, with his red hat on a peg on the wall, and his lion lying peacefully at his feet. The walls of your study were covered with crimson brocade and there was a big oak desk, a Morris chair with a dark blue velvet cushion, and a Moroccan iron filigree lamp hanging on a chain from the ceiling. Stillness and order reigned in the mysterious half-light cast by the lamp's eyes and by the green shade of your desk-light. On your desk a bronze wolf with bared teeth stood, suckling the boy-twins, Romulus and Remus, who sat under their foster mother's dangling breasts, holding up their chubby arms and open mouths. An engraving of Titian's "Sacred and Profane Love" hung over one of the bookcases: two shapely women, one naked and the other modestly swathed from the waist down, are poised on the edge of a rectangular stone well like a sarcophagus. Sacred love—to remind you of marriage? I think of you in your quiet study, presided over by Sacred and Profane Love, by the twin founders of Rome, and by miniatures of your ancestors, going back to your great-great-grandfather Josiah, who rebelled against authority and had an owl's profile.

The books in the bookcases: Goethe, Schiller, Spinoza, Kant, Macauley, Gibbon, Emerson, etc. were your daily bread. You read contemporary books with a kind of reluctance, for they depressed you, and the three I remember are all about the same subject. There were Thomas Mann's *Buddenbrooks*, *The Late George Apley* by Van Wyck Brooks, and *The Last Puritan* by George Santayana. After reading each one, you sank into a profound depression, for each writer was speaking of the disintegration of your most cherished values and was showing the rottenness at their core. You were cast down by any suggestion that our world, like the Roman Empire, was declining. January 31, 1929: You write to Margaret from Sunnyrest Sanatorium, where you were recovering from tuberculosis and the "nervous prostration" caused by your trip with MRBM. "Arthur I. sends an article by a man who says that human beings are all so mean now-a-days that it is impossible even for a great modern genius to write a real tragedy like those of Sophocles and Shakespeare." This had "excited and irritated" you so much that you write two long letters to AIM and propose John Masefield's *Dauber* as a "modern tragedy that made you feel that humanity still had fine traits." As if it isn't worry enough to defend the times, you worry because you have put aside other things to write Arthur. "Does that show a very jumpy mind?" you ask Margaret, and you ask her to make out a sensible schedule for you.

I feel such yearning sympathy for you there, heaped with blankets in your frigid, glass-enclosed room, worrying about our moral and intellectual decline, worrying about your jumpy mind, never for an instant relaxing into the luxury of time without obligations. If Margaret crammed her days so that no time was left for thought, you tortured yourself with thoughts that penetrated deep under your skin, festered and made you sick. Your letters from Washington are full of minute worries; you worry that the model-Ts won't start, you worry that Margaret will scold you. You relate all the good and useful things you have done in the house and garden to propitiate her, and to propitiate the gods in you who impose guilt and demand burnt offerings. How did you accumulate all the negative forces in you that destroyed you: fear of other people's anger, the guilt that comes from fear, the wild oscillations between hope and despair?

Knowing you better now than I did when you were alive, I go back in time and try to find the point at which the beautiful young man with the haughty expression lost faith in himself. Farther back still, to the infant Edward with huge troubled eyes—yes, that look which I see repeated in a baby picture of one of your granddaughters, of trouble to come. A sensibility that turns on itself. You looked to Margaret for help but her strength both lifted you up and increased your dependence on her. I recall your letter in 1919 about a play you had just seen—*He and She* by Rachel Crothers, the story of two artists, man and wife, who live happily together until they enter a competition for a $100,000 frieze, which the wife wins. But she gives up executing the frieze because she has to break up a romance between her daughter and the chauffeur by taking the daughter to Europe (why couldn't she have left that job to her husband, I wonder?). "I went home," you say, "with a rather frightened and uncomfortable feeling that you could easily beat me at scientific work or writing popular articles (!?) if you only wanted to. Could you?" There you go again! "Frightened and uncomfortable." Worrying your mind with a poisonous thought, a brand-new one—that Margaret is perhaps holding back, just as she holds back to let you win games, having seen your ego crumpling like a punctured balloon. The wife in *He and She* is probably scared to death by her victory and uses her daughter as a heaven-sent way of getting out of her dilemma, i.e. the dilemma of being a better artist than her husband. But Margaret was not threatening to you in any way, except that she was discouragingly competent, and it was typical of the perverse machinations of your mind to use the play to lower your self-esteem. You did the same thing with AIM and our declining times, with *Buddenbrooks, The*

Late George Apley, and *The Last Puritan.* You prepared your defences, for the writers seemed to be attacking you personally, and it made you sick. Books made me sick, too: Freud's *Interpretation of Dreams,* the last chapter of *Ulysses,* books that reminded me of the omnipresence of sex. The threat by something we don't want to admit. And for you it was the precariousness of your inherited world; you were like a gentle domestic animal stranded on a little island in a raging flood, or fleeing before a tide of flame.

After your stay in the sanatorium you lived for eleven years, growing thinner and thinner and weakened every winter by long bouts of flu. "I don't think Father was assailed by the thought that he was going to die of tuberculosis," Wister writes me in a recent letter. It was typical of those discreet times that the evidence of serious illness could be staring everybody in the face but there was a general agreement not to look at it. "I am sorry to learn that you are having trouble with your digestion, but hope it will be only temporary," your boss writes you at Sunnyrest Sanatorium. And Wister goes on to say, "It's worth remembering that Father's illness occurred during a period when the news media were totally excluded from medical reports about people in public office." How disgusted you and Mother would be now by the details in the press about the American President's sojourns in the hospital! So you kept the secret of your death sentence and mourned in secret the curtailment of your work and your daydreams. And if we didn't have a sufficient sense of alarm as we watched you fade away in front of our eyes, it was because it was your brave intention—to keep us from worrying.

The year you died your brown tweed suit hung on your bones. I have a vision of you sitting in your study at Woods Hole, doing nothing, perhaps trying not to think about the closeness of death. I tap at the screen door and you give me a glad welcome; your face flushes, your eyes gather blue light. When I ask how you feel, you answer, "Pretty well." I scarcely hear the yearning in your words, "Come and see me any time." (The doctor has forbidden you to eat with the family.) You are speaking out of your loneliness, out of a wish to know better this daughter who is flesh of your flesh and into whom your blessing wishes to enter. I accepted your blessing without acknowledging it, in the same way that I took for granted the non-authority of your body with its ambiguous messages. For just as I have never been able to think of myself as a "real" woman, so I have never thought of you as a "real" man. Daughters derive their ideas about men from their fathers, it is said, and my ideal (which led me to fall in love with beautiful bodies that gave no hint of sex) was a man who, except for his general shape, was as little like a "real" man as possible. Sometimes I think that your terrible depressions (like Margaret's anger) were the price you paid for denying your body, for "the deadly damping down of passion," as Elizabeth Smart says. But I must stop trying to count the cost of your being, finally, what you were. You were like a swan brought up in captivity, released and unable to survive in the company of the wild strangers who struck out confidently across the continent. But now (having read your letters) I can see you when you were young, beating your wings, practising for your long flight, when you felt kinship with all swans, and I want to celebrate that time and stop mourning the long-drawn-out extinction of your dreams.

EBM: Some Letters to Margaret

June 24, 1919: This is not really a postal day, but I love you so much that I have to write a letter. Isn't it funny—I often find it very hard to think of things to say to other people— even to mother—but when I write to you, I always have enough matter for any number of sheets, if I only had time to fill them . . .

June 28, 1919: Today has been perfect, crisp, cool, and breezy—and I have really accomplished a great deal. Indeed, I am beginning to think that I am not naturally lazy—only rather tired most of the time from being a little too hard driven. List of accomplishments: got the trash taken away; brushed and beat automobile rug and put it away in newspapers with moth-balls; inspected all jars, boxes, bottles, etc. in pantry, kitchen and refrigerator room and got rid of all material that I thought would give aid and comfort to the enemy (cockroaches); this included a rotten banana in the refrigerator and various bones and other articles too much decomposed for recognition in the coal scuttle; put padlock on back gate; took off fly-scum and put shutters on dining-room window; spread numerous pieces of paper with roach poison and strewed them around; got my bureau including

215

top and drawers completely in order . . . It was a happy day. Of course you were with me in spirit all the time, my darling (I can imagine how you would have encouraged me and found more little things for me to do if you had been here in the flesh); and the nursery seemed still inhabited by the two sweet girls; and the yard, by the two bad boys. Various radishes and cucumbers still growing made me think of Arthur, and the brick castle in the sand box brought up vividly the picture of a sunny hour which Wister and I spent together not long ago. Give them all kisses from me and take a lot for yourself.

October 12, 1921: I got back just a few minutes ago from my session at U. of Minn. It was a meeting to organize a branch of the Society of Experimental Biology and Medicine in N.Y. and I felt quite proud of being called upon to make the opening speech at the birth of the new society. In fact I am afraid I shall come back with a decidedly swelled head, for they made more or less of a lion of me—talked about distinguished visitors, brought me all the way back here in a motor, etc.; and were altogether most kind and cordial.

April 9, 1922: I thought I had better go out to Beltsville this morning and see how things were coming along; and I found that the disease, whatever it is, had attacked another of my cows and several more victims in the West Wing. So I just cut the silage off altogether from my cows—I do not know what else to do. I know I ought to be able to take it all more calmly, but this is my work—the only thing I am good for, if I am good for anything at all—and to see it cut into the way it has been, with a prospect of indefinitely more damage if I make the wrong guess, is pretty disturbing . . .

April 26, 1922: The boys are crazy about "Treasure Island", and we are having a great deal of fun wondering whether Long John Silver is a pirate or an honest man. Even little Wis takes in the situations through a word of explanation which I give him here and there. What a lot of things there are and will be to enjoy in life, if only I can keep away from the dumps and the fantods for a reasonable fraction of the time that yet remains to me.

October 17, 1922: Miss Balfour took the twins to the Embassy to tea this afternoon, and saw Lady Geddes, who wishes to know when you will be home so that she can talk to you about the proposed dancing class for small children. Do come back pretty soon and arrange all these important matters, and incidentally bring a little sunshine to your old husband.

November 11, 1923: . . . Mr. Wilson's Armistice Day speech on the radio. Someone prompting him all through it. The substance of the speech was bitter, the theme being that our country had dishonored itself by turning its back on its obligations after the peace treaty. When I think of the wonderful speeches that Mr. Wilson used to make and the way in which he lifted the country above itself, I fall into a very low state of depression. . . . I had more or less of a fight with Arthur this morning about his habit of being late for meals.

August 10, 1924: My trouble is that I feel closer to the scientific people . . . than I do to the department nabobs, in spite of being in the same organization with them. What do you think of it all? I know that you think that I am a good deal of a blab, you dear old thing, and I do not expect you to be unduly prejudiced in my favor; but what on earth am I to talk about to my scientific colleagues except my scientific ambitions, adventures, and troubles and theirs!

> Warum ziehst du mich (Wherefore drawst thou me)
> unwiderstehlich, (irresistibly)
> Ach! in jener Pracht? (Ah! in yonder brilliant light?)
> War ich, guter Junge, nicht (Was I, good youth, not)
> so selig (happy enough)
> In der odem Nacht? (In the lovely night?)

September 10, 1924: I can't get out of my head the news that Judge Caverly has sentenced Leopold and Loeb in Chicago to life imprisonment instead of death. I never wished to have anybody executed before, and I would abolish capital punishment immediately in this country if I could; but I really feel tonight as if the devil was defying and jeering at all of us in the persons of those two.

June 8, 1928 [MWM, her four children and Miss Balfour are en route to Europe]: You must be getting somewhere near the British Coast by this time and—still more important—it is our wedding day—a good time to think and try to express how much I love you and how much I have come to be dependent on you. We don't seem to see so terribly much of each other when we are in Washington together, and we certainly each seem to have enough interests of our own to fill up a human life—and yet through all these seven weeks I feel as if a band had been stretching and stretching until it must certainly break or bring us together with a snap.

December 5—Pennsylvania Hospital [EBM has been told he has tuberculosis]: This afternoon there was a loud step in the passage and a loud knock on the door which I immediately recognized as my distinguished brother—and I was more than delighted to see him, as you can imagine. . . . He was just as kind and comforting as he has been right along—one's troubles certainly do have the good feature of bringing out the good qualities of one's relations.

December 21: If it got to be generally known how pleasant a rest cure is, I am afraid everybody would find a spot on their lung or some other excuse, and the business of the world would come to a stop.

December 31—White Haven, Pa. Sunnyrest: Last night there was a tremendous wind which came blustering around every side of my little glass house, and today has been gloriously clear and crisp, and pretty cold. I feel more intimate with the weather than I ever did in my life before.

January 17, 1929: You need not worry at all about my suffering from the cold. I was perfectly warm the night it went to ten below zero, though I had only 5 of my 7 blankets over me . . . So please save yourself this one of the many things that you have to worry about. . . .

February 20: I had been more or less worried about some

218

work of Mitchell in feeding alfalfa and timothy hay to sheep, the results of which seemed to be more or less out of harmony with ours. . . . he found that the sheep would not eat enough of his timothy ration to keep them at uniform body weight, and gave the alfalfa sheep a correspondingly inadequate ration. The result was that a considerable proportion of both lots died before the end of the experiment. It certainly seems a funny way to test the relative values of the two hays for practical purposes.

I got news from Beltsville yesterday which cheered me up a great deal—probably unreasonably. Of the three cows getting alfalfa and timothy combined, two were rather under the weather toward the end of January, but they are now all doing quite well. Of course it is just another bump surmounted in the long road toward finding a ration which will keep dairy cows near their best for an indefinite number of years . . .

February 28: While I was lying awake in my rest hours yesterday, it occurred to me all of a sudden that I should be, as Mary says, "terribly glad to get up". It seemed to me that it would be, if not supreme happiness, at least the greatest relief to be able to do just the least bit of what normal people do—a little shopping in White Haven, knocking a box together to plant some seeds in, or perhaps taking an automobile trip to Hazelton—anything to let me use my arms and legs a little and see some other prospect than what appears from the three sides of this bungalow. . . . Do you suppose that you could stay up here a little longer sometimes, and amuse the baby [himself] by taking it out for a walk or a drive?

Postlude

I am old and she is a ghost. Who are so
unforgiving as the dead? It is useless to ask
them to forgive.

Journey from the North:
The Autobiography of Storm Jameson

In the last few seconds of her life, my mother's left hand tightened around my sister Sarah's hand. She was in a coma, had stopped the harsh breathing that had racked her for two days and nights; her temperature had shot up with the last valiant effort the body makes to keep on living. Yet her hand knew how to tighten its hold on Sarah's hand. The need for love; isn't it greater than any other? "All I know is that I love you," she said to me one day. She had been sitting silently in her wheelchair, dozing and thinking her thoughts. It was unusual for a sentence to come out with such clarity. This was one of the moments of revelation in my life when a warm drop of love has fallen on my heart and melted it so that it can scatter its own drops. My unreliable memory remembers each of these moments that mark the giving and receiving of love, and dissolve the hard pellets of unforgiving

220

resentment, impurities that lodge in our vital organs.

Sometimes during my mother's illness, I took one of the nurse's eight-hour shifts. The effort of lifting my mother on to the toilet from her wheelchair made us both laugh, locked as we were in an uncharacteristic embrace, my arms clasped tightly around her waist and my cheek touching hers. It was the first time in my life that I had seen her body naked, and now I saw that her skin was as smooth and white as a young girl's. Her body was like that of Suzanna in Rembrandt's painting, innocently voluptuous in its classical curves and volume; I can still feel the softness of her skin, like a baby's, and her weight in my arms.

Another memory: my mother and I are sitting in the living-room of the house in Woods Hole, with a fire burning in the fireplace. She is close to the hearth in her wheelchair. I put on a log and go upstairs, come down after a few minutes and find that the fire has blazed up hotly, and my mother is gesticulating with her left hand and making sounds of alarm. I move her away, cursing my stupidity, feeling suddenly the painful knowledge of what it is to be trapped inside a body that has lost the power to command movement. Now the memory of my mother's helplessness, of my power to move her out of reach of the fire, merges with the mixed pain and love of writing this book. For three years I've been shut into the world of the box closet and every available surface in my work-room is still covered with packages of letters, labelled with names and dates, and diaries, piled up in front of me in an irregular column. I've been forced to think harder about my grandparents, my parents, my uncle and aunts than I did when they were alive. I've had to think about their world of certainties, about them and us, their children, and our complicity in their world. At times I've wanted to disown them with their received ideas and blind spots; at other times, I've loved them with a ferocious love. Don't you dare criticize them! I feel like saying to any non-family member. Cast the mote out of your own eye! And how do *I* dare to criticize them or think that our eyes are less full of motes or that we (their collective children) know more than they did? "How sharper than a serpent's tooth it is to have a thankless child," my father used to quote—humorously. In the course of writing this book, I have sometimes felt like a serpent's tooth and sometimes as though I were holding a wounded bird cupped in my hands.

"The long-legged cranes, the solemn pelicans and white-winged paddy birds," Margaret wrote in her diary in 1897. She was in

221

Egypt with her family; her bright, curious eyes took in everything. She felt sorry for the mummies, "which are really people's dead bodies"; "shelves and shelves of them." She thought the dead deserved more respect. She was that same observant child her whole life long. I've been working away at a big jigsaw puzzle. There are many more pieces of Margaret than of anyone else; I have an almost complete view of her whole life, but the pieces of the secrets she kept from herself will never be found. I have no pieces of Edward's childhood, only photographs to stare at, from his infancy almost to his death. The parts of the puzzle that are finished show me that their happiest lives were lived before we were born, when they were dreaming dreams of the future, before they had taken the marriage-shape and the parent-shape. We were four intruders, who jumped up and down on the fragile web of their happiness and changed the shape of their lives. Serpent's teeth at times.

Dearest Father and Mother,

Think of it, your four children are old (our average age is seventy-three!) and we have become like you in ways that would amaze you, would perhaps make you laugh. We are all both of you with our sudden bright nodding, yes! yes! and slow speech that trails into a murmur, our hesitations and endless musings. A tall white-haired quartet with an air of always being ready to apologize for something, diffidently bowing and nodding and saying thank you with our identical smiles. Enough to make a passerby turn and smile, too. Like you, for I remember the two of you brightly and shyly nodding as though your long marriage had made you alike. To find you again I look at us, gathered together for our annual meeting, thirty-two years after Mother's death, forty-six years after Father's death: our air of old-fashioned refinement, our unnecessary modesty, our politeness, irritability, depressions, excitement, argumentativeness, our anxiety and fears, our aches and pains, high blood pressure and dyspepsia. Mea culpa, Mother—my impatience when we went to Europe together. You were seventy-two; I was thirty-six. How slowly you moved, with little steps, holding my arm for support. How dreamily you thought aloud, gathered thoughts like straying sheep, careful not to frighten them into a stampede. As we drove along, I liked to get you started on set memory pieces, the Kings of France, for instance, which you could reel off without faltering. Now I'm

222

familiar with the state in which the mind is full of a soft darkness like a summer night without moon or stars, when the slightest pressure drives memories deeper into their starless night. And now that I've begun to do things with great deliberation I see my impatience with you in other people's eyes.

Each of us has both of you, they say, in equal parts, and I seem programmed to imitate your movements, Mother, when you were growing old; I see your smile when I look at my own in a photograph, and I think with Father's maddening logic. Yet each of us is a burning glass that has collected light which has passed through you from thousands of forbears, each is the unique mixture of herself and himself, acted upon by history and by the lives we have chosen. And I am more than ever the daughter who was inside your world with you, and outside, looking in at you and at myself. At this moment (February 13, 1987, 10 a.m.) I look at a photograph, taken in Woods Hole in 1938, the summer of the great hurricane. I see you, Mother, looking directly at me with a kind, relaxed and happy smile on your face, sending out the quiet energy of your smile. And Father—you are standing with your hands in the pockets of your tweed knickerbockers, looking down toward a tangle of dead flowers, smiling painfully, your eyebrows drawn together, but you send a message of courage and patience. You both seem as alive as your children still are, and with great ease I imagine a meeting (now! in this second that has already passed) between the six of us; I see and feel and hear us falling into each other's arms and crying with joy.